THE DOLMEN ARCH
A STUDY COURSE IN THE DRUID MYSTERIES

VOLUME I
THE LESSER MYSTERIES

THE
DOLMEN ARCH
A STUDY COURSE IN
THE DRUID MYSTERIES

VOLUME 1
THE LESSER MYSTERIES

COMPILED BY
JOHN MICHAEL GREER

AZOTH
PRESS™

2021

First Paperback Edition
published 2021 Azoth Press
ISBN 978-1-935006-91-6

First Limited Hardcover Edition
published 2020 Azoth Press

Azoth Press
Portland, OR
USA
www.azothpress.com

Printed in the United States of America.

CONTENTS

LIST OF ILLUSTRATIONS

INTRODUCTION

W HEN I WAS A CHILD, before the advent of container ships, freighters carrying goods across the ocean sometimes lost portions of their cargo to the sea, sometimes by accident, sometimes when severe weather forced the captain to choose between jettisoning cargo or going down with all hands. When my family vacationed on the desolate but beautiful Pacific coast of Washington State, where the great North Pacific currents come sweeping against the shore, it happened from time to time that we found lying on the sand pieces of flotsam and jetsam that had once belonged to some unknown freighter's cargo. I used to wonder, as I watched the little crabs scuttle over the seaweed and sand, about the events that had sent these fragments of modernity drifting up onto the shelving beaches of Grayland and North Cove.

I thought of those days more than once in the years that followed my election as Grand Archdruid of the Ancient Order of Druids in America (AODA) in 2003. AODA was founded in 1912, as part of a great wave of interest in occultism and alternative spirituality that's nearly forgotten today; when I joined it, after most of a decade as an active member of the Order of Bards Ovates and Druids (OBOD), it had fewer than a dozen members, and was on the verge of extinction. The elderly members who brought me into it and then made me its head hoped that I could rescue it, and fortunately—with a great deal of help from other people—their hopes were not misplaced.

As word spread in various odd corners of the American occult community that I had been elected AODA's seventh Grand Archdruid, however, something else began to happen. I was contacted repeatedly by an assortment of people, some of them members or former members of AODA or certain other organizations that shared longstanding ties with it, some of them with no connection to AODA I know of. What each of them had to say was some variation on

"Since you're now the Grand Archdruid, you ought to have this." What "this" included varied in each case, but usually centered on a collection of old documents from the early- to mid-twentieth century American occult scene, often but not always related to AODA or its sister orders.

The great majority of the material I received has never been published, and most of what was published is long out of print and difficult to obtain. It ranges across a dizzying spectrum of occult and esoteric traditions, from Druidry, through Hermetic and Rosicrucian occultism, to Gnostic and Essene teachings. All of it was passed on to the current Grand Archdruid of AODA when I stepped down in 2015, after twelve eventful and exhausting years. Some of what I received belongs to traditions that still exist, and in some cases copies have been quietly passed on to the current custodians of those traditions. Other parts belong to traditions that have apparently gone extinct, and I intend to publish these in due time.

To me, at least, the most intriguing thing I received in this profusion of material took the form of a thin stack of documents, mimeographed on flimsy onionskin paper, that belonged to a correspondence course in Druid occultism. The collection included portions of two lessons, neither of them complete, and exactly how they got into a stack of unrelated papers on Hermetic occultism I have no idea—the person who sent them to me didn't include a return address on the bulky manila envelope that brought them to me, or a cover letter inside. Each lesson included instructions to read certain sections of published books, as well as material set out in detail. The name of the course was The Dolmen Arch.

I have not been able to trace the course or the organization that sponsored it, but one clue followed promptly once I used search engines on distinctive passages: important parts of the course were either written by, or plagiarized from, William Walker Atkinson, one of the leading lights of American occultism around the turn of the last century. Atkinson wrote under a flurry of pen names. He was the "Yogi Ramacharaka" who wrote books on Hindu philosophy and breathing exercises, the "Theron Q. Dumont" who published books on mentalism and the powers of the mind, and the "Three Initiates" responsible for *The Kybalion*, still among the most popular works of occult philosophy today.

Two of Atkinson's books were included among the required reading for students of the correspondence course, and a great deal of the philosophical material in the course echoed the central themes, ideas, and idiosyncrasies of Atkinson's work. It is entirely possible that the correspondence course was issued by Atkinson himself, but it is at least as possible that the course's authors simply cribbed large sections of their text from him.

I found the material intriguing and its incomplete state frustrating. After brooding over the matter for some time, I decided to write a course following the lines sketched out by the fragmentary material that had come to me. Several of Atkinson's books and correspondence courses provided me with additional inspiration and raw material, and I also included rituals, exercises, and practices from the AODA teachings, which meshed smoothly with what I could extract from the fragmentary lessons. The result is not the original course; it's not even my best guess as to what the original course might have been—but it turned out to be a workable and effective system of training in old-fashioned Druid Revival occultism. In 2009, having completed the course of training myself, I began teaching it to students by correspondence. Once other calls on my time made it difficult for me to continue mentoring personal students in this material, I decided to publish it in book form.

The Dolmen Arch course is organized in seven lesson packets, each of which corresponds to a grade of initiation; the sheer volume of material (more than 200,000 words) has required its division into two volumes. The practical work of each of the first four grades takes at least three months to complete, while the three remaining grades will take somewhat longer. Students should expect to spend a short period every day in meditation and ritual practice, and a session of study once or twice a week, in order to take advantage of the material the course provides. The subjects covered include ritual, energy work, meditation, philosophy, the stories and symbolism of the Mabinogion, memory training, spiritual healing, and initiation.

I wish to thank, in closing, Dr. John Gilbert, who was instrumental in bringing me into the Ancient Order of Druids in America and introducing me to the half-forgotten and utterly fascinating world of traditional American occultism; Gordon Cooper, my successor as Grand Archdruid, whose ready help during my years in charge of AODA was as reliable as it was welcome, and whose willingness to step up to the Northern Chair when it was time for me to step down made what could have been a difficult transition much easier; my wife Sara, who served AODA as Grand Almoner, Archdruid of the East, and Archdruid of the West successively, and whose support was as essential to that as to everything else I've accomplished; and especially to the students who enrolled in the Dolmen Arch course during the years when I ran it by correspondence, and whose comments, criticisms, and unfailing enthusiasm were a constant inspiration to me. My thanks go with all.

John Michael Greer

GRADD Y NEWYDDIAN

THE GRADE OF THE NOVICE

INTRODUCTION
TO THE GRADE

ELCOME TO THE FIRST of the seven grades of the Dolmen Arch study course! You have been accepted into this first stage of the training offered in this course. If you devote the necessary time and effort to studying and practicing the material taught in this course, you may confidently expect to proceed step by step through its grades, learn its lessons, and complete the journey as an initiate of the Dolmen Arch.

Most of the material you will encounter in this and future lessons has never before been published. It is a reconstruction, from surviving fragments, of a course of study offered by an American Druid tradition in the early years of the twentieth century. In its original form, the study course consisted of mimeographed papers and a list of readings, and was fleshed out with oral instruction from teacher to student, given individually or in grove meetings.

Some of the practices given in this course have appeared in my book *The Druid Magic Handbook* (Weiser, 2008), but served a different purpose there, as elements in a system of practical magic; and in that book, they were also combined with material from other Druid Revival traditions. The versions of these practices in this course are different, as you will see, and their purpose is different as well: to serve as the curriculum for a Druid mystery school.

A mystery school is a means by which individuals may be assisted to awaken and experience their own individuality. You may wish to read over this sentence several times, for it expresses the heart and essence of all that is involved in this study course. Some mystery schools carry out this work in a setting of grand temples, ornate rituals of initiation, gorgeously clad hierophants, and complicated sequences of grades and levels. Others use much simpler means. In each case the goal is the same, and the means are simply those that are best suited to a given place, time, and set of circumstances.

Every culture around the world and throughout time, indeed, has had its own mystery schools. Among tribal peoples who make their living by hunting wild game and gathering wild plants, rites of initiation have always been much practiced, and all the most important of the traditional lore of any such tribe is only known to the initiates of its mysteries. As human societies grew more complex and explored different means of living in the world, secret knowledge and the rites of initiation that accompanied its transmission persisted and took on similar complexity and differentiation. Each of the ancient civilizations had its own mysteries and mystery teachings. Yet a common thread of wisdom united all these traditions; ancient writers spoke learnedly of teachings held in common by the mysteries of many lands, and it was no rare thing for the wise of one nation to travel abroad to receive the mystery teachings of another.

The ancient Druids were among those priesthoods who were famous in the ancient world for their mystery teachings, and the great Pythagoras, among the most influential teachers of the mysteries the world has known, is said to have traveled to Gaul and become an initiate of the Druid mysteries, after he had been initiated into those of Egypt, Babylon, and Greece. When the founders of the Druid Revival began their labors in the eighteenth century of our era, the connections between the Druid mysteries and those of other lands were explored and studied in as much detail as the available sources permitted, and this study played a vital role in shaping the renewed Druidry that rose out of the Revival. Today the Druid mysteries are among the living mystery traditions of the western world, and offer the aspirant an effective path to the awakening of the higher potentials of the self.

The Druid mysteries as presented in this course have their roots in a long history of past schools of thought. The teachings of the ancient Celtic Druids in their original form were lost forever when Rome's imperial expansion, followed by the spread of early and too often intolerant forms of Christianity, brought an end to Druidry as a living tradition among the Celts. Folklore and poesy in all the Celtic countries, however, are held by many scholars to have preserved many fragments of the ancient Druid lore. These fragments were zealously gathered up by the founders of the Druid Revival in the eighteenth and nineteenth centuries of our era.

The teachings of the ancient Druids, however, were considered by Greek and Roman scholars in ancient times to be very closely related to those of the

Pythagorean Brotherhood. This was a mystic order founded in the sixth century BCE by the same Pythagoras mentioned above, who was a brilliant mathematician as well as an initiate of the mystery schools of his time. The accounts of Pythagoras' life written in ancient times claim that he received his training and initiation in the temple schools of Egypt, and certainly the closest resemblance exists between the Pythagorean teachings and those of the Hermetic tradition, which was born in the Land of the Nile and drew substantially on its ancient wisdom.

The founders of the Druid Revival in the eighteenth century of the common era thus turned to the teachings of the Pythagoreans and the Neoplatonists, who derived much of their system from Pythagorean sources, and also from the *Corpus Hermeticum* and other Hermetic documents, to fill out the fragmentary teachings handed down to them from Celtic antiquity. The result was a coherent and effective method of inner development sharing much in common with other esoteric traditions of the West, but with a unique character of its own.

Different branches of the Druid Revival formulated their teachings in different ways. The study course to which this grade is an introduction has been adapted from one such formulation, which descends from a particular set of American Druid traditions originating in the first decades of the twentieth century. Those familiar with the occultism of that period will recognize many similarities, amounting in some cases to direct borrowings, between the material in this course and the lessons offered by some of the most respected American occult teachers of the time.

We are speaking now of the historical view of the subject, rather than the perspective of esoteric symbolism and tradition. The received traditions of Druidry, speaking from this latter standpoint, hold that the Druid teachings are one expression of a perennial wisdom as old as humanity itself. According to the creation myth recorded in *Barddas* by Iolo Morganwg, that indefatigable collector (and sometime "improver") of ancient Welsh lore, the Druid mystery teachings have their source in the Three Rays of Light beheld by Einigan the

Fig. 1. Three Rays of Light from Awen beheld by Einigan

Giant, the first of all created beings, in the beginning of time. Those three rays descended from Awen, the principle of creation that underlies all things, and so they contained all the wisdom that ever was or will be.

The wisdom in the Rays, according to the lore, was written by Einigan in the form of lineal marks on three rowan staves, and these, after Einigan's death, were found to have miraculously taken root in Einigan's skull and grown into living saplings, on which the teachings written by Einigan were partly visible and partly obscured. Menw the Old, who discovered the three staves, is said to have copied down such of the writing as could still be read, and this became the foundation of the Druid wisdom. This is clearly symbolism rather than history, but it reflects the undoubted fact that mystery teachings similar to those of the Druids can be found throughout the world and across the ages, witnesses to a common perception of spiritual truth.

Fig. 2. Title page of BARDDAS *(1862) by Iolo Morganwg*

If you have studied other Druid traditions, you will find many differences between the teachings you receive under the Dolmen Arch and what you have learned elsewhere. Like the similarities you will also find, these differences are not accidental, for the teachings of the Druid mysteries are not meant to satisfy idle curiosity about the Cosmos, or to provide abstract information. Nor is it required that you accept them by what is so often misnamed "faith," and might better be called blind opinion.

They have, instead, a practical purpose. If you become a student of this course, it will be your task to learn to see the world "as though" they were true—to accept the teachings as a perspective whereby to experience and understand the Cosmos and all that exists in it. It is immaterial whether or not you choose to believe the teachings; what matters is that you learn to use them.

This lesson packet contains seven instructional papers:

These papers may best be studied in the order given. The first six cover the practices and teachings you should plan on studying. The Completion Exercises for this grade, given in the final paper, are to be practiced only after you have finished working with the other papers.

It deserves repetition that the material in this grade is to be studied and practiced, not merely filed away for future reference. You will gain nothing out of the further lessons unless you complete the practical work given in this one. This will require you to set aside some time for practice every day—perhaps twenty minutes—as well as additional time for study one or two times a week.

You should also plan on keeping a practice journal during the time you spend working on the lessons of this grade. In your journal, record each practice you do, noting the date, time of day (a general time such as "evening" is sufficient), what you did, how well or poorly the practice went, and what if anything you learned from it.

Even given a willingness to perform daily practices, it will take you at least three months to do an adequate job of working with the exercises given in this lesson, and for most people, it will take longer. Take the lessons at whatever speed works best for you; it's much more productive to take your time and get the most from the course than to rush through and learn less.

Wishing you all the best in your journey on the Path of the Druid Mysteries,

 *John Michael Greer*

THE SEVEN CANTREFS

NE, THREE, AND SEVEN are the great symbolic numbers of the Druid tradition. One denotes the Law of One, which teaches that all things are One, sharing and participating in One Life. Three denotes the three creative principles or Three Rays of Light that proceed from the One. Seven denotes the fulfillment or permutation of the Three; if there are three factors—call them A, B, and C—the whole range of possibilities inherent in them, alone or in combination, is seven: A, B, C, AB, BC, AC, and ABC.

Seven is thus the number of completeness and wholeness. Mystery traditions from around the world teach that seven planets, principles, spirits, or rays symbolize the fullness of existence. By learning and using these sevenfold patterns, the initiate of the mysteries is able to grasp the fundamental patterns of being, and wield that knowledge in many practical ways. The tradition of Druid mystery teaching on which this course is based likewise uses a sevenfold symbolism, called the Seven Cantrefs.

In old Wales a *Cantref* (pronounced CAHN-trev) was part of a kingdom; the word means "a hundred towns," though this was a figure of speech rather than a strict definition. Several of the old Welsh kingdoms were divided into seven Cantrefs, and this may have inspired the founders of this system to use the symbolism of a kingdom of seven provinces for their map of the Cosmos.

The Seven Cantrefs can be understood as the seven basic modes of the One Life. They fall out naturally into two groups of three, with one as the bridge or transition between them. Traditionally, the first three are considered subjective, as they express the possibilities of the One Life as an immanent presence within each created being; the last three are traditionally considered objective, as they express the possibilities of the One Life as a transcendent presence surrounding and conditioning each created being. The fourth is the point of contact between these two modes of existence, and faces both ways.

These are the Seven Cantrefs:

The First Cantref: Awyr

This Cantref is symbolically situated in the eastern quarter of the world, the place where the sun rises, and this sense of light shines throughout the Cantref and its imagery. It is the Cantref of inspiration and illumination, of mind and consciousness. Morning, springtime, and every other image of newborn light and life

Fig. 3. The Cantref Awyr

correspond to this Cantref, and so does inspiration and illumination of every kind. Its symbol is a circle with a line extending up from its top. This represents light and air being born from the infinite potential of Spirit. Its name is pronounced AH-wur.

Among elements, it is Air.	Among planets, the Sun.
Among seasons, Spring.	Among directions, East.
Among times of day, morning.	Among colors, yellow.
Among beasts, the hawk.	Among trees, the birch.
Among gods, Hu the Mighty.	Among angels, Raphael.
Among days, Sunday.	Among powers, thought.
Among laws, the Law of Unity.	Among grades, Newyddian (Novice).

The Second Cantref: Dŵr

This Cantref is symbolically situated in the western quarter of the world, and the West in the Druid tradition has meanings not shared by other magical systems. It is the Cantref of growth, learning, and enlargement, as well as that of emotions and of all things watery. Wisdom in the old Celtic lore is symbolized

Fig. 4. The Cantref Dŵr

by a salmon who dwells in a sacred pool over which hazel branches hang, and through this symbol water has close symbolic connections to trees and other growing things. Its symbol is the triangle pointing down, representing water's downward movement. Its name is pronounced DOO-r.

Among elements, it is Water.

Among seasons, Autumn.

Among times of day, evening.

Among beasts, the salmon.

Among gods, Esus chief of tree-spirits.

Among days, Wednesday.

Among laws, the Law of Balance.

Among planets, Mercury.

Among directions, West.

Among colors, blue.

Among trees, the hazel.

Among angels, Gabriel.

Among powers, memory.

Among grades, Damcaniwr (Theoretician).

The Third Cantref: Ufel

This Cantref is symbolically situated in the southern quarter of the world, and it represents every force and factor that energizes and transforms, making the many into one. It teaches us that no barrier separates us from the creative energies that weave the world into being, just as no barrier separates our energies from their broader context in the universe around us. In the

Fig. 5. *The Cantref Ufel*

unawakened self, it is passion; in the awakened self, it is intentionality. Its symbol is the triangle pointing up, representing the upward movement of flame. Its name is pronounced IH-vel.

Among elements, it is Fire.

Among seasons, summer.

Among times of day, noon.

Among beasts, the stag.

Among gods, Sul of the Sun.

Among days, Tuesday.

Among laws, the Law of Polarity.

Among planets, Mars.

Among directions, South.

Among colors, red.

Among trees, the holly.

Among angels, Michael.

Among powers, will.

Among grades, Ymarferiwr (Practitioner).

The Fourth Cantref: Daear

This Cantref is the realm of manifestation, the firm material basis that allows the other elemental powers to take form in the universe of our experience. In the individual, it is the body, and every form of embodiment and structured manifestation. In nature, it takes the shape of soil and the other materials of Earth's surface; the realm of Earth's far depths belongs to the Fifth Cantref instead. The symbol of this Cantref is the creative circle of spirit with a line descending downward into manifestation. Its name is pronounced DYE-ar.

Fig. 6. The Cantref Daear

Among elements, Earth.	Among planets, Venus.
Among seasons, Winter.	Among directions, North.
Among times of day, midnight.	Among colors, green.
Among beasts, the bear.	Among trees, the apple.
Among gods, Elen of the roads.	Among angels, Uriel.
Among days, Friday.	Among powers, sensation.
Among laws, the Law of Causation.	Among grades, Athroniwr (Philosophizer).

The Fifth Cantref: Maen

This Cantref is the power of Spirit Below, the chthonic and telluric current, and its closest representation in the world of ordinary human experience is the deep places of the earth. The world that human beings inhabit consists of four overlapping spheres, one each of fire, air, water, and earth—the upper atmosphere corresponding to fire; the lower atmosphere to air; the seas, rivers, lakes and groundwater to water; and the solid crust of the planet, to earth. Below that lies a realm as alien to human life as the furthest reaches of outer space, a realm of unimaginable heat, pressure, and energy that drives the continents across the face of the planet and sets the land trembling with earthquakes. The symbol of this Cantref is the circle of Spirit with the cross of

Fig. 7. The Cantref Maen

balanced manifestation below it; in ritual practice, the plain circle of Spirit is used. Its name is pronounced MINE.

Among elements, Spirit Below.

Among seasons, time past.

Among times of day, night.

Among beasts, the white dragon.

Among gods, Cêd the Earth-mother.

Among days, Saturday.

Among laws, the Law of Vibration.

Among planets, Saturn.

Among directions, Below.

Among colors, orange.

Among trees, the yew.

Among angels, Sandalphon.

Among powers, intuition.

Among grades, Gwyddon y Ffordd (Loremaster of the Path).

The Sixth Cantref: Nef

This Cantref is the power of Spirit Above, the solar and celestial current, and its nearest representation in human terms is the universe beyond the limits of the earth. Just as the world we inhabit, with its four elemental spheres, stops a few miles below our feet where the earth's crust gives way to the mantle, it stops a few miles above our heads at the borders of space. Beyond

Fig. 8. The Cantref Nef

these are the vast reaches where stars and planets circle through the void. The symbol of this Cantref is the circle of Spirit with the cross of balanced manifestation above it; in practical work, it shares the same symbol as Spirit Below, the plain circle of Spirit. Its name is pronounced NEV.

Among elements, Spirit Above.

Among seasons, time to come.

Among times of day, day.

Among beasts, the red dragon.

Among gods, Celi the Hidden One.

Among days, Thursday.

Among planets, Jupiter.

Among directions, Above.

Among colors, purple.

Among trees, the oak.

Among angels, Metatron.

Among powers, inspiration.

Among laws, the Law of Correspondence.	Among grades, Gwyddon y Cylch (Loremaster of the Circle).

The Seventh Cantref: Byw

The Seventh and last Cantref represents the presence of life and spirit within everything in the world, including you and me. Where some religions see human beings as something set apart from the rest of the world and equally far from the divine, Druidry recognizes that human beings are part of one great reality, along with stones, trees, gods, and everything else there

Fig. 9. The Cantref Byw

is. The symbol of the Seventh Cantref is the circle of Spirit with the cross of balanced manifestation in its center; in practice, its symbol is nothing other than yourself. Its name is pronounced BE-oo.

Among elements, Spirit Within.	Among planets, the Moon.
Among seasons, eternity.	Among directions, Center.
Among times of day, this moment.	Among colors, white.
Among beasts, the human being.	Among trees, the mistletoe.
Among gods, Mabon.	Among angels, the guardian angel.
Among days, Monday.	Among powers, imagination.
Among laws, the Law of Circularity.	Among grades, Gwyddon Rhydd (Free Loremaster).

The Cantrefs and their correspondences have their own poetic logic, which will be found to differ from those of other systems of correspondence, such as are used in other mystery schools. This expresses an important truth. The correspondence that binds the First Cantref to yellow among colors, air among elements, and the Sun among the planets of ancient astrology, for example, is not negated by the fact that certain other systems relate the Sun to fire rather than air, and that still others assign to the Sun the color orange rather than yellow. Each traditional system of correspondence is a world unto itself, and debating the truth of a correspondence from one system against that of one from another is as futile as might be a debate between an Englishman, a Frenchman and a

German concerning whether the four-legged animal barking at all three is "a dog," "un chien," or "ein Hund."

In every school of the mysteries, symbols are paramount. The human mind can only grasp the meaning of things through symbols. Gaze upon a tree, and the image that appears in your mind is a symbol of the tree, not the tree itself; think about the tree, and your thoughts wield symbols as tools to craft more symbols in which your understanding of the tree clothes itself; know the tree in its essence, and you will grasp the truth that the tree in all its vibrant life and solidity is a symbol—one expression of Nwyfre, the One Life. Each of the Seven Cantrefs is a basic division of existence expressed in symbols. No one of the symbols assigned to the Cantrefs exhaust its meaning; rather, that meaning is to be grasped in a transrational fashion by meditation and other practices using the Cantrefs and their symbols.

You will be working with the Seven Cantrefs in many different ways in the months and years to come. For now, take some time each day to think through the Cantrefs. Try to understand the poetic logic that unites the correspondences, and make sure you commit to memory the names, colors, and directions of the Cantrefs, so that (for example) you know at once that the First Cantref corresponds to the East and the color yellow. It can be helpful to make a game of it: when you see anything yellow, for example, remind yourself of the Cantref and the direction to which it corresponds. Do the same with the other six colors. Add in other correspondences once you find that you can do this easily.

It is also useful to make time to observe the elements that correspond to the Cantrefs, and weave those into your unfolding grasp of the symbolism. Air, Fire, Water, and Earth surround us at every moment, and are also found within us: the breath of our lungs, the warmth of our bodies, the fluids that move through us and the earthy solidity of our bodies express the same four elements. Spirit Below, Spirit Above, and Spirit Within also surround and penetrate us at every moment, but we are less aware of them. For the time being, think of Spirit Below as the deep substance of the planet on which we live, distinct from the soil and stone of elemental Earth; think of Spirit Above as outer space, with its shining stars and wheeling lights, distinct from the winds and skies of elemental Air; and think of Spirit Within as the life force within you. You will gain a clearer sense of the three forms of Spirit as you progress in the course.

THE SPHERE OF PROTECTION

HE MYSTERY SCHOOLS of every age and nation have always taught ritual as one of the keys to wisdom and power, and the tradition of Druid philosophy and practice embodied in this course is no exception to this longstanding rule. As you proceed through the grades of the Dolmen Arch, you will learn a sequence of ritual workings that work with nwyfre, the One Life that flows through all lives, beginning with simple forms and proceeding step by step to more complex and powerful ones.

In pursuing these studies, two mistakes must be avoided. The first is the mistaken belief that rituals have power irrespective of the person who performs them. The second is the equally mistaken belief that rituals have no power at all.

The teaching of the mysteries has ever been that ritual forms are tools; like any other tool, they receive the force that passes through them from the workman who uses them; like any other tool, they direct that power to some definite end, with greater or lesser effectiveness depending on the skill with which the tool is designed and constructed.

In learning the art of ritual, you are in the position of an apprentice who must learn to use the tools of his trade. The wise master starts his apprentices on the simplest tools first, and proceeds to those more difficult to use in due time. Thus the ritual form assigned to students of this first grade of the Dolmen Arch is the simplest form of the Sphere of Protection, the fundamental ritual working of this system. The Sphere of Protection begins with a ceremonial act called the Elemental Cross, and ends with another called the Circulation of Light. These two you will learn in this grade; the remainder of the ritual, the Calling of the Elements, will be studied in the following grade.

Before you can begin the Elemental Cross, you will need to choose four names and symbols of spiritual power that, between them, define the universe for you. The traditional rule here is to choose two gods, one elder and one younger, and two goddesses, one elder and one younger. The two gods form a vertical axis, the elder above and the younger below; the two goddesses form a horizontal axis, the elder to the right and the younger to the left.

The Druid tradition has always held it as inviolable that individuals must be free to invoke the powers in whom they put their trust, by whatever names or symbols are appropriate to those powers. One whose faith is in the Welsh Druid gods might invoke Hu the Mighty, the high god of Welsh Druid tradition, above; Hesus, the chief of tree-spirits, who sits in the first fork of the sacred oak, below; Ceridwen, the old wise goddess of the sacred cauldron, to the right; and Niwalen, the young goddess of springtime greenery, to the left. One who reveres Irish deities might invoke the Dagda, Lugh, Danu, and Brigid instead, while a Christian Druid might choose, from among the saints specially revered by the old Celtic Church, St. Peter, St. John the Evangelist, St. Brigid, and St. Mary Magdalene. One who prefers to work with animal powers might invoke the Hawk above, the Bear below, the Stag to the right and the Salmon to the left. Another, who prefers impersonal symbols, might invoke the sky above, the land beneath, the fire to the right and the water to the left. All these and more are appropriate.

Once you have chosen the powers you will invoke, stand facing south with your feet parallel to one another, with the length of one of your feet between them. Divide your weight evenly between your feet, and bend your knees very slightly. Keep your spine upright but not stiff, as though you were suspended from the top of your head.

Standing in this position, you will make the same gestures as in the Christian sign of the Cross, but with different words, images, and intentions.[1] Perform the ritual as follows:

1. Touch your forehead, and say the name of the elder of the two gods, or the first of the four powers you've chosen to invoke: for example "Hu the Mighty, great Druid god." As you do this, imagine that the sun is far above your head, radiating golden light downwards toward you. See a ray of golden light descending to the crown of your head and passing within, to a point at the center of your head, where it forms a sphere of brilliant

---

1. I have suggested an alternative set of gestures, for those who find the sign of the Cross inappropriate, in my book *The Druid Magic Handbook*; you may use either set, depending on your preferences.

light a few inches across. Feel the warmth of the light radiating outwards through your head.

2. Draw your hand down to your solar plexus, the space just below where the two sides of your ribcage separate. Say the name of the younger god, or the second power: for example, "Hesus of the Oaks, chief of tree spirits." Meanwhile, imagine that the ray of golden light descends further, creating a second sphere of brilliant light at your solar plexus. From there, as you invoke your second power, the ray extends straight down through the midline of your body into the ground beneath you, extending all the way down to the heart of the Earth. Visualize this as a brilliant sphere of silvery-green light, the color of sunlight on moving water, as large and bright as the sun but located far below you.

3. Bring your hand up to heart level, and then out to your right shoulder, and say the name of the elder goddess, or the third power: for example, "Ceridwen the Wise, keeper of the cauldron." Imagine a second ray streaming out to the right from the sphere of light at your solar plexus, flowing through your right side in a straight line out to infinite distance. Hold this image as you invoke your third power.

4. Draw your hand across to your left shoulder, and say the name of the younger goddess, or the fourth power: for example, "Niwalen of the Flowers, child of spring." Imagine a third ray streaming out to the left from the sphere of light at your solar plexus, flowing through your left side and across the palm of your left hand in a straight line out to infinite distance. Hold this image as you invoke your fourth power.

5. Cross your hands over your chest, right over left, and say, "May the powers of nature bless and protect me, now and always." Here imagine two more rays of light streaming out from the sphere at your solar plexus. One of them goes straight ahead of you into infinite distance, the other straight out behind you into infinite distance. At this point the sphere of light in your solar plexus is the meeting place of six rays of light extending above, below, to your left, to your right, ahead of you, and behind you. Hold this image as you say the final invocation.

The Circulation of Light

As soon as you finish the Elemental Cross, pause, and be aware of the sphere of light at your solar plexus. Then imagine the sphere enlarging until it surrounds you on all sides, extending out as far as you choose. With practice, you can make this any space you decide to protect—a room, a building, a valley, a bioregion, the entire Earth—but to begin with, make it a sphere around ten feet across, centered on your solar plexus and surrounding you on all sides. Concentrate on the image of the sphere of light around you, and concentrate likewise on the idea that no hostile or unwanted influence can pass into the light from outside.

Once you have established this image solidly, the next step is to spin the sphere around you in three directions. The first circulation goes over your head, down in front of you, under your feet and up behind you. The second goes around from left to right in front, and from right to left behind you; the third goes from above down to your right, under your feet, and then up to your left to return to above you.

Begin these circulations with the first, up from behind and down from in front. Make the motion slow at first, and then gradually speed it up until the sphere is whirling around you in a blur of speed. As it spins, add the second circulation, around you in a clockwise motion. Imagine it moving slowly at first, then faster and faster, until the second rotation also becomes a blur of speed. Then add the third circulation, from above, down and to the right and from below, up and to your left, slowly at first again and then faster and faster, until you see yourself surrounded by a sphere of white light spinning in all directions at once. Imagine all three circulations reaching infinite speed, so that the sphere around you appears to be perfectly still.

At this point, close the ritual by crossing your arms in front of your chest and saying "I thank the powers for their blessings," or any other words of thanks you prefer.

Perform the Elemental Cross followed by the Circulation of Light once each day during the time you spend on this course. By the end of the first two weeks, you should have committed the entire rite to memory, so that you can perform it without having to refer to these instructions. Thereafter, concentrate on making the imagery as clear and intense as possible.

INTRODUCTION TO MEDITATION

THE PRACTICAL CORE of the system of training imparted by these lessons, and of the spirituality of the Druid Revival as a whole, is meditation. The methods of meditation practiced in the Druid mysteries, however, are not the same as those practiced in the mystery temples of the East. While many people in recent years have learned the art of meditation from Eastern schools, it is too rarely realized that the West has traditions of meditation of their own, and that these differ in important ways from those of the Orient.

At the heart of those differences stands a variance in attitudes toward the ordinary thinking mind. In most of the mystical traditions of the East, the mind is conceived as being the enemy of the spirit: "The mind is the slayer of the Real; slay thou the slayer." Accordingly, most Eastern meditative practices seek to silence the mind, by chanting sacred syllables, building up pictures in the imagination, or focusing on paradoxical statements such as the koans of Zen Buddhism.

The meditative ways of the West take a different path. They recognize that the mind can be the enemy of the spirit, but it need not be; disciplined and harnessed to the work of the spirit, it can become a powerful ally. Thus most Occidental traditions of meditation seek to train the thinking mind and not merely to silence it. From the standpoint of Druidry, the thinking mind is seen as a natural part of human existence, and like all things natural, it embodies a grand potential for good, if only it is used rightly. Meditation is the way of learning how to use it rightly.

Preliminaries for Meditation

Meditation begins when the mind enters a state of relaxed concentration. The word "relaxed" deserves special attention here. Too often, the word "concentration" suggests an inner struggle: teeth clenched, eyes narrowed, the whole body taut with useless tension. This is the opposite of the state that is to be reached here. A triad of the Druid mysteries explains the proper state:

> *Three keys to meditation: body without tension, breath without hurry, mind without distraction.*

Begin learning to reach this state by choosing a place to meditate that is quiet and sheltered from bright light. It may be outdoors or indoors, but in either case should not expose you to interruptions or disturbances. A chair with a straight back and a seat of such a height that you can rest your feet flat on the floor, while keeping your thighs level with the ground, is also needed, along with a clock or watch, placed so you can see it easily without moving your head.

Sit on the chair with your feet and knees together or parallel to one another, whichever you find most comfortable. Allow your back to straighten but do not stiffen it. Your hands rest on your thighs, and your head rises gently upwards as though a string fastened to the crown of your skull pulls upwards on it. Your eyes may be open or closed as you prefer; if open, they should look ahead of you but not focus on anything in particular. This is the posture for meditation that will be used throughout this course.

Exercise 1: Relaxation

Put yourself in the meditation position, and then spend ten minutes being aware of your physical body. Start at the soles of your feet, your contact point with the earth, and work your way slowly upward to the crown of your head. Take your time, and notice any tensions you feel. Don't try to force yourself to relax; simply be aware of each point of tension. Over time this simple act of awareness will dissolve your body's habitual tensions by making them conscious, and bringing up the rigid patterns of thought and emotion that form their foundations. Like so much in meditation, though, this process has to unfold at its own pace.

While you're doing this exercise, let your body become as still as possible. You may find yourself wanting to fidget and shift, but resist the temptation. Whenever your body starts itching, cramping, or reacting against stillness in some other way, simply be aware of it, without responding to it. These reactions often become very intrusive during the first month or so of meditation practice, but bear with them. They show you that you're getting past the levels of ordinary awareness. The discomforts you're feeling are actually present in your body all the time; you've simply learned not to notice them. Now that you can perceive them again, you can relax into them and let them go.

Exercise 2: Breathing

Do the first exercise ten minutes daily for one week, or until the posture starts to feel comfortable and balanced. At this point, bring in the next dimension of meditation practice, the dimension of breath. Start this phase of the practice by taking your meditation position and going through the first exercise quickly, as a way of settling into a comfortable and stable position. Then turn your attention to your breath. Draw in a deep breath, and expel it in a series of short puffs through pursed lips, as though you were blowing out a candle.

When every last puff of air is out of your lungs, hold the breath out while counting slowly and steadily from one to four. Then breathe in through your nose, smoothly and evenly, counting from one to four. Hold your breath in, counting from one to four; hold the breath in by keeping the chest and belly expanded, not by closing your throat. Breathe out through your nose, smoothly and evenly, again counting from one to four. Continue breathing at the same slow steady rhythm, counting in the same way, for ten minutes. The "puffing" breath is called the cleansing breath, and the rhythmic breath that follows it is called the fourfold breath. These are the first of a number of special breathing methods taught in this course.

While you're breathing, your thoughts will likely try to stray onto some other topic. Don't let them. Keep your attention on the rhythm of the breathing, the feeling of the air moving into and out of your lungs. Whenever you notice that you're thinking about something else, bring your attention gently back to your breathing. If your thoughts slip away again, bring them back again. With practice, you'll find it increasingly easy to keep your mind centered on the simple process of breathing, and at that point, the positive effects of meditation will start to show themselves.

Exercise 3: Meditation

Do the second preliminary exercise for ten minutes daily for one week, or until you start to achieve a state of mental clarity in the fourfold breath. At this point, bring in the third dimension of meditation, the dimension of mind, by proceeding to meditation itself.

The work of meditation begins with what the traditional Western meditation literature calls a theme—that is, a concept, symbol, or saying that you desire to understand more fully. The choice and sequence of themes for meditation is central to training in a mystery school. The themes to be used for your meditations will be discussed in the next paper in this lesson packet.

When you have selected your theme, sit down in the meditation posture, and spend a minute or two going through the first preliminary exercises, being aware of your body and its tensions. Then begin the fourfold breath, and continue it for five minutes by the clock. During these first steps, don't think about the theme, or for that matter anything else. Simply be aware of your body and its tensions, then of the rhythm of your breathing, and allow your mind to clear.

After five minutes, change from the fourfold breath to ordinary, slow breathing. Call the theme to mind, repeat it silently to yourself three times, and begin thinking about what it means. Consider the theme in a general way. Then, out of the various thoughts that come to mind as you think about the theme, choose one and follow it out step by step, thinking about its meaning and implications, taking it as far as you can.

As an example, let us suppose that you have taken the triad given earlier in this paper as a theme for meditation. After relaxing your body and stilling your thoughts, you call the triad to mind and repeat it silently to yourself three times. Then, with your body relaxed, your breath steady, and your mind focused, begin thinking about the triad. Go through it word by word, thinking about what each word means and how they relate to one another. Note any questions that the triad brings to mind, and when you feel ready, choose one of them and follow it out.

In the course of this meditation, let us suppose, you are struck by the figure of speech that describes states of body, breath and mind as "keys." What is a key? A device to open a lock. What are the locks that these keys open? What doors do those locks seal? What might lie beyond them? What might the author of the triad have meant by choosing the figure of speech he did, rather than some other? Think about these things with a focused mind for the duration of your meditation session, and then repeat the cleansing breath once more to end the meditation.

As you meditate, unless your mind is already well trained, your thoughts will likely wander from the theme again and again. Do not simply leave off and go back to the theme; instead, follow your thoughts back through their wanderings until you reach the point where they left the theme. Whenever your mind strays from the theme, bring it back up the track of wandering thoughts in this same way.

Let us say you chose the same figure of speech just referenced as a theme for meditation. Some minutes into your practice, you find that you are no longer thinking about keys in any sense, but instead about some unhappy memory from childhood—say, an experience at school. Instead of returning at once to your chosen theme, ask yourself what it was that started you thinking about that experience. You might discover that you had been thinking about the neighborhood of the school you attended at that time. What started you thinking about the neighborhood? You thought of a childhood friend named Tom, who lived there. What started you thinking of Tom? Another Tom, one of your fellow workers in your present employment. What brought that Tom to mind? His habit, a subject of much humor at your work, of losing his keys. With this memory, of course, you have returned to the theme.

This habit of retracing the flow of thought has at least two advantages. First of all, you will learn much about the workings of your mind, the flow of its thoughts and the sort of associative leaps it makes; this will be important to the work of future grades. Second, it develops the habit of returning to the theme, and with practice you'll find that your thoughts run back to the theme just as enthusiastically as they run away from it. Time and regular practice will shorten the distance they run, until eventually your mind learns to run straight ahead along the meanings and implications of a theme without veering from it at all.

During the time you spend on this grade, spend ten minutes meditating each day, following the five minutes of relaxation and breathing. You may not be able to make time for meditation every day, but be honest with yourself; there are few days in which fifteen minutes cannot be spared from other business. Like everything else, meditation is learnt through regular practice, and the more time you give to it, the richer will the results be.

You may find it easiest to set a specific time each day for your meditations—in the morning just before breakfast, for example, has proven very convenient for many students, as the cares of the day have not yet filled the mind. Whatever time you choose, plan on meditating at least five days out of every seven to begin with, and work up to a session every day as soon as possible.

THE MABINOGION:
PWYLL PRINCE OF DYFED

HE FOUR BRANCHES of the Mabinogion are among the great legacies of ancient Celtic literature. They were preserved along with other tales in two Welsh manuscripts of the Middle Ages, and a few fragments and references to them may be found in other works of the same age. Their origin and authorship remain unknown, but doubtless they date back long before the writing of the manuscript volumes that preserve them. In the Druid tradition from which these lessons derive, they were held to date in their original form from before the coming of Christianity to Britain, and to embody the deepest secrets of the Druid path.

The meaning of the collective title of these four linked tales, "The Four Branches of the Mabinogion"—*"Pedair Cainc Mabinogi"* in Welsh—remains a subject of controversy among scholars. In the old Druid Revival lore, however, the word *Mabinogi* is held to derive from two words, *Mabon* and *Og*. Mabon is the same as the *Maponus* recorded by the Romans, and its meaning is "son" or "child," while Og is the same as the *Ogmios* recorded by the Romans, the Sun-hero or Hercules of the Celts, who is also the god of eloquence. The Four Branches recount the life of one who begins as Mabon the marvelous child, and ends as Og the solar hero-god.

The Druid lore asserts further that these are titles rather than names, and that they—and indeed the Four Branches as a whole—map out the transformations of the human soul as it passes from its mortal state of repeated rebirth to its immortal condition of solar radiance. The central character of the Four Branches accordingly has two names; as Mabon he is called Pryderi, and as Og he is called Llew. Students familar with Welsh tradition will recall that in the legend of Taliesin, the central character is named Gwion before he passes through the initiatory ordeal of knowledge, death, and rebirth that makes him Taliesin, the great wizard-bard of Druid legend.

Such patterns may be found throughout Celtic myth and story. The teachings of the ancient Druids, according to tradition, were communicated in the form of teaching narratives that each student was caused to study and interpret for himself. In these modern Druid lessons, the same approach is preserved. It is your task in this grade, using the tools of meditation, to learn as much as you can from the First Branch of the Mabinogion, the tale of Pwyll Prince of Dyfed, which is also the story of the conception, birth, and childhood of Pryderi the Mabon.

This is best done in the following way. First, read through the tale itself several times, and familiarize yourself with its characters and events. Then, before you begin meditation, choose a theme from the beginning of the tale. Any phrase, sentence, image, name, or personage may serve as a theme, and you will find with practice that the more specific the theme, the more you will get from it.

When you begin the meditation, after relaxation and breathing, imagine the theme you have chosen in its setting in the tale. Supposing that you have chosen the name of Pwyll, which means "sense," "perception," or "intelligence," as your theme, begin by imagining Pwyll himself in his court at Arberth, surrounded by the chieftains of Dyfed. Make the image as lifelike and complete in your imagination as you can. Allow yourself to experience the scene as though you were there; see the colors, hear the voices, put every sense to its use. Then begin meditating on the name itself and its meanings. What are sense, perception, intelligence? What does it suggest to you that the central personage in the story should have this as his name?

As you proceed through the story, one theme after another, you will find that small details often open the door to important realizations. You will also find that the story has more than one set of meanings, and any given detail may itself have more than one meaning. The traditions of the Druid Revival teach that each of the ancient legends has three meanings: a bardic meaning, which describes the life and deeds of a hero or heroine of ancient times, and teaches wise conduct; an ovate meaning, which describes in symbolic form the cycles of the seasons and the heavens, and teaches the sciences that were known in the days of the ancient Druids; and a Druid meaning, which describes the transformations of the soul on its journey from ignorance to wisdom along the path of the mysteries, and teaches spirituality. Neither of these is higher or lower than any other, but they do form a sequence.

You may find it useful to explore each of the themes you choose with this division in mind. Still, do not expect to unravel the riddles of the Mabinogion at a single glance! There will doubtless be many sessions of meditation ahead of you in which you find yourself as baffled at the end of the session as you were at the beginning. These also have their value. Those themes that you do not understand at once are seeds; planted in your mind by the act of meditating on them, they will sprout and bear fruit in their proper season.

The version of the First Branch that follows is a slightly edited version of the English translation of Lady Charlotte Guest, which was used in the original form of these lessons; the details left out of this translation, due to the Victorian attitudes with which Lady

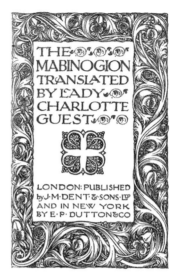

Fig. 10. Title page of Lady Charlotte Guest's translation of THE MABINOGION

Guest had to contend, have been restored. There are other translations, and if you prefer one of these you may certainly do so; if you have a knowledge of Welsh, of course, you may certainly use the original instead. However, it is not appropriate to perform this work with a novel based on the Mabinogion, such as those of Kenneth Morris or Evangeline Walton; these make enjoyable reading, but do not follow the original closely enough to be of value in the work that is before you.

Pwyll Prince of Dyfed

Pwyll,[2] Prince of Dyfed,[3] was lord of the seven Cantrefs of Dyfed; and once upon a time he was at Arberth[4] his chief palace, and he was minded to go and hunt, and the part of his dominions in which it pleased him to hunt was Glyn

---

2. *Pwyll*: "Sense," "Perception," or "Intelligence."

3. *Dyfed*: the westernmost part of south Wales. Notice how the action of this Branch proceeds toward the east.

4. *Arberth*: "Above the Hedge." Cf. *Gwent-ys-Coed* further on, "Gwent below the forest."

Cuch.[5] So he set forth from Arberth that night, and went as far as Llwyn Di-arwyd.[6] And that night he tarried there, and early on the morrow he rose and came to Glyn Cuch; when he let loose the dogs in the wood and sounded the horn, and began the chase. And as he followed the dogs, he lost his companions; and whilst he listened to the hounds, he heard the cry of other hounds, a cry different from his own, and coming in the opposite direction.

And he beheld a glade in the wood forming a level plain, and as his dogs came to the edge of the glade, he saw a stag before the other dogs. And lo, as it reached the middle of the glade, the dogs that followed the stag overtook it and brought it down. Then looked he at the color of the dogs, staying not to look at the stag, and of all the hounds that he had seen in the world, he had never seen any that were like unto these. For their hair was of a brilliant shining white, and their ears were red; and as the whiteness of their bodies shone, so did the redness of their ears glisten. And he came towards the dogs, and drove away those that had brought down the stag, and set his own dogs upon it.

And as he was setting on his dogs he saw a horseman coming towards him upon a large light-grey steed, with a hunting horn round his neck, and clad in garments of grey woollen in the fashion of a hunting garb. And the horseman drew near and spoke unto him thus.

"Chieftain," said he, "I know who thou art, and I greet thee not."

"Peradventure," said Pwyll, "thou art of such dignity that thou shouldest not do so."

"Verily," answered he, "it is not my dignity that prevents me."

"What is it then, O Chieftain?" asked he.

"By Heaven, it is by reason of thine own ignorance and want of courtesy."

"What discourtesy, Chieftain, hast thou seen in me?"

"Greater discourtesy saw I never in man," said he, "than to drive away the dogs that were killing the stag and to set upon it thine own. This was discourteous, and though I may not be revenged upon thee, yet I declare to Heaven that I will do thee more dishonour than the value of an hundred stags."

"O Chieftain," he replied, "if I have done ill I will redeem thy friendship."

"How wilt thou redeem it?"

"According as thy dignity may be, but I know not who thou art?"

"A crowned King am I in the land whence I come."

---

5. *Glyn Cuch*: "Scowl Valley."

6. *Llyn Diarwyd*: "Grove without Vice."

"Lord," said he, "may the day prosper with thee, and from what land comest thou?"

"From Annwn,"[7] answered he; "Arawn,[8] a King of Annwn, am I."

"Lord," said he, "how may I gain thy friendship?"

"After this manner mayest thou," he said. "There is a man whose dominions are opposite to mine, who is ever warring against me, and he is Hafgan,[9] a King of Annwn, and by ridding me of this oppression, which thou canst easily do, shalt thou gain my friendship."

"Gladly will I do this," said he. "Show me how I may."

"I will show thee. Behold thus it is thou mayest. I will make firm friendship with thee; and this will I do. I will send thee to Annwn in my stead, and I will give thee the fairest lady thou didst ever behold to be thy companion, and I will put my form and semblance upon thee, so that not a page of the chamber, nor an officer, nor any other man that has always followed me shall know that it is not I. And this shall be for the space of a year from tomorrow, and then we will meet in this place."

"Yes," said he; "but when I shall have been there for the space of a year, by what means shall I discover him of whom thou speakest?"

"One year from this night," he answered, "is the time fixed between him and me that we should meet at the Ford; be thou there in my likeness, and with one stroke that thou givest him, he shall no longer live. And if he ask thee to give him another, give it not, how much soever he may entreat thee, for when I did so, he fought with me next day as well as ever before."

"Verily," said Pwyll, "what shall I do concerning my kingdom?"

Said Arawn, "I will cause that no one in all thy dominions, neither man nor woman, shall know that I am not thou, and I will go there in thy stead."

"Gladly then," said Pwyll, "will I set forward."

"Clear shall be thy path and nothing shall detain thee, until thou come into my dominions, and I myself will be thy guide!"

So he conducted him until he came in sight of the palace and its dwellings. "Behold," said he, "the Court and the kingdom in thy power. Enter the Court, there is no one there who will know thee, and when thou seest what service is done there, thou wilt know the customs of the Court."

---

7. *Annwn*: "Unworld," the Welsh land of the dead.

8. *Arawn*: from *ar*, "ploughed land, ground," and *awen*, the spirit of inspiration.

9. *Hafgan*: "Summer White."

So he went forward to the Court, and when he came there, he beheld sleeping-rooms, and halls, and chambers, and the most beautiful buildings ever seen. And he went into the hall to disarray, and there came youths and pages and disarrayed him, and all as they entered saluted him. And two knights came and drew his hunting dress from about him, and clothed him in a vesture of silk and gold. And the hall was prepared, and behold he saw the household and the host enter in, and the host was the most comely and the best equipped that he had ever seen. And with them came in likewise the Queen, who was the fairest woman that he had ever yet beheld. And she had on a yellow robe of shining satin; and they washed and went to the table, and sat, the Queen upon one side of him, and one who seemed to be an Earl on the other side.

And he began to speak with the Queen, and he thought, from her speech, that she was the seemliest and most noble lady of converse and of cheer that ever was. And they partook of meat, and drink, with songs and with feasting; and of all the Courts upon the earth, behold this was the best supplied with food and drink, and vessels of gold and royal jewels.

And when it came time for sleep, Pwyll and the Queen went to bed, and no sooner had they come unto the bed but he turned his face to the wall and his back to the Queen, nor spoke he another word to her until daybreak. The next day all was tenderness and affection between them, but however kindly the day was spent, not a single night during that year did he spend in other wise than the first.

And the year he spent in hunting, and minstrelsy, and feasting, and diversions, and discourse with his companions until the night that was fixed for the conflict. And when that night came, it was remembered even by those who lived in the furthest part of his dominions, and he went to the meeting and the nobles of the kingdom with him. And when he came to the Ford, a knight arose and spake thus.

"Lords," said he, "listen well. It is between two Kings that this meeting is, and between them only. Each claimeth of the other his land and territory, and do all of you stand aside and leave the fight to be between them."

Thereupon the two Kings approached each other in the middle of the Ford, and encountered, and at the first thrust, the man who was in the stead of Arawn struck Hafgan on the center of the boss of his shield, so that it was cloven in twain, and his armour was broken, and Hafgan himself was borne to the ground an arm's and a spear's length over the crupper of his horse, and he received a deadly blow.

"O Chieftain," said Hafgan, "what right hast thou to cause my death? I was not injuring thee in anything, and I know not wherefore thou wouldest slay me. But, for the love of Heaven, since thou hast begun to slay me, complete thy work."

"Ah, Chieftain," he replied, "I may yet repent doing that unto thee, slay thee who may, I will not do so."

"My trusty Lords," said Hafgan, "bear me hence. My death has come. I shall be no more able to uphold you."

"My Nobles," also said he who was in the semblance of Arawn, "take counsel and know who ought to be my subjects."

"Lord," said the nobles, "all should be, for there is no King over the whole of Annwn but thee."

"Yes," he replied, "it is right that he who comes humbly should be received graciously, but he that doth not come with obedience, shall be compelled by the force of swords." And thereupon he received the homage of the men, and he began to conquer the country; and the next day by noon the two kingdoms were in his power. And thereupon he went to keep his tryst, and came to Glyn Cuch.

And when he came there, the King of Annwn was there to meet him, and each of them was rejoiced to see the other.

"Verily," said Arawn, "may Heaven reward thee for thy friendship towards me, I have heard of it. When thou comest thyself to thy dominions," said he, "thou wilt see that which I have done for thee."

"Whatever thou hast done for me, may Heaven repay it thee."

Then Arawn gave to Pwyll Prince of Dyfed his proper form and semblance, and he himself took his own; and Arawn set forth towards the Court of Annwn; and he was rejoiced when he beheld his hosts, and his household, whom he had not seen so long; but they had not known of his absence, and wondered no more at his coming than usual. And that day was spent in joy and merriment; and he sat and conversed with his wife and his nobles. And when it was time for them rather to sleep than to carouse, they went to rest. And when Arawn and his Queen had come unto the bed, at once he began to speak to her, to hold her and to caress her as husband ought.

Not for a year had she been so treated, and she thought to herself, "By heaven, how otherwise is he this night than heretofore."

Long she thought, and when he woke and spoke to her once, again, and yet a third time, she made no answer.

"Why is it," he asked, "that you answer me not?"

"I tell you," said she, "that for twelvemonth I have spoken no word here."

"Wherefore not, as we have always spoken together in bed?"

"May shame be upon me," said she, "if since twelvemonth from yester night this bed hath witnessed speech or tenderness betwixt us, nor so much as your turning your face toward me."

Then Arawn bethought himself, "By heaven, a faithful comrade indeed did I take for a friend!" Then to his wife he said, "Lady, blame me not, for this twelvemonth past I have not lain or slept beside you."

And he related to her the whole, and she said, "May Heaven witness that it was a firm fellowship indeed, for your friend to have overcome temptation and so kept faith with you."

"That indeed was my thought, Lady," said he, "when I spoke not."

"I wonder not," said she.

Pwyll Prince of Dyfed came likewise to his country and dominions, and began to inquire of the nobles of the land, how his rule had been during the past year, compared with what it had been before.

"Lord," said they, "thy wisdom was never so great, and thou wast never so kind or so free in bestowing thy gifts, and thy justice was never more worthily seen than in this year."

"By heaven," said he, "for all the good you have enjoyed, you should thank him who hath been with you; for behold, thus hath this matter been." And thereupon Pwyll related the whole unto them.

"Verily, Lord," said they, "render thanks unto Heaven that thou hast such a fellowship, and withhold not from us the rule which we have enjoyed for this year past."

"I take Heaven to witness that I will not withhold it," answered Pwyll.

And thenceforth they made strong the friendship that was between them, and each sent unto the other horses, and greyhounds, and hawks, and all such jewels as they thought would be pleasing to each other. And by reason of his having dwelt that year in Annwn, and having ruled there so prosperously, and united the two kingdoms in one day by his valour and prowess, he lost the name of Pwyll Prince of Dyfed, and was called Pwyll Chief of Annwn from that time forward.

Once upon a time, Pwyll was at Arberth his chief palace, where a feast had been prepared for him, and with him was a great host of men. And after the first meal, Pwyll arose to walk, and he went to the top of a mound that was above the palace, and was called Gorsedd Arberth.[10]

"Lord," said one of the Court, "it is peculiar to the mound that whosoever sits upon it cannot go thence, without either receiving wounds or blows, or else seeing a wonder."

"I fear not to receive wounds and blows in the midst of such a host as this, but as to the wonder, gladly would I see it. I will go therefore and sit upon the mound."

And upon the mound he sat. And while he sat there, they saw a lady, on a pure white horse of large size, with a garment of shining gold around her, coming along the highway that led from the mound; and the horse seemed to move at a slow and even pace, and to be coming up towards the mound.

"My men," said Pwyll, "is there any among you who knows yonder lady?"

"There is not, Lord," said they.

"Go one of you and meet her, that we may know who she is."

And one of them arose, and as he came upon the road to meet her, she passed by, and he followed as fast as he could, being on foot; and the greater was his speed, the further was she from him. And when he saw that it profited him nothing to follow her, he returned to Pwyll, and said unto him, "Lord, it is idle for any one in the world to follow her on foot."

"Verily," said Pwyll, "go unto the palace, and take the fleetest horse that thou seest, and go after her."

And he took a horse and went forward. And he came to an open level plain, and put spurs to his horse; and the more he urged his horse, the further was she from him. Yet she held the same pace as at first. And his horse began to fail; and when his horse's feet failed him, he returned to the place where Pwyll was. "Lord," said he, "it will avail nothing for any one to follow yonder lady. I know of no horse in these realms swifter than this, and it availed me not to pursue her."

"Of a truth," said Pwyll, "there must be some illusion here. Let us go towards the palace." So to the palace they went, and they spent that day. And the next day they arose, and that also they spent until it was time to go to meat. And after the first meal, "Verily," said Pwyll, "we will go the same party as yesterday to the top of the mound. And do thou," said he to one of his young men, "take

---

10. *Gorsedd Arberth*: "High Seat of Arberth."

the swiftest horse that thou knowest in the field." And thus did the young man. And they went towards the mound, taking the horse with them.

And as they were sitting down they beheld the lady on the same horse, and in the same apparel, coming along the same road.

"Behold," said Pwyll, "here is the lady of yesterday. Make ready, youth, to learn who she is."

"My Lord," said he, "that will I gladly do." And thereupon the lady came opposite to them. So the youth mounted his horse; and before he had settled himself in his saddle, she passed by, and there was a clear space between them. But her speed was no greater than it had been the day before. Then he put his horse into an amble, and thought that notwithstanding the gentle pace at which his horse went, he should soon overtake her. But this availed him not; so he gave his horse the reins. And still he came no nearer to her than when he went at a foot's pace. And the more he urged his horse, the further was she from him. Yet she rode not faster than before. When he saw that it availed not to follow her, he returned to the place where Pwyll was.

"Lord," said he, "the horse can no more than thou hast seen."

"I see indeed that it avails not that any one should follow her. And by Heaven," said he, "she must needs have an errand to some one in this plain, if her haste would allow her to declare it. Let us go back to the palace." And to the palace they went, and they spent that night in songs and feasting, as it pleased them.

And the next day they amused themselves until it was time to go to meat. And when meat was ended, Pwyll said, "Where are the hosts that went yesterday and the day before to the top of the mound?"

"Behold, Lord, we are here," said they.

"Let us go," said he, "to the mound, to sit there. And do thou," said he to the page who tended his horse, "saddle my horse well, and hasten with him to the road, and bring also my spurs with thee." And the youth did thus.

And they went and sat upon the mound; and ere they had been there but a short time, they beheld the lady coming by the same road, and in the same manner, and at the same pace.

"Young man," said Pwyll, "I see the lady coming; give me my horse." And no sooner had he mounted his horse than she passed him. And he turned after her and followed her. And he let his horse go bounding playfully, and thought that at the second step or the third he should come up with her. But he came no

Fig. 11. The Mabinogion • Pwyll Beholds Rhiannon from Afar

nearer to her than at first. Then he urged his horse to his utmost speed, yet he found that it availed nothing to follow her.

Then said Pwyll, "O maiden, for the sake of him whom thou best lovest, stay for me."

"I will stay gladly," said she, "and it were better for thy horse hadst thou asked it long since." So the maiden stopped, and she threw back that part of her head dress which covered her face. And she fixed her eyes upon him, and began to talk with him.

"Lady," asked he, "whence comest thou, and whereunto dost thou journey?"

"I journey on mine own errand," said she, "and right glad am I to see thee."

"My greeting be unto thee," said he. Then he thought that the beauty of all the maidens, and all the ladies that he had ever seen, was as nothing compared to her beauty.

"Lady," he said, "wilt thou tell me aught concerning thy purpose?"

"I will tell thee," said she. "My chief quest was to seek thee."

"Behold," said Pwyll, "this is to me the most pleasing quest on which thou couldst have come; and wilt thou tell me who thou art?"

"I will tell thee, Lord," said she, "I am Rhiannon,[11] the daughter of Hefeydd Hen,[12] and they sought to give me to a husband against my will. But no husband would I have, and that because of my love for thee, neither will I yet have one unless thou reject me. And hither have I come to hear thy answer."

"By Heaven," said Pwyll, "behold this is my answer. If I might choose among all the ladies and damsels in the world, thee would I choose."

"Verily," said she, "if thou art thus minded, make a pledge to meet me ere I am given to another."

"The sooner I may do so, the more pleasing will it be unto me," said Pwyll, "and wheresoever thou wilt, there will I meet with thee."

"I will that thou meet me this day twelvemonth at the palace of Hefeydd. And I will cause a feast to be prepared, so that it be ready against thou come."

"Gladly," said he, "will I keep this tryst."

"Lord," said she, "remain in health, and be mindful that thou keep thy promise; and now will I go hence." So they parted, and he went back to his hosts and to them of his household. And whatsoever questions they asked him respecting the damsel, he always turned the discourse upon other matters.

---

11. *Rhiannon*: from *rhiain*, "maiden."

12. *Hefeydd Hen*: from *haf*, "summer," and *hen*, "old."

And when a year from that time was gone, he caused a hundred knights to equip themselves and to go with him to the palace of Hefeydd Hen. And he came to the palace, and there was great joy concerning him, with much concourse of people and great rejoicing, and vast preparations for his coming. And the whole Court was placed under his orders.

And the hall was garnished and they went to meat, and thus did they sit; Hefeydd Hen was on one side of Pwyll, and Rhiannon on the other. And all the rest according to their rank. And they ate and feasted and talked one with another, and at the beginning of the carousal after the meat, there entered a tall auburn-haired youth, of royal bearing, clothed in a garment of satin. And when he came into the hall, he saluted Pwyll and his companions.

"The greeting of Heaven be unto thee, my soul," said Pwyll, "come thou and sit down."

"Nay," said he, "a suitor am I, and I will do mine errand."

"Do so willingly," said Pwyll.

"Lord," said he, "my errand is unto thee, and it is to crave a boon of thee that I come."

"What boon soever thou mayest ask of me, as far as I am able, thou shalt have."

"Ah," said Rhiannon, "wherefore didst thou give that answer?"

"Has he not given it before the presence of these nobles?" asked the youth.

"My soul," said Pwyll, "what is the boon thou askest?"

"The lady whom best I love is to be thy bride this night; I come to ask her of thee, with the feast and the banquet that are in this place."

And Pwyll was silent because of the answer which he had given.

"Be silent as long as thou wilt," said Rhiannon. "Never did man make worse use of his wits than thou hast done."

"Lady," said he, "I knew not who he was."

"Behold this is the man to whom they would have given me against my will," said she. "And he is Gwawl the son of Clud,[13] a man of great power and wealth, and because of the word thou hast spoken, bestow me upon him lest shame befall thee."

"Lady," said he, "I understand not thine answer. Never can I do as thou sayest."

"Bestow me upon him," said she, "and I will cause that I shall never be his."

---

13. *Gwawl son of Clud*: "Radiance son of Burden."

"By what means will that be?" asked Pwyll.

"In thy hand will I give thee a small bag," said she. "See that thou keep it well, and he will ask of thee the banquet, and the feast, and the preparations which are not in thy power. Unto the hosts and the household will I give the feast. And such will be thy answer respecting this. And as concerns myself, I will engage to become his bride this night twelvemonth. And at the end of the year be thou here," said she, "and bring this bag with thee, and let thy hundred knights be in the orchard up yonder. And when he is in the midst of joy and feasting, come thou in by thyself, clad in ragged garments, and holding thy bag in thy hand, and ask nothing but a bagful of food, and I will cause that if all the meat and liquor that are in these seven Cantrefs were put into it, it would be no fuller than before. And after a great deal has been put therein, he will ask thee whether thy bag will ever be full. Say thou then that it never will, until a man of noble birth and of great wealth arise and press the food in the bag with both his feet, saying, 'Enough has been put therein;' and I will cause him to go and tread down the food in the bag, and when he does so, turn thou the bag, so that he shall be up over his head in it, and then slip a knot upon the thongs of the bag. Let there be also a good bugle horn about thy neck, and as soon as thou hast bound him in the bag, wind thy horn, and let it be a signal between thee and thy knights. And when they hear the sound of the horn, let them come down upon the palace."

"Lord," said Gwawl, "it is meet that I have an answer to my request."

"As much of that thou hast asked as it is in my power to give, thou shalt have," replied Pwyll.

"My soul," said Rhiannon unto him, "as for the feast and the banquet that are here, I have bestowed them upon the men of Dyfed, and the household, and the warriors that are with us. These can I not suffer to be given to any. In a year from tonight a banquet shall be prepared for thee in this palace, that I may become thy bride."

So Gwawl went forth to his possessions, and Pwyll went also back to Dyfed. And they both spent that year until it was the time for the feast at the palace of Hefeydd Hen. Then Gwawl the son of Clud set out to the feast that was prepared for him, and he came to the palace, and was received there with rejoicing. Pwyll, also, the chief of Annwn, came to the orchard with his hundred knights, as Rhiannon had commanded him, having the bag with him. And Pwyll was clad in coarse and ragged garments, and wore large clumsy old shoes upon his feet. And when he knew that the carousal after the meat had begun, he went towards the hall, and when he came into the hall, he saluted Gwawl the son of Clud, and his company, both men and women.

"Heaven prosper thee," said Gwawl, "and the greeting of Heaven be unto thee."

"Lord," said he, "may heaven reward thee, I have an errand unto thee."

"Welcome be thine errand, and if thou ask of me that which is just, thou shalt have it gladly."

"It is fitting," answered he. "I crave but from want, and the boon that I ask is to have this small bag that thou seest filled with meat."

"A request within reason is this," said he, "and gladly shalt thou have it. Bring him food." A great number of attendants arose and began to fill the bag, but for all that they put into it, it was no fuller than at first.

"My soul," said Gwawl, "will thy bag be ever full?"

"It will not, I declare to Heaven," said he, "for all that may be put into it, unless one possessed of lands, and domains, and treasure, shall arise and tread down with both his feet the food that is within the bag, and shall say, 'Enough has been put herein.'"

Then said Rhiannon unto Gwawl the son of Clud, "Rise up quickly."

"I will willingly arise," said he. So he rose up, and put his two feet into the bag. And Pwyll turned up the sides of the bag, so that Gwawl was over his head in it. And he shut it up quickly and slipped a knot upon the thongs, and blew his horn. And thereupon behold his household came down upon the palace. And they seized all the host that had come with Gwawl, and cast them into his own prison. And Pwyll threw off his rags, and his old shoes, and his tattered array; and as they came in, every one of Pwyll's knights struck a blow upon the bag, and asked, "What is here?"

"A badger," said they. And in this manner they played, each of them striking the bag, either with his foot or with a staff. And thus played they with the bag.

Every one as he came in asked, "What game are you playing at thus?"

"The game of Badger in the Bag," said they. And then was the game of Badger in the Bag first played.

"Lord," said the man in the bag, "if thou wouldest but hear me, I merit not to be slain in a bag."

Said Hefeydd Hen, "Lord, he speaks truth. It were fitting that thou listen to him, for he deserves not this."

"Verily," said Pwyll, " I will do thy counsel concerning him."

"Behold this is my counsel then," said Rhiannon; "thou art now in a position in which it behoves thee to satisfy suitors and minstrels, let him give unto them in thy stead, and take a pledge from him that he will never seek to revenge that which has been done to him. And this will be punishment enough."

"I will do this gladly," said the man in the bag.

"And gladly will I accept it," said Pwyll, "since it is the counsel of Hefeydd and Rhiannon."

"Such then is our counsel," answered they.

"I accept it," said Pwyll. "Seek thyself sureties."

"We will be for him," said Hefeydd, "until his men be free to answer for him." And upon this he was let out of the bag, and his liegemen were liberated.

"Demand now of Gwawl his sureties," said Hefeydd, "we know which should be taken for him." And Hefeydd numbered the sureties.

Said Gwawl, "Do thou thyself draw up the covenant."

"It will suffice me that it be as Rhiannon said," answered Pwyll. So unto that covenant were the sureties pledged.

"Verily, Lord," said Gwawl, "I am greatly hurt, and I have many bruises. I have need to be anointed, with thy leave I will go forth. I will leave nobles in my stead, to answer for me in all that thou shalt require."

"Willingly," said Pwyll, "mayest thou do thus." So Gwawl went towards his own possessions.

And the hall was set in order for Pwyll and the men of his host, and for them also of the palace, and they went to the tables and sat down. And as they had sat that time twelvemonth, so sat they that night. And they ate, and feasted, and spent the night in mirth and tranquillity. And the time came that they should sleep, and Pwyll and Rhiannon went to their chamber and spent the night as befits husband and wife.

And next morning at the break of day, "My Lord," said Rhiannon, "arise and begin to give thy gifts unto the minstrels. Refuse no one today that may claim thy bounty."

"Thus shall it be gladly," said Pwyll, "both today and every day while the feast shall last." So Pwyll arose, and he caused silence to be proclaimed, and desired all the suitors and the minstrels to show and to point out what gifts were to their wish and desire. And this being done, the feast went on, and he denied no one while it lasted. And when the feast was ended, Pwyll said unto Hefeydd, "My Lord, with thy permission I will set out for Dyfed tomorrow."

"Certainly," said Hefeydd, "may Heaven prosper thee. Fix also a time when Rhiannon may follow thee."

"By Heaven," said Pwyll, "we will go hence together."

"Willest thou this, Lord?" said Hefeydd.

"Yes, by Heaven," answered Pwyll.

And the next day, they set forward towards Dyfed, and journeyed to the palace of Narberth, where a feast was made ready for them. And there came to them great numbers of the chief men and the most noble ladies of the land, and of these there was none to whom Rhiannon did not give some rich gift, either a bracelet, or a ring, or a precious stone. And they ruled the land prosperously both that year and the next.

And in the third year the nobles of the land began to be sorrowful at seeing a man whom they loved so much, and who was moreover their lord and their foster-brother, without an heir. And they came to him. And the place where they met was Preseleu,[14] in Dyfed.

"Lord," said they, "we know that thou art not so young as some of the men of this country, and we fear that thou mayest not have an heir of the wife whom thou hast taken. Take therefore another wife of whom thou mayest have heirs. Thou canst not always continue with us, and though thou desire to remain as thou art, we will not suffer thee."

"Truly," said Pwyll, "we have not long been joined together, and many things may yet befall. Grant me a year from this time, and for the space of a year we will abide together, and after that I will do according to your wishes." So they granted it.

And before the end of a year a son was born unto him. And in Arberth was he born; and on the night that he was born, women were brought to watch the mother and the boy. And the women slept, as did also Rhiannon, the mother of the boy. And the number of the women that were brought into the chamber was six. And they watched for a good portion of the night, and before midnight every one of them fell asleep, and towards break of day they awoke; and when they awoke, they looked where they had put the boy, and behold he was not there.

"Oh," said one of the women, "the boy is lost!"

"Yes," said another, "and it will be small vengeance if we are burnt or put to death because of the child."

---

14. This is Prescelly, a site of ancient sanctity, and the source of the Stonehenge bluestones.

Said one of the women, "Is there any counsel for us in the world in this matter ?"

"There is," answered another, "I offer you good counsel."

"What is that?" asked they.

"There is here a staghound bitch, and she has a litter of whelps. Let us kill some of the cubs, and rub the blood on the face and hands of Rhiannon, and lay the bones before her, and assert that she herself hath devoured her son, and she alone will not be able to gainsay us six." And according to this counsel it was settled.

And towards morning Rhiannon awoke, and she said, "Women, where is my son?"

"Lady," said they, "ask us not concerning thy son, we have nought but the blows and the bruises we got by struggling with thee, and of a truth we never saw any woman so violent as thou, for it was of no avail to contend with thee. Hast thou not thyself devoured thy son? Claim him not therefore of us."

"For pity's sake," said Rhiannon; "the Lord God knows all things. Charge me not falsely. If you tell me this from fear, I assert before Heaven that I will defend you."

"Truly," said they, "we would not bring evil on ourselves for anyone in the world."

"For pity's sake," said Rhiannon, "you will receive no evil by telling the truth." But for all her words, whether fair or harsh, she received but the same answer from the women.

And Pwyll the chief of Annwn arose, and his household, and his hosts. And this occurrence could not be concealed, but the story went forth throughout the land, and all the nobles heard it. Then the nobles came to Pwyll, and besought him to put away his wife, because of the great crime which she had done.

But Pwyll answered them, that they had no cause wherefore they might ask him to put away his wife, save for her having no children. "But children has she now had, therefore will I not put her away; if she has done wrong, let her do penance for it."

So Rhiannon sent for the teachers and the wise men, and as she preferred doing penance to contending with the women, she took upon her a penance. And the penance that was imposed upon her was, that she should remain in that palace of Arberth until the end of seven years, and that she should sit, every day near unto a horseblock that was without the gate. And that she should relate the story to all who should come there, whom she might suppose not to know it already; and that she should offer the guests and strangers, if they would permit her, to carry them upon her back into the palace. But it rarely happened that any would permit. And thus did she spend part of the year.

Now at that time Teyrnon Twryf Liant[15] was lord of Gwent-ys-Coed,[16] and he was the best man in the world. And unto his house there belonged a mare, than which neither mare nor horse in the kingdom was more beautiful. And on the night of every first of May she foaled, and no one ever knew what became of the colt.

And one night Teyrnon talked with his wife: "Wife," said he, "it is very simple of us that our mare should foal every year, and that we should have none of her colts."

"What can be done in the matter?" said she.

"This is the night of the first of May,"[17] said he. "The vengeance of Heaven be upon me, if I learn not what it is that takes away the colts." So he caused the mare to be brought into a house, and he armed himself, and began to watch that night.

And in the beginning of the night, the mare foaled a large and beautiful colt. And it was standing up in the place. And Teyrnon rose up and looked at the size of the colt, and as he did so he heard a great tumult, and after the tumult behold a claw came through the window into the house, and it seized the colt by the mane. Then Teyrnon drew his sword, and struck off the arm at the elbow, so that portion of the arm together with the colt was in the house with him. And then did he hear a tumult and wailing, both at once.

And he opened the door, and rushed out in the direction of the noise, and he could not see the cause of the tumult because of the darkness of the night, but he rushed after it and followed it. Then he remembered that he had left the door open, and he returned. And at the door behold there was an infant boy in swaddling-clothes, wrapped around in a mantle of satin. And he took up the boy, and behold he was very strong for the age that he was of.

Then he shut the door, and went into the chamber where his wife was. "Lady," said he, "art thou sleeping?"

"No, lord," said she, "I was asleep, but as thou camest in I did awake."

---

15. *Teyrnon Twryf Liant*: from *teyrn twrf lliant*, "monarch of the host of the sea."

16. *Gwent-ys-Coed*: "Gwent below the forest." Gwent is the easternmost province of south Wales.

17. This is the eve of *Calan Mai* or Beltane, one of two days in Welsh tradition when the gates of the Otherworld stand open.

"Behold, here is a boy for thee if thou wilt," said he, "since thou hast never had one."

"My lord," said she, "what adventure is this?"

"It was thus," said Teyrnon; and he told her how it all befell.

"Verily, lord," said she, "what sort of garments are there upon the boy?"

"A mantle of satin," said he.

"He is then a boy of gentle lineage," she replied. "My lord," she said, "if thou wilt, I shall have great diversion and mirth. I will call my women unto me, and tell them that I have been pregnant."

"I will readily grant thee to do this," he answered.

And thus did they, and they caused the boy to be baptized with the baptism that was used in that time; and the name which they gave unto him, was Gwri Wallt Euryn,[18] because what hair was upon his head was as yellow as gold. And they had the boy nursed in the court until he was a year old. And before the year was over he could walk stoutly. And he was larger than a boy of three years old, even one of great growth and size. And the boy was nursed the second year, and then he was as large as a child six years old. And before the end of the fourth year, he would bribe the grooms to allow him to take the horses to water.

"My lord," said his wife unto Teyrnon, "where is the colt which thou didst save on the night that thou didst find the boy?"

"I have commanded the grooms of the horses," said he, "that they take care of him."

"Would it not be well, lord," said she, "if thou wert to cause him to be broken in, and given to the boy, seeing that on the same night that thou didst find the boy, the colt was foaled and thou didst save him?"

"I will not oppose thee in this matter," said Teyrnon. "I will allow thee to give him the colt."

"Lord," said she, "may Heaven reward thee; I will give it him." So the horse was given to the boy. Then she went to the grooms and those who tended the horses, and commanded them to be careful of the horse, so that he might be broken in by the time that the boy could ride him.

And while these things were going forward, they heard tidings of Rhiannon and her punishment. And Teyrnon Twryf Vliant, by reason of the pity that he felt on hearing this story of Rhiannon and her punishment, inquired closely concerning it, until he had heard from many of those who came to his court.

---

18. *Gwri Wallt Euryn*: *Gwri* is from *gwr*, "man;" *Wallt Euryn* is "Golden Hair."

Then did Teyrnon, often lamenting the sad history, ponder within himself, and he looked steadfastly on the boy, and as he looked upon him, it seemed to him that he had never beheld so great a likeness between father and son, as between the boy, and Pwyll, the chief of Annwn. Now the semblance of Pwyll was well known to him, for he had of yore been one of his followers. And thereupon he became grieved for the wrong that he did, in keeping with him a boy whom he knew to be the son of another man.

And the first time that he was alone with his wife, he told her that it was not right that they should keep the boy with them, and suffer so excellent a lady as Rhiannon to be punished so greatly on his account, whereas the boy was the son of Pwyll, the chief of Annwn. And Teyrnon's wife agreed with him, that they should send the boy to Pwyll.

"And three things, lord," said she, "shall we gain thereby. Thanks and gifts for releasing Rhiannon from her punishment; and thanks from Pwyll for nursing his son and restoring him unto him; and thirdly, if the boy is of gentle nature, he will be our foster-son, and he will do for us all the good in his power." So it was settled according to this counsel.

And no later than the next day was Teyrnon equipped, and two other knights with him. And the boy, as a fourth in their company, went with them upon the horse which Teyrnon had given him. And they journeyed towards Narberth, and it was not long before they reached that place. And as they drew near to the palace, they beheld Rhiannon sitting beside the horse-block.

And when they were opposite to her, "Chieftain," said she, "go not further thus, I will bear every one of you into the palace, and this is my penance for slaying my own son and devouring him."

"Oh, fair lady," said Teyrnon, "think not that I will be one to be carried upon thy back."

"Neither will I," said the boy.

"Truly, my soul," said Teyrnon, "we will not go."

So they went forward to the palace, and there was great joy at their coming. And at the palace a feast was prepared, because Pwyll was come back from the confines of Dyfed. And they went into the hall and washed, and Pwyll rejoiced to see Teyrnon. And in this order they sat. Teyrnon between Pwyll and Rhiannon, and Teyrnon's two companions on the other side of Pwyll, with the boy between them. And after meat they began to carouse and to discourse. And Teyrnon's discourse was concerning the adventure of the mare and the boy, and how he and his wife had nursed and reared the child as their own.

"And behold here is thy son, lady," said Teyrnon. "And whosoever told that lie concerning thee, has done wrong. And when I heard of thy sorrow, I was troubled and grieved. And I believe that there is none of this host, who will not perceive that the boy is the son of Pwyll," said Teyrnon.

"There is none," said they all, "who is not certain thereof."

"I declare to Heaven," said Rhiannon, "that if this be true, there is indeed an end to my trouble."

"Lady," said Pendaran Dyfed,[19] "well hast thou named thy son Pryderi,[20] and well becomes him the name of Pryderi son of Pwyll, Chief of Annwn."

"Look you," said Rhiannon, "will not his own name become him better?"

"What name has he?" asked Pendaran Dyfed.

"Gwri Wallt Euryn is the name that we gave him."

"Pryderi," said Pendaran, "shall his name be."

"It were more proper," said Pwyll, "that the boy should take his name from the word his mother spoke when she received the joyful tidings of him." And thus was it arranged.

"Teyrnon," said Pwyll, "Heaven reward thee that thou hast reared the boy up to this time, and, being of gentle lineage, it were fitting that he repay thee for it."

"My lord," said Teyrnon, "it was my wife who nursed him, and there is no one in the world so afflicted as she at parting with him. It were well that he should bear in mind what I and my wife have done for him."

"I call Heaven to witness," said Pwyll, "that while I live I will support thee and thy possessions, as long as I am able to preserve my own. And when he shall have power, he will more fitly maintain them than I. And if this counsel be pleasing unto thee, and to my nobles, it shall be that, as thou hast reared him up to the present time, I will give him to be brought up by Pendaran Dyfed, from henceforth. And you shall be companions, and shall both be foster-fathers unto him."

"This is good counsel," said they all. So the boy was given to Pendaran Dyfed, and the nobles of the land were sent with him. And Teyrnon Twryf Vliant and his companions set out for his country, and his possessions, with love and gladness. And he went not without being offered the fairest jewels and the fairest horses, and the choicest dogs; but he would take none of them.

---

19. *Pendaran Dyfed*: "Chieftain of Dyfed."

20. *Pryderi*: "Anxiety" or "Trouble."

Thereupon they all remained in their own dominions. And Pryderi, the son of Pwyll the Chief of Annwn, was brought up carefully as was fit, so that he became the fairest youth, and the most comely, and the best skilled in all good games, of any in the kingdom. And thus passed years and years, until the end of Pwyll the Chief of Annwn's life came, and he died.

And Pryderi ruled the seven Cantrefs of Dyfed prosperously, and he was beloved by his people, and by all around him. And at length he added unto them the three Cantrefs of Ystrad Tywi, and the four Cantrefs of Ceredigion; and these were called the Seven Cantrefs of Seissyllwch.[21] And when he made this addition, Pryderi the son of Pwyll the Chief of Annwn, desired to take a wife. And the wife he chose was Cigfa,[22] the daughter of Gwynn Gloyw,[23] the son of Gloyw Wallt Lydan,[24] the son of Prince Casnar,[25] one of the nobles of this Island.

And thus ends this First Branch of the Mabinogion.

---

21. *Ystrad Tywi* is the valley of the Tywi River; *Ceredigion* and *Seissyllwch* are names for regions of Wales east of Dyfed. Note that Pryderi has gained a second sevenfold rulership east of his sevenfold rulership of Dyfed.

22. *Cigfa*: "House of Flesh," a metaphor for the physical body.

23. *Gwynn Gloyw*: "White the Splendid."

24. *Gloyw Wallt Lydan*: "Splendor of the Wide Hair."

25. *Casnar*: "Ruler." Note that these latter three names are all titles of the Sun.

FOUNDATIONS OF
DRUID PHILOSOPHY

HE FOLLOWING LECTURE deserves careful study. Its contents
may be found abstract and dry at first reading, but there is more
here than meets the eye: "The wisest of the ancients considered
what is not too explicit as the fittest for instruction, because it rous-
es the faculties to act," wrote William Blake, and his advice has been followed by
Druid teachers throughout the history of the Revival. The nine triads given in
this lecture, in particular, may be taken as suitable themes for meditation once
work with the First Branch of the Mabinogion has been concluded.

It is among the curious differences between the ancient and modern worlds that
the manner of instruction in ancient times is the reverse of that which prevails
today. Students in schools of our present day begin, as it were, at the lowest
point, with particulars that they are gradually taught to assemble into more and
more universal understandings. In the ancient world, students began from the
highest point, with universal principles, and gradually learned to apply those
principles in more and more particular settings. Each method has its strengths
and its weaknesses, and each is appropriate to different purposes.

The instruction offered in mystery schools follows the ancient method, as
that is most appropriate to the distinctive purposes of education in the mysteries. Thus the novice in Druid philosophy begins with the highest and most universal principles of that philosophy. The following triads and the commentary
appended to them are to be studied carefully by the student.

The Druid teachings begin from the fundamental postulate of a transcendent creative principle, which is the cause and reason of the Cosmos and all

the manifestations contained therein—all that humanity calls "the universe." Greater than the galaxies, this same principle is at one and the same moment present to each individual being within the universe as a source of inspiration and insight. This principle is known in the Druid teachings as Awen, and it is represented by the symbol of the three rays of light: / | \

Awen cannot be represented adequately by words or symbols; its name and the emblem of the three rays of light are concessions to the human inability to grasp the transcendent without name and form. Awen is not a deity, a person or a being; rather, it is an absolute and impersonal creative principle. It does not manifest itself in a universe of shapes and forms, by separating itself into the many, as the absolute is held to do in certain philosophies. Instead, it causes universal being to proceed from infinite not-being—it causes the Cosmos to arise from chaos—it causes manifestation to arise from the unmanifest—it causes everything to arise from infinite nothing. It is the source of all pattern, all meaning, and all existence, but it is not patterned, meaningful, or even existent. Awen is not being, but the cause of being. It cannot even be said to "be," in any ordinary sense. Instead, it is that which causes the verb "to be" to have meaning.

It is important not to confuse Awen with the beings that come into being because of it, however great those beings may be, or to think of the human soul as a fragment or aspect of Awen. The absolute can never become the relative; thus Awen can never separate itself into bits of "you and me." Nor do Druids regard the Cosmos as a nightmare, dream, meditation, illusion, delusion, or imagination of the Absolute, as some philosophical schools suggest. Awen does not dream, meditate, imagine, or think; nor can it be deluded, or subject to illusion, delusion or ignorance. These are qualities belonging to beings; Awen is above beings, and even above Being.

We begin with four triads concerning Awen.[26]

Triad I.

Three things which are not: that which is beyond Awen, that which is before Awen, and that which is above Awen.

---

26. None of the triads found in this course can be found in the standard Welsh collections of triads, and it is believed that they were created for the purpose of this course.

Triad II.

Three truthful sayings concerning Awen: Awen is; Awen transcends; Awen manifests.

Triad III.

Three abiding places of Awen: the unknowable, the unthinkable, and the ineffable.

Triad IV.

Three relations of Awen to created things: it is their first cause, their ideal form, and their efficient reason.

A consideration of these four triads will throw light on the nature of Awen as the Druid mysteries understand it. Let us examine them in detail.

Triad I.

Three things which are not: that which is beyond Awen, that which is before Awen, and that which is above Awen.

This triad sets forth Awen's place at the summit of Druid cosmology. Naught is beyond Awen; that is to say, it is not limited in space. Naught is before Awen; that is to say, it is not limited in time. Naught is above Awen; that is to say, it occupies the highest position in the structure of being. These points also set forth the teaching that Awen was not created, but eternal and self-existent, there being nothing beyond, before, or above it that might have caused or created it.

Note also, though, that each of the sections of this triad can be read in another way. Naught is beyond Awen; that is, it is further away in space than anything else. Naught is before Awen; that is, it is further away in time than anything else. Naught is above Awen; that is, it is further away in degree or kind than anything else. Between this sense and the one previously discussed lies a certain paradox; Awen is at once everywhere and infinitely far off. This paradox and its possible resolution deserves your thorough consideration.

You should also consider the fact that the triad uses the term "not," and our discussion the word "naught," instead of "nothing." The technical meaning of these terms in our philosophy is different. The words "not" and "naught" are used to express an absolute negation; they are positive denials of any existence whatsoever, of any kind, character, or degree, absolute or relative, past, present or future. Further than this, language cannot go. But the words "nothing" and "nothingness," although used in common speech to mean "naught" in the sense just described, have a technical meaning in our philosophy. Throughout these lessons, these words are used in a relative sense. This distinction will be explored further in a later triad.

TRIAD II.

Three truthful sayings concerning Awen: Awen is; Awen transcends; Awen manifests.

Each of the three parts of this triad deserves careful attention. "Awen is;" this simple sentence bears far more meaning than appears at a first or casual glance. Central to the mystery teachings of every age is the distinction between that which is and that which becomes. "What is it that always is and is never becoming," the old riddle asks, "and what is it that is always becoming and never is?" The answer to the riddle conflicts with the ordinary usage of the verb "is." Commonly, when people say that a thing is, they mean that it can be perceived with the senses, and of a thing that cannot be perceived with the senses, they are apt to say that it "is not." Yet those things that are perceived by the senses are ephemeral and subject to constant change. Today's caterpillar is tomorrow's butterfly; today's boy is tomorrow's man, and the next day's corpse. Even a mountain, enduring as it seems from the human perspective, is in the midst of its own coming to being and passing away. All these things, all things perceived by the senses, belong to the realm of becoming and not that of being; they become, but they are not.

Of all the things human beings can know, the things of the sensory realm are furthest in the direction of becoming. More durable than things are feelings—love may endure unchanged while the lover and beloved change almost out of all recognition—and more durable than feelings are ideas—the sum of one and one will continue to equal two so long as beings capable of adding one and one exist in the Cosmos. Beyond ideas, in turn, lies the realm of principles, and the summit of this realm, the absolute principle of existence, is Awen. Here we stand at last in the presence of being. All other things come into existence and pass away; Awen alone is. Only Awen possesses being in this true sense—all other apparent being is becoming, a transitory and phenomenal appearance. In the fullest sense of the word, nothing but Awen is.

"Awen transcends." This sentence hints at a truth scarcely capable of being expressed in words. Let us examine the term and see what it really means. To transcend is to surpass, to surmount, to be above or beyond. Some popular spiritual teachings consider the absolute principle as a being existing on the same level as other beings, rather than as the factor that allows being to be in the first place; or envision it as subject to the conditions of time, space and change. Central to the Druid teaching is the recognition that none of these things are true of Awen. Think of any thing whatsoever, and you may be certain that Awen transcends it. Think of the conditions of time, space, and change, and you may be certain that Awen transcends them as well. Think of the seven cosmic principles that were mentioned in the first introductory letter of this course, and you may be sure that Awen is above them—that they proceed from Awen, rather than Awen being subject to them. Think, finally, of your own conception of Awen, and you may be just as sure that Awen transcends that conception.

"Awen manifests." As the ultimate Being beyond all Becoming, and the transcendent principle beyond all other existences, Awen may seem utterly apart from the realm of created existence. This third part of Triad II counters that misconception with the paradox at the core of all spiritual effort: the ultimate principle, though immeasurably removed from the realm of creatures, yet manifests in that realm. Its manifestations are present in every created being. The manifestation is not the ultimate Reality, but it is as much of the reality as may be communicated at whatever rung upon the great ladder of being it occupies.

Think of the Sun, blazing in unbearable glory in the midst of its court of planets, and then think of the presence of sunlight throughout the world we know. Sunlight is not the Sun; even climbers perched on the tops of the highest earthly mountains can perceive, through the Sun's rays, only a faint glimpse of the whole; in the fogs and mists of the valleys below, the Sun becomes a pallid disk and its light seems faint; at the bottom of the sea it cannot be seen at all, and only the slow rain of animalcules from the waters above, food for the strange creatures of the ocean's depths, provides evidence of the distant source of light and life. To each of these manifestations of the Sun corresponds a manifestation of Awen.

Triad III.

Three abiding places of Awen: the unknowable, the unthinkable, and the ineffable.

Note the subtle distinctions in this triad. The unknowable is that which cannot be grasped by perception; the unthinkable is that which cannot be made into an object of thought; the ineffable is that which cannot be expressed in language.

One meaning of the triad, therefore, is that Awen cannot be perceived, conceived, or expressed—it is utterly beyond the reach of the human mind's three powers. Another meaning is that where these three powers, perception, thinking, and language, have been taken so far that they can go no further, Awen is close at hand.

It may be asked, if Awen is unknowable, unthinkable, and ineffable, why these lessons attempt to inform you about it, and what they might possibly hope to teach you of it. Certainly no attempt is made here to explain the unexplainable to you, or to describe its nature to you. That would be impossible, since no words can express Awen, and no mind is capable of understanding it were it explained.

The reason for the discussion of Awen in these lessons is otherwise. Humanity has built up, around the dim perception of an absolute reality that is the highest truth the human mind can reach, many different conceptions of the nature of that reality. All too often the followers of one or another such conception have confused these accretions with the reality behind them, and condemned and persecuted those who accepted some different conception. Thus arises the need, in any tradition of wisdom—a need too rarely met outside the shrines of initiation and the temples of the mysteries—for such a caution as this. In the same way the great Chinese sage Lao Tze wrote of the Tao, the conception of which corresponds in Taoism to that of Awen in Druidry: "The Tao that can be spoken of is not the eternal Tao; the names that can be given it are not eternal names."

TRIAD IV.

Three relations of Awen to created things: it is their first cause, their ideal form, and their efficient reason.

The three parts of this triad make use of technical terms from philosophy. The first cause of a thing is that which originally sets in motion the course of events that brings that thing into being. The ideal form of a thing is the pattern that is expressed by the thing, as the perfect circle of geometry is expressed in the imperfect circles of the world of becoming. The efficient reason of a thing is the goal or purpose of a thing, that which accounts for or explains its existence.

Thus Awen is understood in the Druid mysteries as that by which created things originate; that on which created things are modeled; and that toward which created things strive. It forms the context or framework for the universe of created things. Note the parallel between this triad and Triad I, which places Awen beyond, before, and above all other things.

The Druid teachings hold that other than Awen, in an ultimate sense, there is only Annwn, which is nothingness. The word Annwn literally means "not-world." The nothingness of Annwn is not nonexistence, but literally "no-thing-ness," the total absence of any thing as distinct from anything else. In Annwn sleeps the latency, possibility, potency, and promise of everything, past, present, and future. In its infinite emptiness, which is equally an infinite fullness, no thing exists in actuality or manifestation, but everything exists in latency and possibility. In the language of mythology, Annwn is imagined as a vast and bubbling cauldron from which Ceridwen, the goddess of wisdom, draws forth whatsoever she wishes.

The following three triads offer a first approximation of the Druid teaching concerning Annwn, the abyss of Nothingness in which the light of Awen is reflected, and from which all created things take their birth.

Triad V.

Three unseen things: that which is not, that which is nothing, and that which is unmanifest.

Triad VI.

Three characteristics of Annwn: infinity, possibility, and space.

Triad VII.

Three things in Annwn before manifestation: latent substance, latent motion, and latent consciousness.

Triad V.

Three unseen things: that which is not, that which is nothing, and that which is unmanifest.

The distinction made earlier between "not" and "nothing" is here further expounded. That which is not has no existence of any kind, as mentioned above. In these Druid teachings, however, the words "nothing" and "nothingness" signify "no-thing" and "no-thingness" respectively. This may seem like metaphysical hairsplitting, but it conveys in words a concept poorly suited to ordinary language. Common words too often fail to express uncommon ideas, and so the wise must redefine common words to express subtle shades of meaning and significance, or else remain silent with their thoughts unshared with their students.

In order to understand "nothingness" and "nothing," you must understand the meaning of the word "thing" to which these words are opposed. A "thing" is "whatever exists as a separate object of sense or thought," manifested in the world of becoming and having apparent qualities such as size, shape, form, etc. It is something connected directly or indirectly with physical appearance, something having a correspondence in experience. Nothingness is then the opposite of thingness, the absence of manifestation in the world of becoming, and of apparent qualities, physical appearance, or correspondence in experience. It is that in which there is no separate existence as an object of sense or thought.

Annwn is nothing, or rather no-thing, in this sense. It contains naught that is apparent to the senses; naught that can be experienced; naught that can be sensed; naught that can be thought of by the intellect, nor pictured in the imagination—in short, nothing that is capable of inducing a mental image in your mind. And yet it exists in a state or condition of latency, possibility, futurity, potentiality, and promise.

Annwn may also be understood as unmanifest, and as the Great Unmanifest. That which is manifest is that which appears or is revealed, that which can be experienced or known. In Triad II you have learned that Awen manifests; it makes itself known to created beings, to the degree that they are capable of knowing it. Annwn, being nothing, does not manifest itself, for to manifest is to become a thing, and whenever something emerges from nothing, then and there, nothing is not. As a future triad will make plain, manifestation emerges from the union of Awen and Annwn; in that manifestation, Awen is partly revealed, but Annwn remains unmanifest.

Triad VI.

Three characteristics of Annwn: infinity, possibility, and space.

This triad offers three positive statements about Annwn, all of which must be considered with some care.

Modern metaphysical teachers have treated the term "infinity" as an attribute of the absolute, and religious theologies commonly consider it as a characteristic of the Divine. From the standpoint of the Druid teachings, neither of these habits of thought is useful. The word "infinite" means boundless; limitless; not circumscribed as to time, space, variety, possibility, combination, shape, form, and so on. The word itself comes from *in*, "not"; and *finitus*, "finished" or "ended." Thus "infinite" means "unfinished; incomplete; capable of limitless manifestation and possibilities." So, while the absolute is that which is established and unchanging, "Infinite" means a state in which the possibilities of manifestation and expression are limitless.

The great thinkers of all times, esoteric and exoteric, have agreed in this idea of the infinite being unlimited possibility. As Schopenhauer says: "It is already a doctrine of Aristotle that Infinity can never be *actu* (actual, given, fixed) but only *potentia* (in possibility, latency, promise, potentiality)." We trust that you now see that the Infinite alone is capable of endless changes in shape, form, variety, in time, space, and number; and contains within itself the promise, possibility, latency, and potentiality of Everything.

Druid teachers once illustrated this to their pupils by the symbols of number. The number 1 stands for Awen, independent, sovereign, and alone. By itself, and in itself it is incapable of multiplying or dividing—multiply anything by 1 or divide anything by 1, and the thing remains unchanged. Multiply or divide 1 by itself, and the answer still is 1, showing that the Absolute cannot be increased or divided, even by itself. Subtract 1 from itself, and the result is 0, showing that if the absolute is removed from consideration there is naught left but the infinite nothingness. Then the Druids called the attention of their pupils to the Zero, or the symbol of infinite nothing, 0. In itself, 0 means nothing. Multiply or divide anything by 0, and the answer is always 0. Multiply 0 by itself, and 0 remains—the infinite cannot increase itself, for in its circle it includes all possibility. But divide 0 by itself—and lo! 0 into 0 goes 1 time: the answer is 1, showing that if the infinite be divided by itself, the absolute is found to be at its center, undisturbed, independent, self-existent. The symbol of infinity, in mathematics, however, is not 0 or unmanifest infinity, but ∞, which indicates manifest infinity, the symbol always indicating endless continuation of action.

The symbol of the infinite nothing becomes infinity in manifestation in this way. Make a string of "os," as follows: 000,000,000,000,000—you see that they still mean nothing. Now place "1" (the symbol of the Absolute), before the string and we have 1,000,000,000,000,000, which we may enlarge to any desired power by the addition of os. Alternatively, place the Absolute 1 behind the string, and we have .000,000,000,000,000,1, a very small decimal, which may be carried to infinitesimal smallness by the addition of os. Thus we see, by symbols, that the action of the absolute on infinite nothingness produces greatness and smallness with equal facility.

Let us now examine the idea of space. Space is the mental symbol for infinity. Consider yourself as standing at a fixed point in space; there exists an infinite distance or extension in space, from that point, in an infinite number of directions. Leaving out of consideration all objects in space—considering pure empty space—there is an endless extension possible, in innumerable directions—extension without end. Imagine a number of miles represented in a row of figures extending from earth to the most distant star; then multiply that number by itself; and then the product by itself; and so on, for a time equal to the number of years since the Cosmic Day began. Then you would have a number of miles, the written figures of which would fill more space than your mind is able to conceive. Then think of a being traveling that many miles—would he then be near the end of space? Not at all; the distance traveled by him would be as nothing compared with infinite space. Think of being able to travel for all eternity through space without coming to an end! You cannot come to an end of space, even in thought or imagination. As far as you proceed into space, there must always be infinite space extending in every direction from that point. Space has its center everywhere, and its circumference nowhere.

TRIAD VII.

Three things in Annwn before manifestation: Latent substance, latent motion, and latent consciousness.

Now let us endeavor to imagine the condition or state of Annwn during the Cosmic Night, before the faintest dawn of the new Cosmic Day. The three cosmic principles, substance or *calas*, motion or *gwyar*, and consciousness or *nwyfre*, are resolved into the unmanifest, but are not destroyed—they are "nothing," but not "not." Substance has assumed its most subtle form, infinitely rarer and finer than the finest ether—it is nothing, yet exists in latency, possibility, and promise. Motion has assumed a rate of vibration so high that it is effectively at rest, although not destroyed—it is still motion in latency. Consciousness has assumed the condition of a deep unconsciousness—a profound dreamless sleep, following upon the attainment of the supreme consciousness in the previous Cosmic Day. It knows nothing; is conscious of nothing—for there is nothing of which it could be conscious, or could know, for all manifestation has ceased until the dawn of the new Cosmic Day. It is even unconscious of Awen, although Awen still reigns over it, and will awaken it once more, as it has many times before, in the eternal chain of Cosmic Days and Nights.

In the language of mythology, the Great Mother sleeps; the turning of the Great Circle has brought her rest after a day of labors and accomplishments; but she will awaken and greet the Great Father at the dawn of the Cosmic Day. From the womb of the Great Mother will proceed the One Life, which will manifest itself in infinitudes of infinitudes of shape, form, and variety, of things, life, and beings. In Her is the promise of all that shall be throughout the coming cycle of manifestation. Thus Annwn is the unmanifest containing all manifestation within it in latency, possibility and futurity.

The Druid teachings hold that time moves in great cycles, far vaster than the human imagination can grasp. At the beginning of each great cycle of time, after the last ripples of the preceding cycle have faded to perfect stillness, Awen is reflected in the symbolic form of three rays of light in the emptiness of Annwn. When this happens the first activities of a new Cosmic Day, or universe, begin to show themselves. The first manifestation of this union of Awen and Annwn is Nwyfre, the One Life. This same teaching is reflected in the language of mythology by the ancient story that Celi, the god of heaven, and Ced, the goddess of the earth, mated and brought forth Hu Gadarn, Hu the Mighty, the personification of Nwyfre.

Nwyfre, the One Life, is the Will-to-Be of the Cosmos. It is the Universal Being, and in the scale of being it is second only to Universal Nonbeing, which is Annwn, and the principle that brings Being into being, which is Awen. From Nwyfre, the world-spirit or universal life principle, emerges the manifest universe of life, energy and form. The universe is alive in every part, and its real nature vests in the One Life, which is ever behind, under, and in, all manifestations of the universal activities, from lowest to highest. Mirroring the threefold rhythm of Awen, Nwyfre differentiates itself in a threefold manner. From Nwyfre itself, which is life, proceeds Gwyar, which is energy, and from Gwyar proceeds Calas, which is form. These become the three Essences of the universe as it comes into being. From the three Essences arise all the infinite variety of combinations which go to make up all the varieties of manifestation in the universe.

The One Life is not eternal. It emerges from the cauldron of Annwn, passes through a sequence of manifestations, and returns again to Annwn at the end of the cycle of manifestation, when the image of Awen is no longer reflected in the waters of Annwn. Between the emergence of the One Life and its return to the "no-thingness" of Annwn, it passes through seven phases, each of which expresses one of seven fundamental patterns or expressions of existence reflected from Awen. These manifest themselves in all three Essences of existence, and in all the combinations of the Essences. From each existence, therefore, all others can be understood.

These seven fundamental patterns are the seven elements of Nature: Air, Water, Fire, Earth, Spirit Below, Spirit Above, and Spirit Within. Do not think of these as merely the material substances that provide them with their names and the rudiments of their symbolism. The seven elements are present in all things, in the highest realms of spirit just as much as in the densest forms of matter. Understand them and their interrelations and you will understand the Cosmos. Understand their expressions in each existing thing and you will understand yourself.

These same seven patterns can also be understood in another way, as seven creative laws or principles. These principles, under various expressions and forms, have been taught in the mystery schools of many lands and times. If you have studied other esoteric teachings you may be familiar with them in a different order, or under different names. The expressions used in this course derive, as mentioned above, from teachings formulated in the early 20th century, and those familiar with the esoteric literature of that time will find close parallels in other traditions, some of them apparently unrelated to Druidry. This is as it should be, for the Druid mysteries are not a thing apart, unrelated to other mystery schools; they are a particular expression, in the language of a given place and time, of insights that transcend place and time and are common to all of humanity.

The following two triads, rounding out the set of nine triads in this lesson, present a first approximation of the Druid teachings of manifestation—the union of Awen and Annwn that gives rise to the One Life, and to all created things.

Triad VIII.

Three conditions of manifestation: the receptivity of Annwn, the superimposition of Awen, and the awakening of the seven laws.

Triad IX.

Three principles of manifestation: substance, motion, and consciousness.

Triad VIII.

Three conditions of manifestation: the receptivity of Annwn, the superimposition of Awen, and the awakening of the seven laws.

This is the Druid teaching regarding the process whereby the Unmanifest becomes manifest; the latent becomes active; the possible becomes actual; the potential becomes real; the promise becomes fulfilment.

At the extreme swing of the pendulum of rhythm, the point of the cycle in which end fades into beginning—the climax of the Cosmic Night is reached in the form of absolute rest. Then begin the first stirrings of the new Cosmic Day, just as the first stirrings of summer can be traced at the sun's turning at midwinter, and the first stirrings of the new day can be sensed at the moment of midnight.

It is the becoming of Annwn, rather than the being of Awen, that sets the new day into motion—the feminine power, and not the masculine principle, that brings the worlds into manifestation. Awen exerts no different degree or kind of power at the period of dawn, than at the period of dusk; no more at the period of noon, than at the period of midnight. During the Cosmic Day and Cosmic Night, Awen is unchangeable and constant in its power and influence.

The difference is caused by the presence of cyclic movement in the Cosmos itself, manifest or unmanifest. Awen is over and above Circularity, or any of the Seven Principles, and it is changeless. The Cosmos, on the contrary, is under the Seven Laws which are the manifestations of Awen, and is changeable—indeed, constantly changing. The difference in the effect of Awen is due to the changing receptivity of the infinite Abyss.

Were the Cosmos and infinity not to exist, Awen would not be changed in any way whatsoever. Its absoluteness raises it above relations. Still, while this is so, the constant outpouring of the power of Awen causes the Cosmos to be affected by it. According to rhythm, the degree of power received by the Cosmos must vary, but Awen changes not. The seven principles which produce these changes in the Cosmos are a part of the action of Awen, as experienced by the Cosmos.

The Triad speaks of "the superimposition of Awen." What is meant by "superimposition"? "Super" means "over or above," and "impose" means "to lay or place upon." "Superimpose" means "to place upon from above," or as used in the Triad, "to influence from above." In other words, the infinite nothingness, or unmanifest Cosmos, owing to the influence of the principle of circularity, begins once more to experience the active radiation of the power of Awen, which serves to vitalize and energize it, and thus begins the dawn of the new Cosmic Day, and the awakening of the One Life.

This first stirring of cosmic activity has been symbolized by the first stirring of the embryo within its temporary home, in which it has lain quietly since its conception, or by the first signs of sprouting within the little acorn that will become a mighty oak. It is the weird and crepuscular light which precedes the first glimmer of the rising sun. Creation is beginning. The birth of the new Cosmos is approaching. The One Life is arousing itself. Infinity is preparing to become manifest. The Zero is evolving into the One.

In the manifestation of the Cosmos there is exhibited an infinitude of variety, degrees, shapes, form, and combinations of the three principles of manifestation—substance, motion, and consciousness. It almost staggers the imagination to think of the fact that in the entire Cosmos there are never two things precisely alike. In view of this fact, is it not obvious folly to endeavor to force all human beings to adhere to any single standard?

And yet through the entire Cosmos there is ever manifest the Law of Unity. Everything in the Cosmos is part of one tremendous whole and shares One Life. Nothing and no one has an existence apart from others. Every part is part of a whole, and the whole of a greater whole, all manifesting throughout the eternal patterns of Awen. Thus the Druid axiom: "From one thing, know all things."

And through the entire Cosmos there is ever manifest the Law of Polarity. Everything has its opposite pole and its other side. Light and dark, hot and cold, good and evil, beauty and ugliness are inseparable from one another; they cannot be known without one another, and they appear together or not at all.

And throughout the entire Cosmos is ever manifest the Law of Balance. Everything has something balancing and counterbalancing it. Everything has its compensation. Nature always maintains its balance and requires its compensation. We must pay our price for everything—we cannot have our penny and our cake at the same time. We can never get something for nothing.

And throughout the entire Cosmos is ever manifest the Law of Causation. Everything proceeds in an orderly manner from cause to effect. There is no cause without an effect, and no effect without a cause. There is nothing truly random in the Cosmos; what seems random or disorderly to us is simply shaped by laws too complex or subtle for our minds to grasp.

And throughout the entire Cosmos is ever manifest the Law of Vibration. Everything vibrates. Everything moves from one pole to the other—from one extreme to the opposite. Everything has its vibratory rate. Everything swings like a pendulum between its polarities. Summer gives way to winter, and winter in turn to summer; night yields to day and then returns in day's place.

And throughout the entire Cosmos is ever manifest the Law of Correspondence—that law which ever manifests a correspondence and agreement between all things on all planes. If we discover certain principles in one thing we may reason by analogy regarding other things, and thus discover the unknown quality.

And throughout the entire Cosmos is ever manifest the Law of Circularity. Everything moves in circles or spirals. Worlds, nations, peoples, and individuals travel in circles—the wise convert the cycles into spirals, and rise and rise by the same law that binds others to rise and fall.

To many people, these laws seem like abstractions removed from the realities of daily life, but it is important to move beyond this misjudgment and grasp the principles as the tools they are. Each of the principles has direct practical application; any one of them, put to use in the life of the initiate, will lead to remarkable transformations in the self and the world; all of them taken together, embraced by a mind trained according to the methods of the Druid wisdom, will throw open portal after portal, opening onto unimaginable vistas.

All seven of the laws are meant to be used, and used in the realm of ordinary life. By learning them, understanding them, and putting them to use, the initiate learns to recognize his or her oneness with sources of power and life throughout the Cosmos; master the hidden energies and processes of generation and regeneration; balance opposing forces against one another to achieve inner and outer poise; take advantage of causality and thus become fate's master rather than her slave; learn to attune to healing and empowering patterns of vibration, instead of those that bring frustration and unhappiness; read the language of correspondences written throughout the worlds of matter, life, and mind, and decode their messages; and convert circles in life into rising spirals that will take you to places and experiences undreamt of.

TRIAD IX.

Three principles of manifestation: substance, motion, and consciousness.

In order to understand the awakening of the Cosmos, which dwells latent within the womb of Annwn, consider the three principles of the Cosmos, from which all forms, shapes, combinations and varieties of manifestation arise. These principles are substance, motion, and consciousness. These three principles are unmanifest during the Cosmic Night, but awaken into nascency and activity with the first light of the dawn of the new Cosmic Day. In the end, and at the last, these three must be considered as phases of One. But that One, in itself, is but the reflection, so to speak, of Awen, although not by any means to be considered a "quality" or "phase" of Awen. Awen has no "qualities" or "phases"—it is over and above these things, which are but the aspects of Annwn, or the Cosmos.

The three principles are fundamental to all manifestations of the Cosmos, from the simplest to the most complex. Wherever is found any manifestation of the Cosmos, there is found the presence of the three principles in some degree of development or activity. If you prefer, you may think of the Cosmos as consisting of merely these three principles, manifest or unmanifest. The three principles we can never know of themselves—we know them only through and by their manifestations. Let us consider them in detail, by the light of the Druid wisdom.

I. Substance or *Calas*, as the term is used in the Druid teachings, means the underlying body of things—their material quality. Everything that is manifested in the Cosmos has its body or material quality. Substance includes all that we may think of as matter, in its various degrees of solidity, from the hardest steel or granite, to the most rarefied gas or vapor known to science. It includes all that science considers as material body, and much that lies beyond those conceptions.

The field of substance recognized by science, compared with the real extent of the principle of substance, is no more than a hairline drawn across a yardstick. There are forms of matter as much more dense than steel or granite, as the latter are more dense than hydrogen gas.[27] At the other end of the scale there are forms of substance that are so nearly akin to nothing that our language cannot describe them.

Between these two extremes there lies a bewildering number of degrees. That which science calls electricity and other subtle forms of energy, are not energy at all, but motion manifesting through subtle forms of substance, which act as its body. There are forms of substance many times finer and rarer than even these. There are bodies worn by beings on higher planes which are finer and rarer than electricity. Even the ordinary astral bodies of beings on our own plane and stage of development, are far rarer and finer than is electricity, or the finest rays of light or magnetism. These bodies are just as real as is the piece of the hardest steel, through which they may pass as easily as the X-ray passes through stone. The universal ether, which science assumes to be the extreme limit of subtle tenuity and fineness, is solid and compact when compared with many of the higher forms of substance. So much for manifest substance.

Unmanifest substance is held by the Druids to be identical with pure space. A preceding triad explains that space is one of the qualities of the Nothing that is Annwn. This Nothing is merely the extreme limit of the rarefaction of substance. Space is not a mere idea—it is substance carried to its highest limit. One of the old Druids, it is said, was once asked by a high king of Britain: "What would exist were there no universe, nor gods, nor anything else?" His answer was "Space." And this pure space is Annwn, and also the unmanifest Cosmos, in its aspect or principle of substance.

II. Motion or *Gwyar*, as the term is used in Druid teachings, means the principle of change in all things, and their quality of action. Motion is the principle in which is gathered the cause of all that we know under the names of change, activity, attraction, repulsion, coming into being and passing out of being, in all their kinds and degrees. Without motion there could be no change or alteration of any kind. In modern times we are taught to think of the counterpart of substance as energy, and divide up the general concept of energy into such subenergies as gravitation, cohesion, chemical affinity; light, heat, electricity, magnetism, and so forth. In the Druid teaching, by contrast, these are under-

---

27. At the beginning of the twentieth century, when this was written, ultradense forms of matter such as the substance of neutron stars had not yet been discovered by scientists. It is interesting that they were anticipated by the Druids of that time. Further foreshadowings of today's advanced physics will be found in the paragraphs that follow.

stood as the effects of motion in various kinds of substance, some denser and some subtler. Motion in denser substances produces denser effects, that can be known by the material senses. Motion in subtler substances produces subtler effects, that can be known by other senses, which all beings possess but few know how to use.

There are finer forces not dreamt of by even the most daring scientist. Motion, like substance, is found in each and every manifestation of the Cosmos. Wherever there is substance there is motion. In its highest form of manifestation motion manifests in vibrations of such exceedingly high degree and effect that there seems to be a condition of absolute rest. This condition is the one existing before the first stirrings of the dawn of the new Cosmic Day. Motion is then motionless, to all intents and purposes—but it has not perished or been destroyed. It is motion in latency. There is no such thing as absolute rest in the manifest Cosmos, but in the unmanifest Cosmos there is motion of so high a degree that it seems motionless and at rest. Thus do extremes meet, in Annwn. When the Cosmos becomes manifest, motion decreases its rate of action or vibration, and manifestation is really a lowering in the scale of motion; just as manifestation is a lowering in the scale of substance. There must first be involution before there is evolution, of both substance and motion.

III. Consciousness or *Nwyfre*, as the term is used in Druid teachings, means the principle of awareness of things—their quality of becoming aware of other things, inner and outer. We are familiar with the form and degree of consciousness manifested in ourselves and other human beings, and we recognize different shades and degrees in this. We know a little about consciousness in the lower animals, in varying degrees. Some of us know of the degrees of consciousness in plants, in varying degrees. Those who have studied along occult lines have become aware of the existence of mind and consciousness in so-called inanimate objects—the minerals, metals, etc., and even in the atoms—and finally in the ether. Everything in the manifest Cosmos has some degree of consciousness. There are many higher and lower degrees of consciousness alongside those just mentioned. From the unconscious consciousness of the Cosmic Night, when the Cosmos is conscious of Nothing, because there is only Nothing of which it may be conscious; to the moment of the Noon of the Cosmic Day, when the Cosmos is fully conscious of itself as a whole—the extreme of Cosmic Consciousness—there is a scale impossible for man to grasp by reason or imagination. There are degrees and planes of consciousness awaiting the soul which transcend any possible dream or picture. Humanity has just begun to manifest consciousness worthy of the name. It is just beginning to awaken to the glorious possibilities of Cosmic Consciousness—it is just "beginning to begin."

In the dawn of the new Cosmic Day, then, the three principles of the Cosmos are awakened into activity—substance, motion, and consciousness begin to combine and become active. There is manifested an unrest and tendency to stir into activity the latent possibilities of the Cosmos. Consciousness begins to awaken from its slumber of ages, and strives to know itself, and to realize its being. This imparts activity to motion, which lowers its vibrations in its effort to manifest itself. This bestirs substance into changing degrees of being. Thus do the first indications of the Cosmic Day begin to manifest themselves. From thence onward, throughout the Cosmic Day, until its close, there is constant change of form, shape and degree of substance; constant change in manifestation of motion; constant change in manifestation of consciousness.

THE MAGICAL MEMORY: INTRODUCTION

HE ANCIENT DRUIDS, according to those Grecian and Roman writers who expounded upon them, held it inadmissible that their teachings should ever be committed to writing. That ancient prohibition is no longer maintained among Druids in the present day, as the lesson before you bears witness! Yet of the many reasons for the old rule, one remains valid today.

One who merely knows where to find a certain item of knowledge, does not know that item of knowledge. If a student must constantly refer to a book for wisdom, the book may be wise but the student is not. It is only when we make knowledge and wisdom our own that they become ours, and we can make them our own only by committing them to memory so that we may use them as tools for thinking and for understanding the world. Nor is memory the simple faculty it is so often thought to be, for it is by memory that each of us creates and imagines the world. Thus the education of the mysteries inevitably includes training of memory.

A part of memory is within immediate reach of our conscious self, but a great deal more is not. It is by learning to call upon the hidden part that the powers of memory are developed.

MEMORY AND THE SUBCONSCIOUS

We can form no clear conception of the nature of memory, or of the rules governing remembrance and recollection, unless we understand something about that great region of the mind known to psychologists as the subconscious. It was taught in the nineteenth century that the mind is necessarily conscious of all that goes on within itself. Among the greatest discoveries, or rather rediscoveries, of the twentieth century was the realization that consciousness forms but a small part of the total of mental processes. Subconscious ideas, impressions, sensations and thoughts play a most important part in the world of thought. It is now understood that in every conscious act there is much that belongs to the region of the subconscious; every conscious act, one may say, is as the figure in a painting, set against a background of subconsciousness.

What is this subconsciousness? It is the part of the self belonging, not to the individual, but to the One Life that embraces every other life. It is by subconsciousness that each person is connected to all others, human and nonhuman. This subconscious realm contains many mysteries. It has been estimated that less than ten percent of the mental operations of everyday life are performed on the conscious plane, the balance of the work being done in the great subconscious regions of the mind. That which we call conscious thought is but the peaks of submerged mountains, the vast body of the mountains being hidden by the waters. We are as if in a forest in the darkest night, our lantern casting around us a little luminous circle, beyond which is a large ring of twilight, and still beyond this is absolute darkness. And in this twilight and in this darkness, work is being done, the results of which, when necessary, are pushed forward into the circle of light which we know as consciousness.

Memory is primarily a function of our subconscious. In the great subconscious region lies the great storehouse of Memory. From the moment we receive an impression, until the moment when it is again brought into the field of consciousness, the subconscious faculties are at work. We receive and store away an impression—where do we store it? Not in the conscious region, else it were always before us—down in the depths of the subconscious storehouse is it stored, placed among other impressions, often so carelessly that we find it almost impossible to find it when again we need it. Where is it kept, during the years that often pass between the storing away of an impression and its subsequent review? In this great storehouse of the subconscious. What process is employed when we wish to recall an impression? Simply an intention going forth from the will, bidding the workers in the subconscious warehouse to find and bring into the light the impression laid away so long ago. And in the degree that these workers have been trained to do their work and accustom themselves to their task, do they succeed in intelligently obeying the orders of the will. And in the measure that they have been taught to carefully store away the things committed to their charge, and to carefully note the locations of the treasures committed to them, are they apt and quick in bringing them to light when they are bidden.

Consciousness cannot be regarded as synonymous with mind. If we treat consciousness and mind as coextensive, and discard the idea of the subconscious, we will be at a loss to explain where, during a particular conscious state, all the rest of the mind is; where are all the other bits of mental furniture other than the particular piece then in use? The field of consciousness at any moment is very limited, and reminds one of looking through a telescope where he sees only that which is within the field of the instrument; all outside of that field being as if it did not exist, for the moment. The mind is constantly filled with ideas, thoughts, impressions, and memories, of which we are totally unconscious until they are brought into the field of consciousness.

It is believed by psychologists that every impression received—every thought that we evolve—every act that we perform—is recorded somewhere in this great subconscious storehouse of the mind, and that nothing is ever absolutely forgotten. Many things that have been apparently forgotten for years, will come into the field of consciousness when summoned there by some association, desire, need or stress. Many mental impressions probably never will be brought again into the field of consciousness, there being no need for such bringing forth, but will remain in the subconscious region silently but powerfully molding our thoughts, ideas and actions. Other impressions will lie hidden in the deep recesses of the mind, awaiting the hour of their renewed use, just as the future oak tree lies hidden in the acorn.

We are at any one time conscious of but a very small part of what is stored away in the mind. Many things which seem to have been forgotten, and which we have often endeavored to recall, will at some time come apparently unbidden into the field of consciousness, as if of their own accord. We often try to recall a thing, but it proves elusive, and we cease our efforts, but after a time, suddenly the idea flashes forth right in the glare of consciousness. It would seem that a desire for recollection often starts into operation the silent workers of the subconsciousness, and long after, when we have almost forgotten the desire, they return triumphantly dragging the desired impression with them. Then again, a chance word uttered by some other person may open up vast fields of memory, of whose existence we may have long since lost sight. Often in a dream we will see long-forgotten faces, and hear and recognize voices whose tones had faded away many years ago. Many events which have been so completely forgotten that no effort of the will seems able to recall them, still seem to be firmly imbedded somewhere in the subconsciousness, and some extraordinary stimulus, strain, or physical condition brings them forth as fresh and vivid as the impression of yesterday.

Persons in the delirium of fever will often speak of things which they had entirely forgotten and fail to recall a single particular after their recovery, but which, upon investigation, proved to have actually occurred in their childhood or youth. It is stated that a drowning man will often recall the events of his past life, and many interesting experiences along this line are related in the standard works on the subject of psychology. Sir Francis Beaufort, after being rescued from drowning, stated that "every incident of my former life seemed to pass before my recollection in a retrograde succession, not in mere outline, but the picture being filled up with every minute and collateral feature, constituting a kind of panoramic view of my entire existence."

Coleridge relates the tale of a young woman who could neither read nor write, who, being seized with a fever, began talking in Latin, Greek and Hebrew. Whole sheets of her ravings were written out, and were found to consist of sentences intelligible in themselves, but having slight connection with each other. Of her Hebrew sayings only a few could be traced to the Bible, and most seemed to be of Rabbinical dialect. The woman was grossly ignorant, and all trickery seemed out of the question, and she was generally believed to be possessed of a devil. A physician who doubted the theory of demoniacal possession determined to solve the mystery, and after much trouble discovered that at the age of nine she had been cared for in the household of an old clergyman. The clergyman was in the habit of walking up and down a passage of the house into which the kitchen opened, reciting to himself passages of the Rabbinical writings, and quotations from the Latin and Greek Fathers. His books were examined and every passage which the girl had uttered was found to be therein contained. The fever had caused the subconscious storehouse to bring forth some of its oldest treasures.

Carpenter relates the story of an English clergyman who visited a castle of which he had no recollection of having ever seen before. But as he approached the gateway he became conscious of a very vivid impression of having been there before, and seemed to not only see the gateway itself, but donkeys beneath the arch, and people on top of it. He was much wrought up over the matter, and some time afterward inquired of his mother whether she could throw any light upon the subject. She informed him that when he was a little child of but eighteen months of age, she had gone with a large party to that particular castle, and had taken him in the pannier of a donkey; that some of the people took their lunch on the roof of the gateway, while the child had been left below with the attendants and donkeys. On the occasion of the second visit the sight of the gateway brought up all the old childish recollection, although it seemed like a dream.

Abercrombie relates the story of a lady dying in a house in the country. Her infant daughter was brought from London to visit her, and after a short interview returned to town. The mother died, and the infant grew into womanhood without the slightest recollection of her mother. When she was a middle-aged woman she chanced to visit the house in which her mother died, and entered the room itself, although not knowing it to be the one in which the mother had passed away. She started upon entering the room, and when a friend inquired the cause of her agitation, said that she had a most vivid recollection of having been in that room before, and of the fact that a lady who lay in that corner, and who seemed to be very ill, had leaned over her and wept. And so the impression stored away in the subconscious storehouse of that baby brain, had remained there unknown, until its owner had grown to middle age, when at the sight of the room the impression was revived and memory gave up some of its secrets.

There are the best possible grounds for asserting that nothing is ever absolutely forgotten, once it has been impressed upon the mind. No impression, once recorded, ever ceases to exist. It is not lost, but merely becomes obscure and exists outside of the field of consciousness, to which however it may be recalled long afterward by some act of the will, or some association, according to the circumstances of the case. It is true that many impressions are never revived, either by volitional effort or involuntarily through association, but the impression is still there and its influence is manifest in our acts and thoughts. If we could reach the depths of the subconscious mentality, we would find there every impression ever received by the mind—records of every thought that had ever been born to us—the memory of every act of our life. All these things would be there—unseen but exerting a subtle influence over us. We are what we are today, because of what we thought, said, saw, heard, felt and did yesterday. Man is a composite of his yesterdays. There is not a single thought or act or impression of our past life that has not had its influence in fixing our present intellectual and moral condition. Our opinion and thoughts today are largely the result of a long succession of little experiences of the past, long since forgotten, perhaps never to be recalled.

In this course, we will train the subconscious to carefully store away, to re-member the location of what they take in charge, and to quickly find and bring forth, at the behest of the will, the desired thing. We will see that the memory is capable of infinite improvement, training and culture. When we realize that nothing is absolutely "forgotten," we begin to see the great possibilities in the direction of improvement in the art of receiving impressions, storing them away, and recalling them. We will see that the more clearly we impress upon the subconscious mentality, the more carefully we store away that impression, the more easily will we be able to bring it again into the field of consciousness. And we will see how wonderfully the subconscious may be trained to seek and find that which we want.

Attention and Concentration

The first key to improving the memory in this way is to recognize that the inten-sity of the original impression determines the degree of the future remembrance or recollection, and that the intensity of the impression is proportionate to the attention given the subject or object producing the impression. The experiences which leave the most permanent impress upon the mind are those upon which the most attention has been bestowed. Attention to the matter in hand is the most important intellectual habit possible to us, and every person has the power to develop a certain degree of genius by developing the power of concentrated attention, which power is capable of almost infinite augmentation by resolute practice. It is the different degrees of attention, rather than any difference in the abstract power of reasoning, which constitutes the great differences noticeable between the minds of different individuals, and that attention constitutes the better half of all intellectual power.

The subconscious part of the mind stores away all impressions received through the senses, whether or not attention is bestowed upon the subject or object, but as such impressions are not ordinarily subject to conscious recall through the memory, they are of very little use to us in the field of conscious-ness, and for this purpose are practically as if they did not exist. So, for our pur-pose, we may assume that without at least some degree of attention no durable impression is stored way. In this sense we may say that it is not sufficient that an object transmit an impression through the avenue of the senses to the brain, but that in order that a thing be remembered attention and consciousness are neces-sary at the time of the primary impression.

To illustrate the difference between conscious attention and the mere receiving of impressions through the senses, let us imagine ourselves in a busy street. Thousands of objects present themselves to our vision—thousands of sounds are transmitted to our brain through our organs of hearing—our sense of smell is receiving impressions—our sense of feeling is likewise doing its work as persons are coming in contact with us or we are brushing up against objects. In the midst of this confusion of sights, sounds, smells, feelings—with every avenue of sense impression open and receiving such impressions, we may be intently occupied with one particular sight, one sound, or even a thought—and all else that is going on around us is as if it were not. And all that we can readily remember of that particular moment is the one thing at which we were intently gazing—the one thing to which we were intently listening—or the particular thought occupying our mind at the moment.

A great proportion of the things we see, hear and feel, are almost immediately forgotten, because we have given them but a trifling degree of attention. It is said that poor memory is practically poor attention, and that the habit of careless observation is the twin of deficient memory.

The best authorities agree that the mind can actually attend to but one thing at a time, but it is able to move from one object to another with wonderful rapidity, which leads one to suppose that he has been directing his attention to two or more objects at the same time. Some very busy men are credited with the ability to do two or more things at the same time, but these men have simply developed an ability to go from one thing to another with the greatest rapidity. Granville, of this practice, says that it is "a sort of mental trapeze-flying, wherein the performer often gets an ugly fall, and may be permanently disabled." Bain sums up the matter when he says: "The fact never to be forgotten is that the human mind can attend to only one thing at a time, although it may shift the attention very rapidly, and thus overtake two or more things by turn."

When the mind is concentrated upon one subject or object, it is often oblivious to other sights and sounds which ordinarily would attract its momentary attention. Thus one who is engrossed in some thing may be oblivious to persons passing through the room, or to the striking of a clock within a few feet of him. If one wishes to devote his closest attention to a subject, he should therefore, if possible, choose a time and place where and when his mind will be free from outside impressions. If you desire to interest a friend in an important matter, you would not see him when he was occupied with other things, and would never dream of submitting the matter to his attention when he was in the midst of other business. You would wait until you could find him comparatively free from other interests, feeling sure that you would then get an attentive hearing. It is only men who have developed the power of concentrated attention who can drop one subject entirely for the moment, and give their undivided attention to a new subject. Of course, the memory follows the attention, and those things are best remembered of which the impressions are received when the mind is at ease and not otherwise employed.

Undivided attention will give remarkably clear impressions, and vastly increases the power of the faculties and gives them a strength which they ordinarily would not possess. A pain becomes more noticeable when the attention is directed toward it. When the attention is firmly directed to any particular portion of the body, a sensation is often experienced at the part. The circulation can be increased in any organ and part of the body by increased attention directed there. If we wish to obtain the fullest and clearest impressions of an object or subject, we should concentrate our attention upon it. Concentration can, of course, be greatly increased by intelligent practice.

People of great intellectual power are noted for their developed power of attention, and on the other hand, imbeciles and idiots[28] are almost destitute of concentrated attention. The sage's mind, consequently, is stored full of strong, intense impressions, which are brought into the field of consciousness in the course of everyday work, while the person of deficient attention has but a small stock upon which to draw, and consequently fails to manifest force and resourcefulness.

What we know about things is simply what we remember about them. This being so, one's knowledge is dependent entirely upon memory. As memory is dependent upon attention, then attention is the prime factor of knowledge. It will pay any man or woman to develop his or her power of attention. Learn to do one thing at a time, and to do that thing as well as you know how. By giving a thing our attention and interest, the task or study will become pleasant and we will be able to do it well. We will learn all that is to be learned about it; and we will remember what we have learned. Well has Chesterfield said: "There is time enough for everything in the course of a day, if we do but one thing at a time; but there is not enough time in a year if you try to do two things at a time." And Lord Burleigh backs him up, saying: "The shortest way of doing many things is

---

28. At the time when this was written, the terms "imbecile" and "idiot" were technical terms used by physicians for levels of developmental disability; only later did they turn into common insults.

to do one thing at a time. When we are attending to business, let us attend to it, and when we are taking our rest or play, let us not allow a thought of business to enter. Let us love business at the office—let us loathe it at home."

Apparently opposed to the above theory of concentrated attention is the fact that many persons are able to do their best thinking when engaged in some light occupation such as light sewing, knitting, cutting the leaves of a book, looking idly at pictures, smoking, etc.; but this apparent exception only proves the rule, the explanation being that the attention wandering from the main thought falls naturally upon the lighter occupation which makes only a minimum demand upon it, and which consequently does not distract the attention to any extent from the main point. The lighter task, in fact, may give the mind a little rest between thoughts. Therefore, if you find it difficult to concentrate your attention upon the subject or object before you, it may help you to take up some light task at the same time. But let the "side" task be light, as any important side issue would invariably divide the attention.

In studying the subject or object we get the best results by directing attention to the various details in succession, rather than by giving our attention to the thing as a whole. We get the best impression of a thing by using our powers of analyzing and abstraction. We can make little progress in intellectual work without exercising this power of analysis. We can best know a thing as a whole by knowing its parts separately. As Dr. Hering says: "Specialization is the mother of proficiency." Before one can learn to perform a complicated motion, he must first learn to perform each part of that motion. When he knows how to perform each part, he knows how to perform the whole. The same principle applies to the perception and acquisition of impressions.

To those who have not been in the habit of concentrating or placing the attention firmly upon an object or subject, the task of forming the new habit will prove difficult and tiresome. But practice will make perfect, and after a time it will be found that the attention will be directed almost automatically, and without effort. All of the desirable qualities of the mind may be so developed by practice that they will unconsciously manifest when needed. Concentrated attention will be given when the subject demands it. Establish a mental habit, and the mind will thereafter follow it. Clear away a mental path, and the mind will thenceforth travel it. The secret of attainment in any form of mental training, therefore, is practice and gradual improvement.

You may easily prove this to yourself. While engaged in whatever reading you ordinarily do for enjoyment, choose one or two paragraphs, and instead of simply reading through the passage in a casual fashion, apply your imagination to the words. Let us suppose you are reading a novel of adventure, and two characters who have been at odds are forced to flee some peril together. Use as many faculties as possible: picture these characters in your mind's eye, not in a vague manner, but in as much detail as possible; imagine their clothing, the items they have with them, etc. Picture also their surroundings, whatever these may be, again in detail; if they speak to one another, imagine their voices, high pitched or low, coarse or refined, as the case may be, and hear also the other sounds that surround them as they make their escape. Be attentive to the thoughts and feelings of the characters and their reactions to each other. Let the entire experience be as vivid as though you fled beside them. The next day, without referring to the book, call the same scene to mind again, and then compare it with another scene from the same book that you did not imagine in this way, and notice the differences between the two memories.

The same differences can be attained, given practice and the use of the subconscious, in less time-consuming ways. The following exercises will build foundations for this achievement.

The following two exercises will begin the process of training the mind and memory. The first should be done during periods of time otherwise wasted—for example, while sitting in a waiting room or standing in line. The second should be done once each evening on retiring.

Exercise 1

Whenever you have nothing to do for a short time, choose some object within your sight, it matters not what, and turn the whole of your attention to it. Note its color, its form, and everything else about it you can determine. See how long you can keep your attention upon it, without letting your thoughts or faculties stray from it to anything else.

When you first essay this exercise, you are likely to find yourself staring at whatever the object might be with a fixed expression and a stiff posture. Learn to control this, until you can attend to a single thing continuously for minutes at a time, without showing any sign of your attentiveness in your expression, your posture, or your movements.

Exercise 2

Each night, when you retire to bed, call to mind the events of the day just ended. Do this in reverse order, beginning with the last thing you did before retiring, proceeding to the thing before that, and so going until your recollection has passed through the whole of the day and reached your first waking actions. With practice, this can be done in a very few minutes.

Some form of this practice is part of the training of most of the mystery schools in the Western world, and some few of these schools make strange claims for it. Its true purpose is simply to teach the mind to make use of that store of memories closest at hand—those that record the events of each day of life. With regular practice, it is true, unexpected capacities commonly open up in the student, but these may best be discussed after they have appeared.

COMPLETION EXERCISES:
ESTABLISHING THE SELF

HESE COMPLETION EXERCISES are meant to be performed as part of the transition from the Novice Grade to the next, or Grade of the Theoretician. When you have learnt the seven Cantrefs, learnt the Elemental Cross by heart and practiced it daily for an extended period, explored the whole of the First Branch of the Mabinogion in your meditations, familiarized yourself intimately with the fundamentals of the Druid philosophy, and made the memory practices just presented a part of your daily life, the following exercises are to be performed. You should continue the completion exercises, along with the Elemental Cross and Circulation of Light and the memory practices, until you begin the next grade.

These completion practices have as their goal the establishment of the self. To "establish" is "to settle or fix firmly; to make steady, firm, or stable; to place upon a firm foundation; to ordain permanently and with authority," and so on. To establish the self imparts the sense and power of firm settlement and steady foundation of consciousness in that reality that goes beyond the realm of Becoming.

The student must develop this awareness of the self by degrees, until at last the consciousness of the self becomes the habitual and natural consciousness, at all times and under all conditions. Once firmly fixed, the consciousness of the self never leaves one. Once found, it becomes a tower of strength in which one may ever take refuge from the trials of the personal life—and from which one may safely defy all outside forces without exception.

Druid teachings draw on terms from the Welsh language to speak more clearly about these matters. The ordinary human personality is called the *hunan*. Druid tradition derives this word from the word *hun*, which means "sleep," and indicates that ordinary human consciousness is to the consciousness of the Individuality as sleep is to waking. Three capacities—*meddwl* or thought, *bryd* or will, and *cof* or memory—make up the triad of personality.

The hunan is not the whole of the ordinary individual; it shares space in the self with the *nwyd* and the *bywyd*. The first of these Welsh words means "passion," and stands for the irrational self, while the second means "life" and represents the basic biological forces and drives present in all living things. The hunan, the nwyd and the bywyd together make up the triad of the ordinary self.

The awakening of reflective consciousness brings a new factor into play, the individuality, which in Welsh is called the *elaeth*. The elaeth comes into being through a process of awakening that many human beings have not yet experienced; an individuality is evolved and earned, not given as a universal birthright of the human race. The elaeth is born from the hunan in much the same way that the hunan was born from the nwyd, collectively in the course of evolutionary time and individually in early childhood, and the nwyd was born from the bywyd further back along either course. Every living thing has a bywyd; every animal has a nwyd; every person has a hunan; but even among men and women, not many have evolved an elaeth. In any generation, many personalities are born, but few individualities are evolved.

The first step in establishing the individuality is that of acquiring a clear, distinct, positive and absolute realization that the self is not limited to the body or physical organism. The following exercises are recommended for this purpose:

Completion Exercise 1

Let the student prepare for the exercise as though for meditation, entering into the posture, relaxing the body, practicing the usual breathing patterns, until he is ready to proceed. Let him then fix his attention upon his physical body; first the body as a whole, and then beginning at the feet let him move the attention upward until the whole body has been included in attention, step by step, until the brain is reached.

During this process the student will become aware, by degrees, that he is a Something inside of the body, viewing and considering the latter in all of its details, instead of being identical with the body. There will be found a dawning realization that the body is but the physical envelope or sheath in which the Self dwells—or a garment which the Self has assumed for the conveniences of physical life. This realization will not come all at once, but will gradually dawn upon and in the consciousness, increasing by practice. When a degree of proficiency and realization of this stage has been acquired, then may the student proceed to the next stage, as follows:

Let the student now concentrate his attention upon his feet, until he is able to regard them as but tools or instruments whereby that which perceives and wills may walk in physical form. Then let him, using his imagination, realize that even if his feet were not there, attached to the body, he would still be fully existent and in being—that, although deprived of useful tools, he would still be himself, unharmed in his essential being.

Then bring the entire lower limbs into attention, and after fixing them firmly in consciousness, let the student realize that these limbs are but instruments for physical movement—useful and important, but not indispensable to the being and reality of the self. Let him see that if these limbs were not there that he would still be complete and fully existent.

Then, let the student bring into attention the pelvic organs (the reproductive organism, etc.) and, after realizing their uses and purposes—important to physical life—let him realize that the integrity and being of the self is in no way dependent upon them. Let him, in imagination, separate himself from them in consciousness, and thus realize that even if that part of the body were removed, and missing, nevertheless he would be fully existent in his entirety of being.

Then let the student, in a similar manner, consider the abdominal organs—the stomach, liver, etc.—and while realizing their value and utility in physical life, let him also realize that they, too, are but physical instruments meant for certain purposes, and that he would dwell unimpaired in being, existence and reality, were they absent.

Then let the student likewise consider the chest organs, the lungs, etc., and while respecting and realizing their usefulness and wonderful adaptability to purpose, also realize that he would be fully existent and real even if these organs or parts of the body were absent.

Then let the student pass on to the consideration of the head, with its various organs of sense; its brain centers and convolutions—the machinery of thought, and then realize that although it would be impossible to live as a physical being in the body without these organs, still if they were absent he would still be himself—complete, existent, in reality, with integrity unimpaired.

Then let the student again consider the whole body, as one organism—the wonderful instrument of the self, adapted for physical life. But let him fully realize that this wonderful machinery is but a created form in and through which he manifests physical life and activity. What is most real is above, independent of and apart from the physical body, in the true sense—for it may dwell apart from, and out of the body.

After performing these mental exercises, throw the mind into and over the entire body and into and through all of its parts—the purpose of this concluding process being to reenergize the physical organism which has, in a measure, become devitalized during the analytical process. You will find that you will be able to recharge the body with vitality and make it stronger and more virile than it was before the exercise, after you once realize that it is but an instrument, or machine, which is used by and directed by something beyond it. The realization of the mastery of the body by the self brings with it a new power of energizing and vitalizing the body or any part thereof. Throwing the attention to parts of the body, after this realization has been gained, tends to direct to the particular parts an increased supply of nwyfre or vital energy.

After having mastered the above exercise to a satisfactory degree, let the student pass on to the following exercise:

Completion Exercise 2

Let the student, in imagination, leave the physical body and gaze upon the latter. A little mental practice will enable one to do this in imagination, thus bringing fully to the mind the realization that it is possible for the self to leave the body and dwell apart from it. When the mind has once grasped this possibility, the body will ever after be recognized as merely a physical machine, sheath covering, of the self—and one will never again commit the folly of identifying the "I" with the physical body.

To those who may object that this is merely an exercise of the imagination, proving nothing, for the reason that "one may imagine anything;" we suggest the trial of the old occult test whereby the student was instructed to try to imagine himself as dead. A trial will show that this is impossible—all that can be imagined in this direction is that the physical body is dead, while the soul either stands apart, fully alive, viewing the body, or else inhabits the dead body—in either case it being the physical body alone which is dead, the self being always alive.

Then let the student imagine himself as leaving behind his physical body, until as Holmes says: "Thou at length are free, leaving thine outgrown shell by life's unresting sea." Let him then imagine himself as occupying other and different bodies, one at a time, in different phases of life and condition, in different ages, etc. This will bring about a realization that the self is something higher and independent of the particular physical expression that it is now using, and which it may have at one time considered identical with itself. Then will the particular body occupied seem, in reality, "my body," instead of "I" or "Me."

It is of course a mistake to despise the body simply because it is not one's self. The body is to be respected and well cared for, for it is a wonderful and necessary instrument for expression at this period of the evolution of the self. Do not make the mistake of so many who have grasped half-truths, and who hold their bodies and all related to them in contempt, because it is not the spirit which it supports and contains. The physical body must not be undervalued; it is as a bridge which is carrying you over a wild stream, and deserves your respect. Treat it well, with loving regard and care, for it is the Temple of the Spirit. Keep it clean and in good condition. Let it be a worthy dwelling place of the One Life.

GRADD Y DAMCANIWR

THE GRADE OF THE THEORETICIAN

INTRODUCTION
TO THE GRADE

CONGRATULATIONS! With this lesson packet you have passed beyond the probationary grade of Newyddian or Novice, and begun work in the Druid mysteries in earnest. Of those who begin a course of this sort, fewer than half complete the work of the first grade of study and proceed beyond it. You are among those few; should you continue to show the same perseverance in the work, the remaining lessons will offer many challenges to you, but no insuperable obstacles.

The seven grades of the Dolmen Arch are divided into a set of four, which represent the Lesser Mysteries, and a set of three, which represent the Greater Mysteries. The first four grades present the fundamentals of theory and practice; they are of necessity preparatory, though certain practical techniques that may be found useful in the student's daily affairs are presented therein. The latter three grades communicate the principal practical methods of the system: the arts of healing, of enchantment, and of initiation.

Your ascent through the four preliminary grades will therefore require a certain degree of patience and perseverance. Those who have not previously worked with the teachings of a mystery school will find much of the practical work unfamiliar, and possibly unwelcome; those who have received training in some other school of the mysteries may feel burdened by being asked to perform exercises which, it may be, they have previously encountered elsewhere.

It must be remembered in this context that the teachings of a mystery school are of two kinds. The first and least important are the ideas, concepts and symbols passed on, for example, in instructional letters such as these. The second and most vital are the ways of understanding the self and the world that are communicated *through* those ideas, concepts, and symbols. The second kind of teachings are, strictly speaking, incommunicable on their own; they can only be passed on secondhand, by way of some set of teachings of the first kind; and it is all too possible for a student of any mystery school to commit every scrap of the teachings of the first kind to memory, to communicate them to others, and even to parrot them to others at every opportunity, without ever grasping the nature—or even the existence—of the teachings of the second kind.

An old Druid legend, already mentioned in this course, speaks of the three rowan staves that were carved by Einigan the Giant at the beginning of time. The carvings on those staves recorded the wisdom that Einigan learnt from the Three Rays of Light that descended from the heavens at the creation of the world. Later, when Einigan showed the staves to others, they worshipped the staves as gods rather than learning the wisdom that was carved upon them. Einigan was so distraught at this that he burst asunder, and so died. A year and a day after the giant's demise, Menw the Old found the skull of Einigan, and saw that the three staves had taken root and were growing through the openings in the skull. Unlike those who had worshipped the staves, Menw recognized the wisdom present in the writings upon them. He communicated this wisdom to his pupils, who according to legend, became the *Gwiddons*, the loremasters of the Celts in the oldest times, before the order of Druids was established.

This is again symbolism rather than history, but it contains a potent truth. Einigan recognized the rays of light, and Menw recognized the staves, as bearers of knowledge. The others who saw the staves failed to grasp the presence of the knowledge, and worshipped the staves instead of learning from them. All those who treat the symbols and stories of religion as objects of blind belief rather than vessels of understanding do the same.

Yet the risk of misunderstanding cannot be avoided. Human beings exist on many different levels of consciousness. Some have not yet grown beyond the state of simple consciousness, and live a life entirely oriented to things outside themselves. Many others have proceeded beyond this to various stages in the realm of personal consciousness, and are aware of the world around them as well as their own thoughts and feelings, but have not yet attained to any knowledge of their own nature. A few have embarked on the grand adventure of individual consciousness, and have begun to know themselves as more than their bodies and their minds.

No one form of spirituality can be appropriate for so broad a diversity of minds and states of consciousness. Those who exist in simple consciousness can conceive of spiritual realities only as things entirely outside themselves, and the appropriate path for them is that of ordinary reverence for the god or gods of their people, supported by a moral law suited to their understandings and the exigencies of their daily lives. From those who have attained to some degree of personal consciousness, spirituality demands more; to them belongs the effortful searching of conscience in prayer and meditation, and the direction of the mind toward some ideal grand enough to provide inspiration for betterment in thought, word, and deed.

For those who are approaching the threshold of individual consciousness, or have passed through it and are beginning to glimpse the splendid vistas beyond, yet another form of spirituality is appropriate. Here reverence is not enough; morality is not enough; the promptings of conscience and the pursuit of an ideal are not enough. The awakening flame of the individuality must be fed with teachings and exercises that foster reflective awareness and the recognition of the powers and possibilities inherent in this higher aspect of the self. These things the mystery schools have offered since time immemorial.

This lesson packet, like the first, contains seven instructional papers:

Like the lessons of the Novitiate Grade, these are to be worked through at your own pace, with the Completion exercises reserved for last. The practical work given in this lesson packet builds on that of the previous grade, and a similar length of time, *i.e.*, at least three months, and possibly more, should be allotted to their completion. Once again, remember that rushing through the exercises benefits no one, least of all yourself. A few extra weeks, or even a few extra months, devoted to mastering some exercise that seems more than usually challenging will pay substantial dividends further along the path.

Wishing you all the best in your journey on the Path of the Druid Mysteries,

 *John Michael Greer*

COLORS AND COLOR BREATHING

O F THE CORRESPONDENCES that pertain to the Seven Cantrefs, the most important to the beginning practitioner of this work is color. There is a philosophy of color, and a symbolism of color, and a practice of color; and one who masters each of these is well advanced on the path of knowledge.

Know first that all color begins from the juxtaposition of white and black, which are Awen and Annwn, the eternal Absolute and the creative Void.

Fig. 12. The Juxtaposition of White & Black, Awen & Annwn

From these proceed the first two colors: yellow, the lightest of all the colors and therefore closest to white, and blue, the darkest of all the colors and therefore closest to black. These two combined yield green, which harmonizes light and darkness and is thus the color of life.

Fig. 13. The Blending of Yellow & Blue to Produce the Green of Life

Yet white and black, by another means, also create red. Take a disk half white and half black, affix it to a spindle like a wheel to an axle, and spin it, slowly at first, and then with increasing speed. When it turns slowly, you will see black and white turning around a common center, and when it turns fast, you will see nothing but a gray blur, but between these two rates of speed, at the edge between white and black, you will see flashes and glimpses of red. Red is thus the color of the primal powers in their direct combination, as distinct from the indirect combination that gives rise to green; it is the color of power, of transformation, and of death.

Red is also the complementary color of green. Yellow and blue also have their complementary colors, and the resulting circle of colors may be placed on the familiar color circle.

Note how these relationships among colors reflect the relationship among the Cantrefs. Yellow and blue, the first two colors, belong to the first two Cantrefs, and represent the expressive and receptive energies as they appear in the manifested world. Red is the color of the Third Cantref, the realm of power and will, and green, which mediates among the colors, is the color of the fourth Cantref, which forms the central pivot of the seven. Orange and violet are

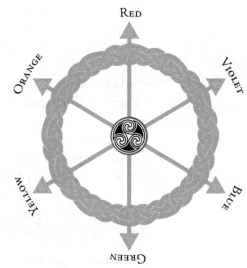

Fig. 14. The Wheel of Complementary Colors

the colors of the Fifth and Sixth Cantrefs, and reflect the same expressive and receptive qualities as their complementary colors, but on another plane; while the Seventh Cantref is symbolized by white, the color of pure creative light.

All these relationships are worthy of meditation and study, as well as practical application. The following exercises will help you begin to learn the last of these.

Exercise 1: Complementary Colors

Take seven white cards, and on them place seven colored circles, one circle on each card, viz.: violet, green, orange, red, blue, yellow, black. The circles can be painted upon the cards, or cut from colored paper and pasted upon the cards, but the color of each circle must be clear, strong, and pure.

When you have done this, seat yourself in a place where you can easily look upon a plain white wall or, failing this, have a sheet of unlined white paper close to hand. Take one of the cards, let us suppose the one bearing a violet circle, and gaze upon it for some minutes, without allowing your eyes to stray from the circle.

After a certain time, which will vary from one student to another, the violet color of the circle will seem to be overlaid with a phantom yellow circle, as it were hovering above the card. When this has been achieved, turn your gaze to the white wall or paper, and you will see the appearance of a yellow circle surrounded by darkness, which will gradually fade from sight.

Perform this practice once each day, varying the card from day to day. You will have better results with this exercise if you practice each day with the color complementary to that of the Cantref that rules the day. Thus the card with the violet circle would be best used on Sunday, the card with the black circle on Monday, and so forth. When you have practiced the foregoing exercise for perhaps three weeks, and can reliably project the phantom of the complementary color and concentrate on it, you may proceed to the following.

Exercise 2: The Ocean of Color

As in Exercise 1, seat yourself and take one of the cards. Gaze on it until the complementary color appears. Then imagine that same complementary color filling all the space that surrounds you. Picture yourself as though immersed in an infinite sea of that color. Strive to make the color as clear and real as the phantom of the color you previously saw projected on the wall or the paper, or even more so. Remain in the sea of color for a few minutes, then deliberately dissolve it, returning the space around you to its normal color.

Perform this practice once each day, varying the color from day to day according to the Cantref corresponding to that day, viz: yellow on Sunday, white on Monday, red on Tuesday, and so forth. When you have practiced this exercise for perhaps three weeks, and can reliably get the impression of being submerged in a sea of color with each of the seven colors, you may proceed to the following.

Exercise 3: Practical Color Breathing

This is practiced during your daily meditation. When you have finished the period of relaxation and done the cleansing breath, imagine yourself surrounded with an ocean of color; the color is again to be taken from that of the Cantref corresponding to that day. As you begin the fourfold breath, imagine that as you breathe air in through your nostrils, you also breathe in color through the pores of your skin. As the color flows in to you through your pores, imagine it flowing in to fill your entire body. As you hold the breath, concentrate on the image of your body filled with color.

As you breathe out, in turn, allow the color to flow back out through the pores of your skin and into the ocean of color that surrounds you. Let every trace of color leave your body. While holding the lungs empty, concentrate on the image of your body as a colorless space surrounded by an ocean of vivid color. Repeat the whole sequence along with the fourfold breath for five minutes, then return to ordinary breathing, dissolve the ocean of color, and begin your meditation.

When you have practiced color breathing often enough that you have no difficulty seeing the ocean of color around you, and experiencing it flowing into and out of your body, you may add the next step, which is to experience—not merely the color—but the whole quality of the Cantref to which it corresponds. Supposing you are practicing on a Sunday, surround yourself not only with the color yellow, but with a yellow that embodies every quality of the First Cantref. Breathe into yourself the essence of morning and of springtime, the radiance of the Sun, the fresh winds of heaven and the spirit of the hawk that circles therein. Do the same with each of the Seven Cantrefs in the cycle of the week.

You may also make use of this same practice in your daily life. Should you need courage and singleness of purpose to face some danger or difficulty, for example, it will be the work of a moment to surround yourself with an ocean of red light, filling it with the qualities of the Third Cantref, and then to breathe those qualities into yourself. In such a case, you will find it helpful to breathe the color into yourself, to retain it on the outbreath, and then to breathe an additional amount of the color into yourself with the next breath. To begin with, seven breaths of a color are as much as you should attempt to breathe into yourself at any one time without breathing them out again.

With practice, this can be increased, but a very real pressure is developed within the body, to which the novice practitioner must become accustomed. After the danger is past, do not neglect to breathe the color back out of yourself, using as many breaths as it took to draw it in; thus, if you breathed the Third Cantref into yourself seven times, draw in seven slow and even breaths, and with each outbreath imagine the red color and the qualities of the Cantref flowing out of you and dispersing into the infinite reservoir of nwyfre that surrounds and fills all things.

THE CALLING OF THE CANTREFS

HE CALLING OF THE CANTREFS consists of seven separate parts, which you will add one at a time, in the order given, between the Elemental Cross and the Circulation of Light. In its complete form, the ritual invokes all seven Cantrefs, and banishes unbalanced energies with the aid of four of them. "Invoke" means to call in, and "banish" means to send away. Thus you are calling in the energies of all the Cantrefs, and sending away certain aspects of the four more material Cantrefs—those of the four material elements of air, fire, water, and earth. The Cantrefs of spirit are always in perfect balance, and nothing that comes from them needs to be banished—though some of their aspects need to be balanced.

The ritual involves a special kind of speech or chanting called *vibration*. Vibration, in occult jargon, is a special way of chanting magically powerful names and words. To learn it, try it with a simple vowel tone like "ah" or "oh." Draw in a deep breath, and chant the sound, stretching it out until you run out of breath. As you make the sound, try changing the shape of your mouth and the quality of the tone until you get a buzzing or tingling feeling in your throat and chest, or elsewhere in your body. The effect may be slight at first, but practice will make it stronger. It will also bring the ability to focus the vibration at various points of the body, and in time to focus it outside the body as well.

Vibration is used only with the names of spiritual powers. In ritual work, you vibrate the name of the god or angel you invoke, and speak all other words in a more ordinary voice.

The Calling of Awyr, the First Cantref

Face east. Using the first two fingers of your right hand, trace the symbol of air in front of you. Start where the circle joins the line, tracing the circle in a clock-

wise direction, and then trace the upward line. This
is the invoking form of the symbol. As you trace the
invoking symbol, imagine that your fingers are drawing it in the air in front of you in brilliant yellow flame.
When you finish and point to the center, imagine the
circle filled with paler, transparent yellow flame.

Fig. 15. The Cantref Awyr

Each of the seven invocations calls on a spiritual
power. In the traditional lore, Hu the Mighty fills this role in the realm of Air.
The "Great Druid God" of Welsh tradition, Hu is the active power of divine
creation in the world. His name is pronounced with the Welsh u; to pronounce
this, purse your lips as though you meant to say "ooooh," and then—without
changing the position of your lips—try to say "eeee" instead. An Irish god appropriate to this Cantref is Aengus Og (pronounced "AHN-gus OHG"), the
youthful god of love and life, while Christian Druids usually invoke St. Raphael
the Archangel (pronounce the name "RA-fa-ell") as the regent of Air.

To invoke the First Cantref in the traditional form, say, "By the yellow gate
of the rushing winds and the hawk of May in the heights of morning, and in the
great name HU, I invoke the Air, its gods, its spirits and its powers." (Christian
Druids typically end this and the other invocations with the phrase "its angels,
its spirits, and its powers.") The name of Hu, or whichever divine name you
choose to use, is the only word vibrated, and it may be extended to a full breath,
letting the vibration resonate all through your body. Then say, "May I receive
the blessings of Air this day and always, that I may attain Gwynfydd in this life.
May my mind be inspired by the ways of Nature."

As you speak these words, concentrate on Air. Picture before you a morning
sky. Feel the wind and smell the fresh air. As you imagine this, feel the powers
and blessings of air flowing into you. Imagine that the yellow light of air flows
into your body through your solar plexus, and feel that you have become so light
and nimble that you could dance on the winds. Then say, "I thank the air for its
gifts."

Hold your hand still for a time, and then trace the symbol of air in its banishing form; first trace the circle in a *counterclockwise* direction, and then draw
the upward line. When banishing, say, "And with the help of the powers of air,
I banish from within me and around me and from all my doings, all harmful
influences and inappropriate thoughts, and every unbalanced expression of Air.
I banish them far away from me." When you thank the air and trace the banishing form of the symbol, release the imagery of air. Concentrate on the idea that

all airy imbalances in your life are swept away by the winds and lost in the vastness of the skies. Take as much time as you need on this visualization.

For the next two or three weeks, include this section in your daily practice. Perform the Elemental Cross, then invoke and banish by air, then perform the Circulation of Light. Practice it until you have this phase of the ritual by heart, and can feel the air respond to the ritual. During the time you spend on this, pay attention to any symbols relating to air that show up in other aspects of your life.

The Calling of Dŵr, the Second Cantref

Fig. 16. *The Cantref Dŵr*

Turn to the west. With the first two fingers of your right hand trace a triangle with one point down, as shown in the diagram, starting at the bottom point and tracing clockwise. Visualize it in blue flame, and then fill it with paler, transparent blue flame. Then say: "By the blue gate of the mighty waters and the salmon of wisdom in the sacred pool, and in the great name ESUS, I invoke the Water, its gods, its spirits, and its powers. May I receive the blessings of Water this day and always, that I may attain Gwynfydd in this life. May my heart be instructed by the ways of Nature."

Esus is the chief of all tree spirits, a god of wisdom who sits in the first fork of the sacred oak. His name is pronounced "EH-suus," with the Welsh "u" again. If you prefer an Irish god, invoke Manannan, the Irish sea god; his name is pronounced "mah-NAHN-un." If you prefer Christian symbolism, St. Gabriel the archangel is invoked in this quarter; pronounce the name "GAH-bree-ell."

Pause for a time, and concentrate on Water. Imagine the ocean reaching out in front of you into infinite distance. Weave the sounds and scents of water into your imagery. As you picture all this, feel the powers and blessings of Water flowing into you through your solar plexus. Imagine your body filled with the blue light of Water, and feel yourself becoming so fluid and responsive that nothing can contain or restrict you.

Then say, "I thank the Water for its gifts," and trace the symbol counterclockwise, again from the bottom of the triangle. Say: "And with the help of the powers of Water, I banish from within me and around me and from all my doings, all harmful influences and mistaken beliefs, and every unbalanced expression of Water. I banish them far away from me." Concentrate on the idea that all unbalanced factors in your life are swept away and drowned in the depths. Take as much time as you need on this visualization.

For the next two or three weeks, include this section in your daily practice: perform the Elemental Cross, then invoke and banish by air, then invoke and banish by water, then perform the Circulation of Light. Practice it until you have this phase of the ritual by heart, and can feel the water respond to the ritual. During the time you spend doing this, pay attention to any of the symbols of the Gate of Water that show up in other aspects of your life.

The Calling of Ufel, the Third Cantref

To call the Third Cantref, turn to the south; this is usually done between the First and Second, so that the Callings can be done in a circle from east around to north. With the first two fingers of your right hand trace a triangle with one point up, as shown in the diagram, starting at the top point and tracing clockwise. Visualize it in red flame, and then fill it with transpar-

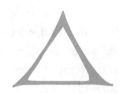

Fig. 17. The Cantref Ufel

ent red flame. Then say: "By the red gate of the bright flames and the white stag in the light of summer, and in the great name SUL, I invoke the Fire, its gods, its spirits, and its powers. May I receive the blessings of Fire this day and always, that I may attain Gwynfydd in this life. May my will be governed by the ways of Nature."

Sul is the ancient British goddess of the hot springs at Bath, a goddess of the sun and also of the fires beneath the earth; her name is pronounced "SUL," with the Welsh "u." If you prefer to work with Irish divinities, Brigid (pronounced "BREEJ"), the goddess of smiths, poets and healers, is a good choice for this element. Christian Druids invoke St. Michael the archangel (pronounce the name "MEE-ka-ell") in this quarter.

Once you have finished the invocation, pause for a time, and concentrate on fire. Imagine the sun blazing down on the hottest day you can imagine, as flames rise from the ground before you. Feel the heat from the sun, the ground, and the flames, and smell the dry air and the tang of smoke. As you picture this, feel the powers and blessings of fire flowing into you through your solar plexus. Imagine your body filled with the red light of fire, and feel yourself become so full of flaming energy that nothing could stand against you.

Then say, "I thank the Fire for its gifts," and trace the symbol counterclockwise, again from the top of the triangle. Say: "And with the help of the powers of Fire, I banish from within me and around me and from all my doings all harmful influences and misguided intentions, and every unbalanced expression of fire. I banish them far away from me." Concentrate on the idea that all unbalanced factors in your life are caught up in the flames and burned away until not even the finest ash remains. Take as much time as you need on this visualization.

For the next two or three weeks, include this section in your daily practice: perform the Elemental Cross, then invoke and banish by Air, then invoke and banish by Fire, then invoke and banish by Water, then perform the Circulation of Light. Practice it until you have this phase of the ritual by heart, and can feel fire respond to the ritual. During the time you spend doing this, pay attention to any of the symbols of the Gate of Fire that show up in other aspects of your life.

The Calling of Daear, the Fourth Cantref

Fig. 18. The Cantref Daear

This Calling follows the same pattern as the others. Turn to the north. With the first two fingers of your right hand trace the symbol of earth. In the invoking mode it is traced starting from the place where the circle meets the line and going around the circle clockwise, then drawing the line downward. Visualize it in green flame, and then fill it with paler, transparent green flame. Then say: "By the green gate of the tall stones and the great bear who guards the starry heavens, and in the great name ELEN, I invoke the earth, its gods, its spirits, and its powers. May I receive the blessings of earth this day and always, that I may attain Gwynfydd in this life. May my body be healed by the ways of Nature."

Elen is the goddess of dawn and springtime, as well as the mistress of the old straight trackways, older than the Romans, that still puzzle wayfarers in the British countryside. She rules the dragon current flowing along the old tracks, and thus is a powerful symbol of life and strength within the earth. Her name is pronounced "ELL-enn." If you prefer to work with Irish deities, Boann, the Irish cow goddess, is a good choice for earth; her name is pronounced "BO-unn." Christian Druids usually invoke St. Uriel the archangel in this quarter; pronounce the name "OO-ree-ell."

When you finish the invocation, pause for a time, and concentrate on earth. Imagine the land in which you live, with whatever vegetation flourishes there growing on it. Be sure to bring in the sounds and scents of the landscape. As you picture this, feel the powers and blessings of earth flowing into you through your solar plexus. Imagine your body filled with the green light of earth, and feel yourself becoming so solid and firm that you could resist the mightiest force in the universe.

Then say, "I thank the earth for its gifts," and trace the symbol in its banishing mode, starting from where the circle joins the line, tracing the circle counterclockwise, and then draw the line downwards. Say the following: "And with the help of the powers of earth, I banish from within me and around me all unbalanced manifestations of earth. I banish them far away from me." Concentrate on the idea that all unbalanced factors in your life are swallowed up by the earth and buried far beneath soil and stone. Take as much time as you need on this visualization.

For the next two or three weeks, include this section in your daily practice: perform the Elemental Cross, then invoke and banish by air, then invoke and banish by fire, then invoke and banish by water, then invoke and banish by earth, then perform the Circulation of Light. Practice it until you have this phase of the ritual by heart, and can feel the earth respond to the ritual. During the time you spend doing this, pay attention to any of the symbols of the Gate of Earth that show up in other aspects of your life.

The Calling of Maen, the Fifth Cantref

To invoke Spirit Below, face south, the same direction you faced during the Elemental Cross. Trace the circle of Spirit in a clockwise manner below and in front of you, as though tracing it over an altar. Visualize your fingers drawing the circle in orange flame, and fill it with paler, transparent orange flame. Imagine the circle descending into the ground below you. Then say: "By

Fig. 19. The Cantref Maen

the bright heart of the Earth Mother, and in the great name CÊD, I invoke Spirit Below, its gods, its spirits, and its powers. May I receive the blessings of Spirit Below this day."

In Welsh Druid lore, Cêd is the goddess of living nature and the source of all life. Her name is pronounced "KEHD," and means "bounty" or "abundance" in Welsh. If you prefer to work with Irish divinities, the goddess Danu, mother of all the gods and goddesses, is a good choice for this element, her name is pronounced "DAH-noo." Christian Druids often invoke the Virgin Mary at this station.

When you finish the invocation, pause for a time and concentrate on Spirit Below. Picture in your mind's eye the ground beneath your feet, the soil and stone that belongs to the element of Earth, and then go deeper, into the heart of the living planet itself. Feel the immense power that drives earthquakes and volcanoes, lifts mountains toward the sky, and moves entire continents across the face of the planet, and sense that same power surging through every living thing from the smallest microbe to the great whales and the tallest trees.

As you picture all this, feel the powers and blessings of Spirit Below flowing into you through your solar plexus. Imagine the rich harvest-orange light of Spirit Below filling your body, and feel the life force of the planet leaping through your veins. Take as much time as seems appropriate for this visualization. Then say: "I thank Spirit Below for its gifts."

For the next two or three weeks, include this section in your daily practice. Perform the Elemental Cross, then invoke and banish by air, fire, water, and earth, then invoke Spirit Below, and then perform the Circulation of Light. Practice it until you have this phase of the ritual by heart, and can feel Spirit Below respond to the ritual. During the time you spend doing this, pay attention to any symbols of the Gate of Spirit Below that show up in other aspects of your life.

The Calling of Nef, the Sixth Cantref

Turn to face the same direction you faced during the Elemental Cross. Trace a clockwise circle above you, visualizing it in violet flame. Fill it with paler, transparent violet flame. Then say: "By the Sun in its glory, the father of light, and in the great name CELI, I invoke Spirit Above, its gods, its spirits, and its powers. May I receive the blessings of Spirit Above this day."

Fig. 20. The Cantref Nef

In Welsh Druid lore, Celi is the hidden god of the heavens, the original source of the three rays of light that brought the worlds into being. His name is pronounced "KEH-lee." If you prefer to work with Irish gods and goddesses, the Dagda is a good choice for this Cantref; his name, pronounced "DOY-da," means "the excellent god," and he is the father of the Irish gods. Christian Druids usually invoke Christ in this station.

When you have finished the invocation, pause for a time, and concentrate on Spirit Above. Picture in your mind's eye the sun at midheaven above you, surrounded by the planets in their orbits, with numberless stars scattered across the infinite heavens beyond. Sense the vastness of space, the cold pure starlight that fills it, and the perfect order that governs all the worlds in their courses.

As you picture all this, feel the powers and blessings of Spirit Above flowing into you. Imagine the intense purple light of Spirit Above filling your body through your solar plexus, and feel your awareness opening outwards so that, for a moment, you seem to understand the whole Cosmos. Take as much time as seems appropriate for this visualization. Then say: "I thank Spirit Above for its gifts."

For the next two or three weeks, include this section in your daily practice: perform the Elemental Cross, then invoke and banish by air, fire, water, and earth, then invoke Spirit Below and Spirit Above, and then perform the Circulation of Light. Practice it until you have this phase of the ritual by heart, and can feel Spirit Above respond to the ritual. During the time you spend doing this, pay attention to any of the symbols of the Gate of Spirit Above that show up in other aspects of your life.

The Calling of Byw, the Seventh Cantref

This is the final Calling of the Sphere of Protection. To call the Seventh Cantref, remain facing the same direction you faced during the Elemental Cross, and be aware of the six powers you have already invoked—air in the east, fire in the south, water in the west, earth in the north, Spirit Below in the land beneath you and

Fig. 21. The Cantref Byw

Spirit Above in the heavens above. See yourself in the midst of these six powers, in the place of perfect balance among them. Then say: "By the six powers here invoked and here present, and in the grand word AWEN, I invoke Spirit Within. May the universe within me and the universe around me be in harmony."

When you finish the invocation, pause for a time, and concentrate on Spirit Within. Be aware of yourself exactly as you are, and strive to see every aspect of yourself as a vessel of infinite powers. Imagine yourself filled with the pure white light of Spirit Within, and feel yourself in harmony with the whole Cosmos. Take as much time as seems appropriate for this visualization. Then say "I thank Spirit Within for its gifts." At this point, focus on the center of energies at your solar plexus, and proceed at once to the Circulation of Light.

Once you have learned the Elemental Cross, the Calling of the Cantrefs, and the Circulation of Light, you have gained one of the great tools of the Druid path, the Sphere of Protection ritual. Plan on practicing it once each day for as long as you follow the way of Druidry. It is best performed immediately before your daily meditation.

MEDITATION: THE SEVEN
WAYS OF THOUGHT

I N THE COURSE of completing your journey through the Novitiate Grade in the Dolmen Arch, you have learned the rudiments of meditation in the Druid way, and have begun to use your thinking mind as a means to attain higher states of awareness. Further progress along this path will require you to gain a thorough understanding of that remarkable but in no way flawless tool—your mind; to capitalize on its strengths, correct for its weaknesses, and give it the skilled handling that any tool must receive if it is to achieve its highest potential.

One important task, on which you have made a beginning, consists in understanding the ways that the thinking mind goes about its work. As you meditated on the personages and events of "Pwyll, Prince of Dyfed," and the triads and concepts of Druid philosophy, you will have witnessed your mind at work: now leaping from one idea to another, now hovering over some compelling image, now diverting itself with some topic of thought unrelated to the work you wished it to do. If you followed the instructions to retrace its movements back to the theme whenever it flees from the latter, you also know something of the kinds of mental leaps it makes habitually in passing from thought to thought.

Annoying as they are, when they lead your mind away from its theme in meditation, these leaps are essential to thought, and even more so to the higher functions of thought meditation seeks to induce. Recall a favorite poem and you will see that such leaps are inseparable from the creative process. When Robert Burns said that his love was like a red, red rose, he made such a leap; the lady who inspired the verse presumably did not have red petals on her head, green skin, and thorns; but her beauty, having an impression on him like that received from a brilliant red rose, inspired the metaphoric phrase.

The ability to make such leaps of thought at will is the precondition of genius. Every human being has the potential for genius—few are they who bring forth that potential into manifestation—but by learning the workings of your mind, and applying that knowledge in meditation, you lay foundations for attainments that, it may be, surpass anything you have as yet imagined.

The Druid teachings trace the movement of thought along seven relationships, which may be thought of as paths by which thought moves from one object of its consideration to another. These are the Seven Ways of Thought:

1. Association. Thought moves readily from any object to any other object associated with it in space or time, as: cup—coffee; horse—rider; noon—luncheon.

2. Sequence. Thought moves readily from any object to any other object that comes before or after it, either in logical sequence or in sequence of time, as: winter—snow; afternoon—evening; spark—flame.

3. Quality. Thought moves readily from any object to any quality that describes that object, and from any quality to an object that expresses it, as: fire—warm; ox—strong; dark—night.

4. Polarity. Thought moves readily from any object to its opposite or complement, as: cat—dog; day—night; teacher—student.

5. Composition. Thought moves readily from any object to any part of that object, and from any part to an object to which it belongs, as: table—leg; tail—dog; sentence—word.

6. Category. Thought moves readily from any object to the logical or conventional category to which it belongs, and from any category to an object included in it, as: cat—mammal; ocean—Atlantic; chair—furniture.

7. Symbolism. Thought moves readily from any object to a symbolic meaning related to that object, and from any meaning to an object that symbolizes it, as: lily—purity; strength—oak; sun—divinity.

You will doubtless have noticed already that the Seven Ways of Thought correspond precisely to the Seven Cantrefs. Meditation on the relations between each Cantref and its corresponding Way of Thought will reveal much.

Not all the distractions that beset you in meditation follow one of these seven paths—there will often come thoughts inspired by the perceptions of your senses, as when rain drumming on a window puts some unrelated thought into your mind; there will also come thoughts inspired by besetting worries or passionate desires on your part, as when thoughts about the prospects of a business deal or the course of a relationship keep drawing your attention away from your theme. Nonetheless, most of the distracting thoughts you encounter in your daily meditations will follow one of these seven ways, and this is well, for by directing your mind's movement along the Seven Ways, you will increase the clarity and depth of your thought in meditation.

Here is an exercise that will help you begin that process.

Exercise 1

Take a sheet of paper and a pen or pencil, and write some word, it matters not what, at the top of the paper. Thereafter, write down as many words as you can think of that relate to the word you have chosen. After each word, before writing the next one, decide which of the Seven Ways of Thought connect it back to the original word at the head of the paper, and write the number of the Way after the word.

Suppose the initial word you chose was "stone," some of the words that might come to mind are "circle" (5), because stones are parts of Druid stone circles; "endurance" (7), because stone symbolizes that quality; "hard" (3), because hardness is a quality possessed by stones; "granite" (6), because granite belongs to the category "stone;" "hoof" (1), because stones are so often caught in horse's hooves; "sand" (2), because stones are worn away to sand by the action of water over time; and "silk" (4), the proverbial softness to stone's hardness.

Perform this exercise half a dozen times during the first few weeks you spend on this grade. After you have done so, expand your work with the Seven Ways using the following exercise.

Exercise 2

This is a variation of the first exercise. Take a sheet of paper and a pen or pencil, as before, and leaving space for a word at the top, divide the paper into seven columns, heading each column with a number. Next, write any word you choose at the head of the paper. Think of seven words related to the chosen word through the First Way of Thought, and write them down in the first column. Then think of seven words related to the chosen word by the Second Way of Thought, and write them in the second column. Proceed until you have written down seven words in each of the seven columns.

As you do the foregoing exercise, teach your mind to return to the chosen word at the top of the paper as soon as it has discovered a word related to it along the Way of Thought you are using. For example, the word you have written at the head of the paper is "flame," and you are filling in the first column, you would think "flame, smoke," and write "smoke" in the first column; "flame, wood," and write "wood" in the same column; "flame, chimney," and so on. In doing this, you are teaching your mind to return to the theme as soon as it has ventured far enough from it to find the thing you desire it to find. This is essentially the same skill you are trying to cultivate, in a more complex form, in meditation.

The foregoing exercises will familiarize you with the Seven Ways of Thought, so that you will be prepared to use them during meditation. When you reach a point in your meditations at which nothing comes to mind in response to the theme, use the following exercise.

Exercise 3

When you wish to use the Seven Ways of Thought in meditation, consider the theme you have chosen, and then ask yourself what things relate to your theme by each of the Seven Ways. What things relate to it by association? By sequence? By quality? By polarity? By composition? By category? By symbolism? Glance along all seven Ways, and very often the words, concepts, or ideas that come to mind as a result of this exercise will spark new insights. Continue to practice this exercise until you have finished the work of this grade.

THE MABINOGION:
BRANWEN DAUGHTER OF LLYR

HIS SECOND BRANCH of the Mabinogion differs from the first in setting and tone, but the same themes of love, conflict, cruelty, and redemption run through both. The imagery and events of "Branwen, Daughter of Llyr" echo the correspondences of Dŵr, the Second Cantref; here the magical cauldron, journeys over water, and westward movement take the place of the First Cantref imagery that pervades "Pwyll, Prince of Dyfed."

It is a curious point that those parts of the Mabinogion which take place in the south of Wales or in what is now England place Pryderi the Mabon at or near the center of the tale, while those parts which take place in the north of Wales or Ireland refer to him in passing or not at all. The Second Branch is a case in point; most of the action takes place in North Wales and Ireland, and it is only when the seven survivors of Bran's expedition to Ireland return to Wales that Pryderi is named among them. Druid tradition has it that the entire Mabinogion is the story of Pryderi the Mabon and his journey of initiation and transformation, but that this story takes place on two planes, which are symbolized by the northern and southern parts of Wales.

Those planes, in one of their senses, may be understood as the earth and the heavens, or alternatively as the sky by day and the sky by night. The Ovate symbolism of the First Branch, to refer back to a distinction made in the first grade of this course, relates primarily to the seasons of nature upon the earth, and to the movement of the sun relative to the earth; it extends, as the narrative hints, from *Calan Gaeaf* (Samhuinn, November 1) to *Calan Haf* (Belteinne, May 1). The equivalent symbolism of the Second Branch covers the same period of time but relates to the night sky and its constellations. For this reason, not all of the

Ovate symbolism can be decoded nowadays, for it hearkens back to an archaic Celtic starlore that has been only imperfectly preserved.

The Second Branch will be your source of themes for meditation while you work your way through the lessons appropriate to this grade. As before, read over the tale two or three times, and then start at the beginning; choose one image or event as a meditation theme, meditate on it, then proceed to the next, and so on until you have meditated on the entire tale. Once again, the translation by Lady Charlotte Guest follows; the footnotes give traditional Druid meanings of the Welsh names.

BRANWEN DAUGHTER OF LLYR

Bran[1] the Blessed, the son of Llyr,[2] was the crowned king of this island, and he was exalted from the crown of London. And one afternoon he was at Harlech in Ardudwy,[3] at his Court, and he sat upon the rock of Harlech, looking over the sea. And with him were his brother Manawyddan[4] the son of Llyr, and his brothers by the mother's side, Nisien[5] and Efnisien,[6] and many nobles likewise, as was fitting to see around a king. His two brothers by the mother's side were the sons of Euroswydd[7] by his mother, Penardun,[8] the daughter of Beli[9] son of Manogan.[10] And one of these youths was a good youth and of gentle nature, and would make peace between his kindred, and cause his family to be friends when

---

1. *Bran:* "Raven."

2. *Llyr:* "Sea."

3. This is in Arfon, the westernmost part of north Wales. Notice in what follows how much of the action of this Branch is oriented toward the west, the symbolic direction of the Second Cantref.

4. *Manawyddan:* "Loremaster (*gwyddon*) of the Land."

5. *Nisien:* "Peaceful."

6. *Efnisien:* "Unpeaceful."

7. *Euroswydd:* "Golden Enemy."

8. *Penardun:* "Beautiful Head."

9. *Beli:* "Bright," the old Celtic god of the Sun.

10. *Manogan:* "Place of Song."

their wrath was at the highest; and this one was Nisien; but the other would cause strife between two brothers when they were most at peace.

And as they sat thus, they beheld thirteen ships coming from the south of Ireland, and making towards them, and they came with a swift motion, the wind being behind them, and they neared them rapidly.

"I see ships afar," said the king, "coming swiftly towards the land. Command the men of the Court that they equip themselves, and go and learn their intent." So the men equipped themselves and went down towards them. And when they saw the ships near, certain were they that they had never seen ships better furnished. Beautiful flags of satin were upon them. And behold one of the ships outstripped the others, and they saw a shield lifted up above the side of the ship, and the point of the shield was upwards, in token of peace. And the men drew near that they might hold converse. Then they put out boats and came towards the land. And they saluted the king.

Now the king could hear them from the place where he was, upon the rock above their heads. "Heaven prosper you," said he, "and be ye welcome. To whom do these ships belong, and who is the chief amongst you?"

"Lord," said they, "Matholwch,[11] king of Ireland, is here, and these ships belong to him."

"Wherefore comes he?" asked the king, "and will he come to the land?"

"He is a suitor unto thee, lord," said they, "and he will not land unless he have his boon."

"And what may that be?" inquired the king.

"He desires to ally himself with thee, lord," said they, "and he comes to ask Branwen[12] the daughter of Llyr, that, if it seem well to thee, the Island of the Mighty may be leagued with Ireland, and both become more powerful."

"Verily," said he, "let him come to land, and we will take counsel thereupon." And this answer was brought to Matholwch.

"I will go willingly," said he. So he landed, and they received him joyfully; and great was the throng in the palace that night, between his hosts and those of the Court; and next day they took counsel, and they resolved to bestow Branwen upon Matholwch. Now she was one of the three chief ladies of this island, and she was the fairest damsel in the world.

---

11. *Matholwch:* from *mathol llwch,* "precious dust."

12. *Branwen:* "White Raven" or "Blessed Raven." Note that this latter meaning is identical with that of Bran's full name, *Bran Fendigeid* (literally, "Raven the Blessed").

And they fixed upon Aberffraw[13] as the place where she should become his bride. And they went thence, and towards Aberffraw the hosts proceeded; Matholwch and his host in their ships; Bran the Blessed and his host by land, until they came to Aberffraw. And at Aberffraw they began the feast and sat down. And thus sat they. The King of the Island of the Mighty and Manawyddan the son of Llyr on one side, and Matholwch on the other side, and Branwen the daughter of Llyr beside him. And they were not within a house, but under tents. No house could ever contain Bran the Blessed.[14] And they began the banquet and caroused and discoursed. And when it was more pleasing to them to sleep than to carouse, they went to rest, and that night Branwen became Matholwch's bride.

And next day they arose, and all they of the Court, and the officers began to equip and to range the horses and the attendants, and they ranged them in order as far as the sea.

And behold one day, Efnisien, the quarrelsome man of whom it is spoken above, came by chance into the place, where the horses of Matholwch were, and asked whose horses they might be.

"They are the horses of Matholwch king of Ireland, who is married to Branwen, thy sister; his horses are they."

"And is it thus they have done with a maiden such as she, and moreover my sister, bestowing her without my consent? They could have offered no greater insult to me than this," said he. And thereupon he rushed under the horses and cut off their lips at the teeth, and their ears close to their heads, and their tails close to their backs, and wherever he could clutch their eyelids, he cut them to the very bone, and he disfigured the horses and rendered them useless.

And they came with these tidings unto Matholwch, saying that the horses were disfigured, and injured so that not one of them could ever be of any use again. "Verily, lord," said one, "it was an insult unto thee, and as such was it meant."

"Of a truth, it is a marvel to me, that if they desire to insult me, they should have given me a maiden of such high rank and so much beloved of her kindred, as they have done."

---

13. Another location in north Wales.

14. Bran was traditionally a giant too large to fit inside a house; however, the passage means more than this.

"Lord," said another, "thou seest that thus it is, and there is nothing for thee to do but to go to thy ships." And thereupon towards his ships he set out.

And tidings came to Bran the Blessed that Matholwch was quitting the Court without asking leave, and messengers were sent to inquire of him wherefore he did so. And the messengers that went were Iddic the son of Anarawd,[15] and Hefeydd Hir.[16] And these overtook him and asked of him what he designed to do, and wherefore he went forth.

"Of a truth," said he, "if I had known I had not come hither. I have been altogether insulted, no one had ever worse treatment than I have had here. But one thing surprises me above all."

"What is that?" asked they.

"That Branwen the daughter of Llyr, one of the three chief ladies of this island, and the daughter of the King of the Island of the Mighty, should have been given me as my bride, and that after that I should have been insulted; and I marvel that the insult was not done me before they had bestowed upon me a maiden so exalted as she."

"Truly, lord, it was not the will of any that are of the Court," said they, "nor of any that are of the council, that thou shouldest have received this insult; and as thou hast been insulted, the dishonour is greater unto Bran the Blessed than unto thee."

"Verily," said he, "I think so. Nevertheless he cannot recall the insult." These men returned with that answer to the place where Bran the Blessed was, and they told him what reply Matholwch had given them.

"Truly," said he, "there are no means by which we may prevent his going away at enmity with us, that we will not take."

"Well, lord," said they, "send after him another embassy."

"I will do so," said he. "Arise, Manawyddan son of Llyr, and Hefeydd Hir, and Unig Glew Ysgwyd,[17] and go after him, and tell him that he shall have a sound horse for every one that has been injured. And beside that, as an atonement for the insult, he shall have a staff of silver, as large and as tall as himself, and a plate of gold of the breadth of his face. And show unto him who it was that did this, and that it was done against my will; but that he who did it is my brother, by

---

15. *Iddig son of Anarawd*: "Lordly son of Eloquent."

16. *Hefeydd Hir*: the same person as Hefeydd Hen in the First Branch, but *Hen*, "Old," is replaced by *Hir*, "Long."

17. *Unig Glew Ysgwyd*: "Only One of the Strong Shoulder."

the mother's side, and therefore it would be hard for me to put him to death. And let him come and meet me," said he, "and we will make peace in any way he may desire."

The embassy went after Matholwch, and told him all these sayings in a friendly manner, and he listened thereunto.

"Men," said he, "I will take counsel." So to the council he went. And in the council they considered that if they should refuse this, they were likely to have more shame rather than to obtain so great an atonement. They resolved therefore to accept it, and they returned to the Court in peace.

Then the pavilions and the tents were set in order after the fashion of a hall; and they went to meat, and as they had sat at the beginning of the feast, so sat they there. And Matholwch and Bran the Blessed began to discourse; and behold it seemed to Bran the Blessed, while they talked, that Matholwch was not so cheerful as he had been before. And he thought that the chieftain might be sad, because of the smallness of the atonement which he had, for the wrong that had been done him.

"Oh, man," said Bran the Blessed, "thou dost not discourse tonight so cheerfully as thou wast wont. And if it be because of the smallness of the atonement, thou shalt add thereunto whatsoever thou mayest choose, and tomorrow I will pay thee the horses."

"Lord," said he, "Heaven reward thee."

"And I will enhance the atonement," said Bran the Blessed, "for I will give unto thee a cauldron, the property of which is, that if one of thy men be slain today, and be cast therein, tomorrow he will be as well as ever he was at the best, except that he will not regain his speech." And thereupon he gave him great thanks, and very joyful was he for that cause.

And the next morning they paid Matholwch the horses as long as the trained horses lasted. And then they journeyed into another commot,[18] where they paid him with colts until the whole had been paid, and from thenceforth that commot was called Talebolyon.[19]

And a second night sat they together.

"My lord," said Matholwch, "whence hadst thou the cauldron which thou hast given me?"

---

18. A commot was a subdivision of a Cantref.

19. A Welsh pun, and also a memory image: *tal ebolyon* in Welsh means "payment of colts."

"I had it of a man who had been in thy land," said he, "and I would not give it except to one from there."

"Who was it?" asked he.

"Llassar Llaesgyfnewid;[20] he came here from Ireland with Cymidei Cymeinfoll,[21] his wife, who escaped from the Iron House in Ireland, when it was made red hot around them, and fled hither. And it is a marvel to me that thou shouldst know nothing concerning the matter."

"Something I do know," said he, "and as much as I know I will tell thee. One day I was hunting in Ireland, and I came to the mound at the head of the lake, which is called the Lake of the Cauldron. And I beheld a huge yellow-haired man coming from the lake with a cauldron upon his back. And he was a man of vast size, and of horrid aspect, and a woman followed after him. And if the man was tall, twice as large as he was the woman, and they came towards me and greeted me.

"'Verily,' asked I, 'wherefore are you journeying?'

"'Behold, this,' said he to me, 'is the cause that we journey. At the end of a month and a fortnight this woman will have a son; and the child that will be born at the end of the month and the fortnight will be a warrior fully armed.'

"So I took them with me and maintained them. And they were with me for a year. And that year I had them with me not grudgingly. But thenceforth was there murmuring, because that they were with me. For, from the beginning of the fourth month they had begun to make themselves hated and to be disorderly in the land; committing outrages, and molesting and harassing the nobles and ladies; and thenceforward my people rose up and besought me to part with them, and they bade me to choose between them and my dominions. And I applied to the council of my country to know what should be done concerning them; for of their own free will they would not go, neither could they be compelled against their will, through fighting.

"And being in this strait, they caused a chamber to be made all of iron. Now when the chamber was ready, there came there every smith that was in Ireland, and every one who owned tongs and hammer. And they caused coals to be piled up as high as the top of the chamber. And they had the man, and the woman,

---

20. *Llassar Llaesgyfnewid*: "Lazarus the Loosener," a plausible name for an otherworld being whose cauldron can bring the dead to life.

21. *Cymidei Cymeinfoll*: "Battler with the Full Belly." She is identical with the Cauldron—note the way that both of them give birth to grown and fully armed warriors. The nature and meaning of the Cauldron is one of the central mysteries of this Branch.

and the children, served with plenty of meat and drink; but when it was known that they were drunk, they began to put fire to the coals about the chamber, and they blew it with bellows until the house was red hot all around them. Then was there a council held in the center of the floor of the chamber. And the man tarried until the plates of iron were all of a white heat; and then, by reason of the great heat, the man dashed against the plates with his shoulder and struck them out, and his wife followed him; but except him and his wife none escaped thence. And then I suppose, lord," said Matholwch unto Bran the Blessed, "that he came over unto thee."

"Doubtless he came here," said he, "and gave unto me the cauldron."

"In what manner didst thou receive them?"

"I dispersed them through every part of my dominions, and they have become numerous and are prospering everywhere, and they fortify the places where they are with men and arms, of the best that were ever seen."

That night they continued to discourse as much as they would, and had minstrelsy and carousing, and when it was more pleasant to them to sleep than to sit longer, they went to rest. And thus was the banquet carried on with joyousness; and when it was finished, Matholwch journeyed towards Ireland, and Branwen with him, and they went from Aber Menei with thirteen ships, and came to Ireland. And in Ireland was there great joy because of their coming. And not one great man or noble lady visited Branwen unto whom she gave not either a clasp, or a ring, or a royal jewel to keep, such as it was honourable to be seen departing with. And in these things she spent that year in much renown, and she passed her time pleasantly, enjoying honour and friendship. And in the meanwhile it chanced that she became pregnant, and in due time a son was born unto her, and the name that they gave him was Gwern[22] the son of Matholwch and, they put the boy out to be foster-nursed, in a place where were the best men of Ireland.

And behold in the second year a tumult arose in Ireland, on account of the insult which Matholwch had received in Wales, and the payment made him for his horses. And his foster-brothers, and such as were nearest unto him, blamed him openly for that matter. And he might have no peace by reason of the tumult until they should revenge upon him this disgrace. And the vengeance which they took was to drive away Branwen from the same chamber with him, and to make her cook for the Court; and they caused the butcher after he had cut up

---

22. *Gwern*: "Alder."

the meat to come to her and give her every day a blow on the ear, and such they made her punishment.

"Verily, lord," said his men to Matholwch, "forbid now the ships and the ferry boats and the coracles, that they go not into Wales, and such as come over from Wales hither, imprison them that they go not back for this thing to be known there." And he did so; and it was thus for not less than three years.

And Branwen reared a starling in the cover of the kneading trough, and she taught it to speak, and she taught the bird what manner of man her brother was. And she wrote a letter of her woes, and the despite with which she was treated, and she bound the letter to the root of the bird's wing, and sent it towards Britain. And the bird came to this island, and one day it found Bran the Blessed at Caer Seiont[23] in Arfon, conferring there, and it alighted upon his shoulder and ruffled its feathers, so that the letter was seen, and they knew that the bird had been reared in a domestic manner.

Then Bran the Blessed took the letter and looked upon it. And when he had read the letter he grieved exceedingly at the tidings of Branwen's woes. And immediately he began sending messengers to summon the island together. And he caused sevenscore and four countries to come unto him, and he complained to them himself of the grief that his sister endured.

So they took counsel. And in the council they resolved to go to Ireland, and to leave seven men as princes here, and Caradawc,[24] the son of Bran, as the chief of them, and their seven knights. In Edeyrnion were these men left. And for this reason were the seven knights placed in the town. Now the names of these seven men were, Caradawc the son of Bran, and Hefeydd Hir, and Unig Glew Ysgwyd, and Iddig the son of Anarawd Gwalltgrwn,[25] and Ffodor the son of Erfyll,[26] and Gwlch Minascwrn,[27] and Llashar the son of Llassar Llaesgyfnewid, and Pendaran Dyfed as a young page with them.[28] And these abode as seven ministers to take charge of this island; and Caradawc the son of Bran was the chief amongst them.

---

23. *Caer Seiont*: This is the modern town of Caernarfon.

24. *Caradawc*: "Beloved."

25. *Gwalltgrwn*: "Ridge of Hair."

26. *Ffodor the son of Erfyll*: "Fugitive the son of Oaths."

27. *Gwlch Minascwrn*: "Steep Bone Lip."

28. Note that Pendaran Dyfed was a grown man in the First Branch; in the Second, now that Pryderi has come to adulthood, he is paradoxically a young page.

Bran the Blessed, with the host of which we spoke, sailed towards Ireland, and it was not far across the sea, and he came to shoal water. It was caused by two rivers; the Lli and the Archan were they called; and the nations covered the sea. Then he proceeded with what provisions he had on his own back, and approached the shore of Ireland.

Now the swineherds of Matholwch were upon the seashore, and they came to Matholwch. "Lord," said they, "greeting be unto thee."

"Heaven protect you," said he, "have you any news?"

"Lord," said they, "we have marvellous news, a wood have we seen upon the sea, in a place where we never yet saw a single tree."

"This is indeed a marvel," said he; "saw you aught else?"

"We saw, lord," said they, "a vast mountain beside the wood, which moved, and there was a lofty ridge on the top of the mountain, and a lake on each side of the ridge. And the wood, and the mountain, and all these things moved."

"Verily," said he, "there is none who can know aught concerning this, unless it be Branwen."

Messengers then went unto Branwen. "Lady," said they, "what thinkest thou that this is?"

"The men of the Island of the Mighty, who have come hither on hearing of my ill-treatment and my woes."

"What is the forest that is seen upon the sea?" asked they.

"The yards and the masts of ships," she answered.

"Alas," said they, "what is the mountain that is seen by the side of the ships?"

"Bran the Blessed, my brother," she replied, "coming to shoal water; there is no ship that can contain him in it."

"What is the lofty ridge with the lake on each side thereof?"

"On looking towards this island he is wroth, and his two eyes, one on each side of his nose, are the two lakes beside the ridge."

The warriors and the chief men of Ireland were brought together in haste, and they took counsel.

"Lord," said the nobles unto Matholwch, "there is no other counsel than to retreat over the Linon (a river which is in Ireland), and to keep the river between thee and him, and to break down the bridge that is across the river, for there is a loadstone at the bottom of the river that neither ship nor vessel can pass over." So they retreated across the river, and broke down the bridge.

Bran the Blessed came to land, and the fleet with him by the bank of the river.

"Lord," said his chieftains, "knowest thou the nature of this river, that nothing can go across it, and there is no bridge over it?"

"What," said they, "is thy counsel concerning a bridge?"

"There is none," said he, "except that he who will be chief, let him be a bridge. I will be so," said he. And then was that saying first uttered, and it is still used as a proverb.[29] And when he had lain down across the river, hurdles were placed upon him, and the host passed over thereby.

And as he rose up, behold the messengers of Matholwch came to him, and saluted him, and gave him greeting in the name of Matholwch, his kinsman, and showed how that of his goodwill he had merited of him nothing but good. "For Matholwch has given the kingdom of Ireland to Gwern the son of Matholwch, thy nephew and thy sister's son. And this he places before thee, as a compensation for the wrong and despite that has been done unto Branwen. And Matholwch shall be maintained wheresoever thou wilt, either here or in the Island of the Mighty."

Said Bran the Blessed, "Shall not I myself have the kingdom? Then peradventure I may take counsel concerning your message. From this time until then no other answer will you get from me."

"Verily," said they, "the best message that we receive for thee, we will convey it unto thee, and do thou await our message unto him."

"I will wait," answered he, "and do you return quickly."

The messengers set forth and came to Matholwch. "Lord," said they, "prepare a better message for Bran the Blessed. He would not listen at all to the message that we bore him."

"My friends," said Matholwch, "what may be your counsel?"

"Lord," said they, "there is no other counsel than this alone. He was never known to be within a house, make therefore a house that will contain him and the men of the Island of the Mighty on the one side, and thyself and thy host on the other; and give over thy kingdom to his will, and do him homage. So by reason of the honour thou doest him in making him a house, whereas he never before had a house to contain him, he will make peace with thee."

---

29. Bran is associated with the alder tree, which does not rot in water and therefore was used to make pilings for bridges.

So the messengers went back to Bran the Blessed, bearing him this message.[30]

And he took counsel, and in the council it was resolved that he should accept this, and this was all done by the advice of Branwen, and lest the country should be destroyed. And this peace was made, and the house was built both vast and strong. But the Irish planned a crafty device, and the craft was that they should put brackets on each side of the hundred pillars that were in the house, and should place a leathern bag on each bracket, and an armed man in every one of them. Then Efnisien came in before the host of the Island of the Mighty, and scanned the house with fierce and savage looks, and descried the leathern bags which were around the pillars.

"What is in this bag?" asked he of one of the Irish.

"Meal, good soul," said he. And Efnisien felt about it until he came to the man's head, and he squeezed the head until he felt his fingers meet together in the brain through the bone. And he left that one and put his hand upon another, and asked what was therein.

"Meal," said the Irishman. So he did the like unto every one of them, until he had not left alive, of all the two hundred men, save one only; and when he came to him, he asked what was there.

"Meal, good soul," said the Irishman. And he felt about until he felt the head, and he squeezed that head as he had done the others. And, albeit he found that the head of this one was armored, he left him not until he had killed him. And then he sang an Englyn:[31]

"There is in this bag a different sort of meal,
The ready combatant, when the assault is made
By his fellow-warriors, prepared for battle."

Thereupon came the hosts unto the house. The men of the Island of Ireland entered the house on the one side, and the men of the Island of the Mighty on the other. And as soon as they had sat down there was concord between them; and the sovereignty was conferred upon the boy. When the peace was concluded, Bran the Blessed called the boy unto him, and from Bran the Blessed the boy went unto Manawyddan, and he was beloved by all that beheld him. And from

---

30. Note the parallel between the building of a house for the giant Bran and the earlier story of the house of iron built for the giants Llassar and his wife Cymidei. Interestingly, Irish legend includes several other accounts of the building and burning of a house as a trap for a king or powerful being.

31. *Englyn*: A traditional Welsh verse form of three lines.

Manawyddan the boy was called by Nisien the son of Eurosswydd, and the boy went unto him lovingly.

"Wherefore," said Efnisien, "comes not my nephew the son of my sister unto me? Though he were not king of Ireland, yet willingly would I fondle the boy."

"Cheerfully let him go to thee," said Bran the Blessed, and the boy went unto him cheerfully.

"By my confession to Heaven," said Efnisien in his heart, "unthought of by the household is the slaughter that I will this instant commit."

Then he arose and took up the boy by the feet, and before any one in the house could seize hold of him, he thrust the boy headlong into the blazing fire. And when Branwen saw her son burning in the fire, she strove to leap into the fire also, from the place where she sat between her two brothers. But Bran the Blessed grasped her with one hand, and his shield with the other. Then they all hurried about the house, and never was there made so great a tumult by any host in one house as was made by them, as each man armed himself.

Then said Morddwydtyllyon,[32] "The gadflies of Morddwydtyllyon's Cow!" And while they all sought their arms, Bran the Blessed supported Branwen between his shield and his shoulder.

Then the Irish kindled a fire under the cauldron of renovation, and they cast the dead bodies into the cauldron until it was full, and the next day they came forth fighting-men as good as before, except that they were not able to speak. Then when Efnisien saw the dead bodies of the men of the Island of the Mighty nowhere resuscitated, he said in his heart, "Alas! woe is me, that I should have been the cause of bringing the men of the Island of the Mighty into so great a strait. Evil betide me if I find not a deliverance therefrom." And he cast himself among the dead bodies of the Irish, and two barefoot Irishmen came to him, and, taking him to be one of the Irish, flung him into the cauldron. And he stretched himself out in the cauldron, so that he rent the cauldron into four pieces, and burst his own heart also.

In consequence of that the men of the Island of the Mighty obtained such success as they had; but they were not victorious, for only seven men of them all escaped, and Bran the Blessed himself was wounded in the foot with a poisoned dart. Now the seven men that escaped were Pryderi, Manawyddan, Gluneu Eil

---

32. *Morddwydtyllyon*: "Pierced Thigh," a title of Bran.

Taran,[33] Taliesin,[34] Ynawc,[35] Grudyen the son of Muryel,[36] and Heilyn the son of Gwynn Hen.[37]

And Bran the Blessed commanded them that they should cut off his head. "And take you my head," said he, "and bear it even unto the White Mount, in London, and bury it there, with the face towards France. And a long time will you be upon the road. In Harlech you will be feasting seven years, the birds of Rhiannon singing unto you the while. And all that time the head will be to you as pleasant company as it ever was when on my body. And at Gwales in Penfro[38] you will be fourscore years, and you may remain there, and the head with you uncorrupted, until you open the door that looks towards Aber Henfelen,[39] and towards Cornwall.[40] And after you have opened that door, there you may no longer tarry, set forth then to London to bury the head, and go straight forward."

So they cut off his head, and these seven went forward therewith. And Branwen was the eighth with them, and they came to land at Aber Alaw,[41] in Talebolyon, and they sat down to rest. And Branwen looked towards Ireland and towards the Island of the Mighty, to see if she could descry them.

"Alas," said she, "woe is me that I was ever born; two islands have been destroyed because of me!" Then she uttered a loud groan, and there broke her heart. And they made her a four-sided grave, and buried her upon the banks of the Alaw.

Then the seven men journeyed forward towards Harlech, bearing the head with them; and as they went, behold there met them a multitude of men and of women.

"Have you any tidings?" asked Manawyddan.

---

33. *Gluneu Eil Taran*: "Jewel, the Second Lightning."

34. *Taliesin*: "Radiant Brow," the great wizard-bard of Druid legend.

35. *Ynawc: yn awch*, "having an edge" or "having an appetite."

36. *Grudyen son of Muryel*: "Murmur, son of Thaw."

37. *Heilyn son of Gwynn Hen*: "Trouble, son of Old Light."

38. *Gwales*: the island of Grassholm. *Penfro*: "Head of the Land."

39. *Aber Henfelen*: "River-mouth of the Old Yellow."

40. That is, toward the south.

41. *Aber Alaw*: "River-mouth of Song."

"We have none," said they, "save that Caswallawn[42] the son of Beli has conquered the Island of the Mighty, and is crowned king in London."

"What has become," said they, "of Caradawc the son of Bran, and the seven men who were left with him in this island?"

"Caswallawn came upon them, and slew six of the men, and Caradawc's heart broke for grief thereof; for he could see the sword that slew the men, but knew not who it was that wielded it. Caswallawn had flung upon him the Veil of Illusion, so that no one could see him slay the men, but the sword only could they see. And it liked him not to slay Caradawc, because he was his nephew, the son of his cousin. And now he was the third whose heart had broke through grief. Pendaran Dyved, who had remained as a young page with these men, escaped into the wood," said they.

Then they went on to Harlech, and there stopped to rest, and they provided meat and liquor, and sat down to eat and to drink. And there came three birds, and began singing unto them a certain song, and all the songs they had ever heard were unpleasant compared thereto; and the birds seemed to them to be at a great distance from them over the sea, yet they appeared as distinct as if they were close by, and at this repast they continued seven years.

And at the close of the seventh year they went forth to Gwales in Penfro. And there they found a fair and regal spot overlooking the ocean; and a spacious hall was therein. And they went into the hall, and two of its doors were open, but the third door was closed, that which looked towards Cornwall.[43]

"See, yonder," said Manawyddan, "is the door that we may not open." And that night they regaled themselves and were joyful. And of all they had seen of food laid before them, and of all they had heard of, they remembered nothing; neither of that, nor of any sorrow whatsoever. And there they remained fourscore years, unconscious of having ever spent a time more joyous and mirthful. And they were not more weary than when first they came, neither did they, any of them, know the time they had been there. And it was not more irksome to them having the head with them, than if Bran the Blessed had been with them himself. And because of these fourscore years, it was called "the Entertaining of

---

42. *Caswallawn*: "Foe-scatterer."

43. That is, the first two of the seven Cantrefs are open, but the third, corresponding to the south, is still shut. This is comparable to the condition of the initiate at this stage in the Dolmen Arch course.

Fig. 22. The Mabinogion • The Entertaining of the Noble Head

the noble Head." The entertaining of Branwen and Matholwch was in the time that they went to Ireland.

One day said Heilyn the son of Gwynn, "Evil betide me, if I do not open the door to know if that is true which is said concerning it." So he opened the door and looked towards Cornwall and Aber Henvelen. And when they had looked, they were as conscious of all the evils they had ever sustained, and of all the friends and companions they had lost, and of all the misery that had befallen them, as if all had happened in that very spot; and especially of the fate of their lord. And because of their perturbation they could not rest, but journeyed forth with the head towards London. And they buried the head in the White Mount, and when it was buried, this was the third goodly concealment; and it was the third ill-fated disclosure when it was disinterred, inasmuch as no invasion from across the sea came to this island while the head was in that concealment. And thus is the story related of those who journeyed over from Ireland.

In Ireland none were left alive, except five pregnant women in a cave in the Irish wilderness; and to these five women in the same night were born five sons, whom they nursed until they became grown-up youths. And they thought about wives, and they at the same time desired to possess them, and each took a wife of the mothers of their companions, and they governed the country and peopled it.

And these five divided it amongst them, and because of this partition are the five divisions of Ireland still so termed. And they examined the land where the battles had taken place, and they found gold and silver until they became wealthy.

And thus ends this portion of the Mabinogi, concerning the blow given to Branwen, which was the third unhappy blow of this island; and concerning the entertainment of Bran, when the hosts of sevenscore countries and ten went over to Ireland to revenge the blow given to Branwen; and concerning the seven years' banquet in Harlech, and the singing of the birds of Rhiannon, and the sojourning of the head for the space of fourscore years.

DRUID PHILOSOPHY:
THE ONE LIFE

L IKE THE PHILOSOPHY LECTURE included in the lesson packet of the Novitiate Grade, of which this is a continuation, the following essay makes difficult reading but contains much that is worthy of meditation. It bears repeating, however, that the material in this course is meant to be understood and used, not believed; or, to use a turn of phrase from another esoteric tradition, it is meant to train the mind, not to inform it.

In the course of describing the Druid teaching of the One Life, the author of this lecture refers to several philosophers and writers who have understood the world in ways similar to those of the Druid Revival—for example, Ralph Cudworth, who was a leading English philosopher of the seventeenth century, one of the Cambridge Platonists, and Honoré Balzac, a famous French novelist of the late nineteenth century. You may find it useful to look up each of the thinkers referenced below, and learn a little about what they thought.

At the same time, the author is at pains to stress the disagreements between the ideas he is trying to communicate and some of the popular beliefs of his own time, many of which are still common in ours. (It is one of the ironies of contemporary life that most of what passes for "advanced thinking" today is identical to the ideas that were given the same label a century ago.) Remember, especially if the belief being criticized is one you hold, that the point of these lectures is to give you ideas it will be useful for you to consider, not doctrines you are expected to believe; try to understand why the differences under discussion are important, and what they imply about the individual and the world.

Once you have finished working your way through the Second Branch of the Mabinogion in meditation, the triads presented in this lecture deserve your close attention. As you consider them and the concepts and images that rise around them, search for those places where all these things relate to the experiences of your own life and the world of nature around you. It is by relating the teachings of this course to your own experience, ultimately, that you will learn best what it has to teach.

This is the Druid teaching regarding Nwyfre, which is the One Life from which arises all life, and action, and shape and form, and change, and appearance, and variety, and manifestation—in fact, all that we include in the term "the Cosmos." Consider the following triads.

TRIAD I.

Three truthful names of Nwyfre: the One Life, the One Being, the One Spirit.

TRIAD II.

Three false names of Nwyfre: God, the Absolute, the Perfect.

TRIAD III.

Three paradoxes of Nwyfre: it is the one that is many, the always-same that is always different, and the supreme that is subordinate.

TRIAD I.

Three truthful names of Nwyfre: the One Life, the One Being, the One Spirit.

One universal living creative principle has been recognized in all the great philosophies of all times and places. From the earliest dawn of philosophical thought, the great thinkers of the human race have postulated the existence of One from which proceeded the Many. Some held the One to be a universal being—even a personal being or deity—while others regarded it simply as a principle. But the underlying conception was the same—a living and creative "something" from which all things emerged—a unity from which proceeded diversity. This principle was often confounded with the Absolute, although others held that it was subordinate.

The Chaldeans and Egyptians held that this universal life principle subdivided itself into the many forms of life and things, in obedience to an inner law of its being. The many schools of Hindu thought held that the One manifested as the Many; one school held that Brahman manifested as the Many in order to enjoy objective existence; another school held that Prakriti, the universal substance, was acted upon by the Purusha, or soul-principle, which it had attracted to itself, and manifestations arose by reason thereof; another school held that Brahman was merely a subordinate creative principle, which was caused to create universes by the power of Parabrahm; another school held that all manifestation was merely an illusory dream of Maya, or Illusion, in the mind of the Supreme Being; other schools held ideas akin to those mentioned, or variations or combinations of them.

The Greeks always held to the existence of the universal life principle, calling it by various names. The very term "the Cosmos" was used by the Stoics and others to represent the idea of the *anima mundi* or "world-soul." Heraclitus held to the "world-spirit," which he symbolized as flame. Pythagoras, in his exoteric or popular teachings, taught the doctrine of the life principle, symbolizing it as light or flame. Other schools recognized the existence of the One Life, calling it "Being," a term which has persisted in modern philosophy.

By some schools, notably the Platonist, the universal life principle was called "the Demiurge," the term literally meaning the "universal worker." The Demiurge was held to be an exalted and mysterious agent, by and through whom the Absolute was supposed to have created the Universe—the life of the Demiurge flowed out into manifold forms, and became the Many. This idea was likewise adhered to by the Gnostics of the early Christian church.

The term "the Logos" was also applied by some of the schools to this universal life principle. The Logos was held to be the creative principle of Nature, objective in the world, giving order and regularity to the universe of shapes and forms which it had manifested. This idea of the Logos was inherent in many ancient religions, and permeated early Christianity. Überweg, in his *History of Philosophy*, says: "The Logos was a being intermediate between God and the world. The Logos does not exist from eternity like God, and yet its genesis is not like our own and that of all other created beings; it is the first begotten son of God, and is for us, who are imperfect, a god. Through the agency of the Logos, God created the world, and has revealed Himself to it."

Ralph Cudworth, the Cambridge Platonist philosopher of the seventeenth century, held the existence of a "Plastic[44] Nature," of which he stated: "It may well be concluded that there is a Plastic Nature, under God, which, as an inferior and subordinate instrument, doth execute that part of his providence which consists in the orderly and regular motion of matter."

Cudworth held that this idea of Plastic Nature was reasonable in view of the fact that "the slow and gradual process in the generation of things would be a vain and idle pomp, or a trifling formality, if the moving power were omnipotent; as also may be noted those errors and bungles which are committed where the matter is inept and contumacious; which argues that the moving power is not irresistible, and that Nature is not altogether incapable of being sometimes frustrated and disappointed by the indisposition of matter. An omnipotent moving power, being able to dispatch its work in a moment, would always act infallibly and irresistibly, as no ineptitude and stubbornness of matter would be able to hinder such a one, or to make Him fumble or bungle in anything."

The Plastic Nature of Cudworth and his followers, was but the old Demiurge, or Logos, of the Gnostics—but another name for the One Life, subordinate to the Absolute.

Modern philosophers and thinkers have held to this idea of the Creative Principle, regarding it rather as a principle than as a being, however. Giordano Bruno held the existence of an *anima mundi*, or world-soul principle; others have held the principle of "Nature"; Arthur Schopenhauer proposed the existence of a universal Will-to-Live, which manifested the universe of shape and form and variety; von Hartman held that there existed an "Unconscious," or creative principle, similar to that of Schopenhauer's "Will"; Wilhelm Wundt suggested a "universal will"; Crusius taught the existence of a universal dominating will; Honoré Balzac upheld a "universal Something, akin to will"; Nietsche proclaimed a "World-Will"; Maurice Maeterlinck affirms a life principle; George Bernard Shaw postulates the existence of a universal creative energy which he calls "the Life Forces."

The Naturalistic school of philosophy postulates the existence of a composite something which it calls "Nature," which acts as the universal creative energy; other thinkers speak of "Nature" in its metonymic sense, as "the agent, producer, or creator of things; the powers which carry on the processes of creation; the

---

44. The word "plastic" meant "taking many shapes" originally; that is why it was given to the artificial substances we call "plastics" today.

powers concerned to produce existing phenomena, whether in sum or in detail; the personified sum and order of cause and effect." Herbert Spencer postulates the existence of an "infinite and eternal energy, from which all things proceed, which transcends our reason and even our imagination." In short, this universal living creative principle is found, under one name or another, in nearly all of the leading philosophies or schools of thought, ancient or modern. The highest reports of the human reason agree in this conception.

TRIAD II.

Three false names of Nwyfre: God, the Absolute, the Perfect.

Yet this universal creative principle is not the highest reality; in the terms used in Druid philosophy, it is not Awen. Many of today's popular philosophies and religions confound these two distinct things, the Absolute and the one principle of life. These claim that the creative principle is God; or the Absolute; or the Perfect—that Deity and Nature are identical—that the Universe is God, and God is the Universe. Herein lies a mistaken conception of the Absolute. The idea of an absolute being, omnipotent and omniscient, being compelled to work its way gradually, haltingly, with mistakes and stumbles, is absurd. Cudworth, who was quoted above, makes this point clear.

How can one claim that an Absolute Being is trying to "gain experience" in this way? How can one claim that the Absolute is "trying to accomplish something" by the universal manifestation? If It has not been able to reach Its goal in all the past of Eternity, after all, It can hardly reach it in all the future of Eternity, for the one is equal to the other. Moreover, the Absolute must of necessity be self-sufficient, and can want nothing to perfect Itself. In short, any attempt to postulate the Absolute, God, Deity or other Supreme Thing as being the struggling, striving, evolving Creative Energy must end in logical impossibility. It is only when it is assumed that this Creative Energy is subordinate to the Absolute, that it becomes logically thinkable.

The Absolute and Nature can never be the same, and the attempt to equate them is simply a failure, on the part of men, to recognise to what degree the Absolute transcends relative existence. Nature is relative, and subordinate to that which is Absolute. The difference is important, and not in an abstract or intellectual sense alone, for on it depends the knowledge of the right relation between the individual, as an expression of the One Life, and the order of the Cosmos, which is from Awen.

One of the most glaring of these fallacies of these systems of thought is that which assumes that the Absolute or the Deity is "trying to" accomplish something—either in the direction of "gaining experience," or "building up" some great universe by continual progression. The idea of an Absolute, which must be Perfect, desiring anything other than it has is a contradiction. The idea of an Absolute Deity who must be All-Wise, trying to "gain experience" or learn something by playing the game of Many Parts, is even more so. The idea of an Absolute or Omnipotent Deity "trying to," or endeavoring to build up universes by slow and arduous labor belongs to the category of child-thought. To think of such a being doing "day work" is ridiculous—and then what could He gain by it, this perfect and self-sufficient being? And the point remains that if all past Time has not been sufficient to accomplish perfect results, then all future Time will fail to accomplish them—for just as future Time has no ending, past Time has no beginning, and existed forever. And then, what did this creative being do in all the eternity before creation, if it be held that creation had its beginning in time?

Thus it is wise to ask these test-questions of any system of thought that blends the Absolute and the relative:

(1) Why does your Absolute Being depart from Its absolute nature, and become relative, manifold, and divisible?

(2) How can the Absolute lose Its absolute nature and become relative?

(3) What becomes of the absolute nature of the Absolute, when the latter transforms Itself into the relative?

(4) How can the Unconditioned take on conditions and limitations?

(5) How can the Changeless change?

(6) How can the Indivisible divide and separate Itself into parts? And if the teaching in question postulates an Absolute Being, with the quality of Omniscience or Absolute Wisdom, ask also this question:

(7) How can an Omniscient All-Wise Absolute Being lose Its wisdom, and display the comparative ignorance of the relative forms?

There are but two possible logical explanations of the relation between absolute and relative: (a) That the Cosmos has no existence except in the imagination of an absolute being—either as a dream, meditation, reverie, or deliberate dramatic representation, lacking all reality; or (b) that the universal creative principle is not absolute, but is subordinate to a transcendent reality. The first is the answer of the philosophies of the East—the second is the answer of the philosophies of the West. Take your choice! If you choose the former, however, then admit that the Absolute creates the illusion for no reason except Its own pleasure, for it is contradictory to hold that the Absolute has anything to gain or lose thereby, for if such were so It would no longer be the Absolute.

Triad III.

Three paradoxes of Nwyfre: it is the one that is many, the always-same that is always different, and the supreme that is subordinate.

The Druid teachings hold that the Cosmos—the sum of all things—is in its last analysis, nwyfre, which is Spirit or the Life Force. By "spirit" is meant "essence"—remember this definition. "Essence" is a term derived from the Latin word *esse*, meaning "to be." Therefore essence or nwyfre means the "beingness" of Being. Nwyfre is the essence of the Cosmos. Nwyfre is the first-born of Annwn—the first thing to be. From nwyfre all the Cosmos proceeds—and at the last the Cosmos is all nwyfre. Back of nwyfre there is naught but Annwn. Over and above nwyfre there is naught but Awen.

All the things in the Cosmos are the products of the creative activities of Nwyfre. Nwyfre is the essence of the Cosmos—the Cosmos is the manifestation of nwyfre. Nwyfre and the Cosmos are the same thing in its inner and outer aspects. By "Life" is not meant that biological state called "life"—this latter is but the expression, in one material manifestation, of the One Life. There are many other expressions, in many other planes and forms of being.

In the One Life are inherent the three principles: substance, motion, and consciousness. In the infinitude of manifestation of these Three Principles by the One Life is found the explanation of the Cosmos or Universe. In their play, and interplay, is found the secret of shape, form, variety and degrees of substance, motion, and consciousness. From these arise manifested life. Thus in considering the Cosmos, in its activities and manifestations, the deeper and more subtle metaphysical and philosophical aspects of nwyfre may be set aside, and the One Life may be seen, in its universal operation and manifestation, as a living universe or cosmic life principle, ever moving, changing, flowing, evolving, proceeding, desiring, attaining, seeking, accomplishing. This is the One Life of the Druid teachings, possessing all the attributes and qualities of Deity except those that pertain only to the Absolute, for greater than the human imagination can conceive it though it be, nwyfre is subordinate to Awen.

In this teaching regarding the One Life, the Druid teaching gives us an intelligible explanation of that most perplexing idea of the Universal Life, which has appeared in various guises and under various names in the philosophies of all times and peoples. That all Life, in the end, is One—that the individual lives are but manifestations of, and centers in, one universal life, has been the truth taught by the illumined of all ages.

At the last analysis, the report of the illumined of the human race will be found to agree with the highest report of the human reason—the report that the One Life can be but Relative; governed by an Absolute Reality that is the source of laws; and thus subject to the seven laws of being, having its ebb and flow; its action and reaction; its rise and fall; its days and nights; its periods of creative activity, and receptive rest.

Triad IV.

Three likenesses of Nwyfre to the mind of man: the principle of substance is as the brain of man, the principle of motion is as the thought of man, the principle of consciousness is as the awareness of man.

Triad V.

Three expressions of Nwyfre: through the principle of substance, matter; through the principle of motion, energy; through the principle of consciousness, thought.

Triad VI.

Three manifestations of Nwyfre in great and small: endless change, endless progression, and endless possibility.

Triad IV.

Three likenesses of Nwyfre to the mind of man: the principle of substance is as the brain of man, the principle of motion is as the thought of man, the principle of consciousness is as the awareness of man.

Many philosophies have held that the universe is mental, in its last analysis, and that the reality behind the appearances is a Universal Mind. Others have held that the universe is merely an imagination, illusion, or dramatization, in the mind of a Supreme Being. Most of these conceptions use the terms "mind" or "mental" as something having no connection with material substance, the latter being an illusion. The Druid teachings, by contrast, recognizes Substance as a reality as actual as Consciousness or Motion—the three being but aspects of the same thing—the three principles which are really One. In giving to Substance and Motion equal places with Consciousness, the "World-Mind" is provided with a "World-Brain." Mind, truly understood, is the product of the three principles—the action of Consciousness upon Substance, by means of the vibrations of Motion. As in the human brain, so in the Cosmic Brain—"as above, so below; as below, so above." Substance and motion are not illusions—they are co-equal with consciousness, as real as any relative existence can be. There can be no consciousness without substance and motion; there can be no substance without consciousness and motion; there can be no motion without consciousness and substance. The three principles are always found together—in everything the three are found. There is no separation among them—they are, and must be, always in threefold combination. And this combination in the Cosmos, gives us that which may be called the World-Mind.

In the World-Mind of the Cosmos arise all natural phenomena. All natural phenomena are but the action and reaction; combination and re-combination; distribution and redistribution of the three principles by the One Life. As in the human brain material changes of form, shape, combination, character, and degree, result from mental activities—organic structural changes accompany mental states—states of consciousness are embodied in forms of material brain, substance—so in the World-Mind, by the action of nwyfre, do thoughts become things; desires take on material form; ideas become manifested; mental images become reproduced in material forms, shapes, and appearances. Mental states precede material form—mental images precede materialization.

This latter concept contains a key to knowledge and power little suspected by the majority of thinkers. Every mental state produces a corresponding material change in the structure and substance of the brain—the brain-cells respond to the faintest mental state. The Druid teaching informs us that the Cosmos, being both mind and brain, is governed by the same law. This being so, we may see how the Cosmos while still being mental may yet manifest in actual material and physical forms and phenomena, under the direction of the One Life. There is mind back of every material and physical form and appearance. Here is the reconciliation between mentalism and materialism—idealism and naturalism. Read the above passage carefully, a number of times; it informs you why and how thoughts become things—mental states produce material forms—mental images cause materialization. Here is a key that will unlock many doors. Can you use it?

TRIAD V.

Three expressions of Nwyfre: through the principle of substance, matter; through the principle of motion, energy; through the principle of consciousness, thought.

What is called "matter" is but the countless centers produced by the One Life in the principle of substance, through the action of the principle of motion. What are called "force and energy" are but the action of the principle of motion upon the principle of substance, induced by the One Life. What is called "thought" is but the action of the One Life upon the principle of consciousness, employing the principles of substance and motion in the operation. In every action of the One Life all three principles are employed and involved, in varying degrees and combinations. The One Life is the motive power behind all manifestation in the Cosmos.

Thus Druid tradition, and the teaching of the mysteries of all lands, states that which the more advanced of modern scientists and philosophers now hold to be a proven fact. Science and philosophy are approaching the point, where they will see that behind the activities and phenomena of the universe there is to be found One Life manifesting in the multitudinous variety of shape, form, life, and action. As a celebrated philosopher-scientist said: "The material universe is but the outer wrapper behind which is hidden a spiritual creative activity; a striving, feeling, sensing, like that which we experience in ourselves." Conation,[45] that is, the voluntary power impelling to effort, is held by Wilhelm Wundt to be the fundamental essence of this activity. Thus Wundt postulates the existing of a Cosmic Will, similar to the One Life of our Druid teaching. A recent paper by an English scientist says: "There is but one substance, and that is Spirit. Matter, so-called, is nothing but rigid places in spirit." Matter is now known to be but combinations of the ions or electrons, which are nothing other than "centers of force" in the ether. Thought without substance and motion is held to be unthinkable. Likewise science now holds that there is life and mind in all material substance, from atom to protoplasm. Science, like Druidry, finds the Three Principles Substance, Motion and Consciousness in everything. And

---

45. *Conation*: the mental power of acting in pursuit of a goal.

science is beginning to see in "energy and force" the evidences of "something akin to conation," that is, to conscious will.

And now for the inevitable question: "Why does this Cosmic Will manifest this energy, activity, desire, longing, striving, seeking and evolution?—what is the necessity of it all?—what is the end sought for?" As difficult as this question may be, and though it has repeatedly been called "unanswerable"—the teachings of the mysteries do not shrink from it, but give the one logical answer.

The One Life, seeking to manifest consciousness as its highest principle, manifests the natural phenomena of the universe. From a state of unconsciousness, through many stages of semiconsciousness; through many degrees of simple consciousness, personal consciousness; individual consciousness; and states still higher in the scale, unimaginable to us, on toward the highest states of cosmic consciousness; the One Life proceeds. Consciousness, in all of its phases, proceeds through change and depends upon constant change. Consciousness always produces activity, and manifests motion. Consciousness always manifests objectively in change and motion in substantial shape and form. In this is to be found the explanation of the phenomena of the involution and evolution of the Cosmos, with all the incidents thereof—in this is found the answer to the ultimate "Why."

The One Life, awakening from its sleep of unconsciousness during the cosmic night in Annwn, seeks consciousness. Consciousness is the essence of life—therefore the Cosmos seeks life itself. The Cosmos manifests in order to gain conscious life. Like the mortal awakening from a profound sleep, almost death-like in its intensity, the Cosmos begins its task of regaining consciousness, which is the essence of its life. And just as to the mortal sleeper, such consciousness comes to it slowly.

TRIAD VI.

Three manifestations of Nwyfre in great and small: endless change, endless progression, and endless possibility.

In order to fully appreciate the meaning of this triad, we must regard the nature and meaning of consciousness. Consciousness, as just explained, proceeds from change and depends upon constant change. The best authorities in modern psychology agree with this statement. To them, consciousness is a stream of changing mental states, with their corresponding physical changes. The textbooks say: "Every act of consciousness involves a change from a past state to a present." A leading authority says, "Consciousness does not appear to itself chopped into bits... It is nothing jointed; it flows. A 'river' or a 'stream' are the metaphors by which it is most naturally described. In talking of it, let us call it the stream of consciousness." Another authority says: "Consciousness results from perpetual change. It is impossible to maintain a uniform conscious state. A uniform sensation of pressure becomes quickly unnoticeable—the pressure must perpetually vary or the sensation will cease, and this is true of all conscious states whatsoever." The One Life which is embodied in the cosmic substance, just as is the mind of man embodied in his brain-substance, must constantly manifest changes within that substance in order that it may be conscious. It must do this constantly, else it becomes unconscious. When it is remembered that states of consciousness are always accompanied by corresponding material and physical changes—that thoughts become brain-things—then we can see the explanation of the constant change in the physical world, which we call natural phenomena.

Consciousness always produces activity, and manifests motion. William James has brought out this point most forcibly in his works. He says, among much else on the same subject: "Using sweeping terms and ignoring exceptions, we might say that every possible feeling produces a movement, and that the movement is a movement of the entire organism, and of each and all its parts ... In short, a process set up in the centers reverberates everywhere, and in some way or other affects the organism throughout, making its activities either greater or less." Is it not plain that, granted the existence of the One Life in its aspect of a World-Brain, every state of consciousness within it must produce activity and motion within it; and must also manifest the corresponding physical and material changes in its substance and organic structure? Does not this, coupled with the fact that consciousness depends upon constant change, give us the explanation of the involution and evolution of the Cosmos, with all that this implies? Does not this explain to us the workings of the Law of Sequence?

In awakening into consciousness the World-Brain creates centers of material shape and form within itself. By slow degrees, more complex forms and combinations appear. Upon the created worlds appear materials appropriate for the manifestation of organic life, and then life as we know it appears and proceeds from simpler to more complex forms: on, and on, and on, ever in an ascending scale of life and being; shape and form; combination and degree.

In the World-Brain, there are many planes of consciousness, just as there are in your own brain and mind. There are the instinctive planes, and those still below—the subconscious, and those above—and the superconscious, and other stages of which man does not as yet dream. Just as the various brain cells perform their several functions, varying in the degree of importance and function—so do the various centers in the World-Brain play theirs, in the same varying importance and degree. Each is a part of the All. And there is a relationship and interdependence between all. None is alone and separate. Separateness is an illusion. All is One. The part played by humanity—by YOU—in this great Cosmic Drama, will be considered in the succeeding parts of this study course. There will be taught the lesson of "Man, Know Thyself!"

Do not think that the possibilities before the One Life are limited to the things of this speck of dust called the Earth. In the Cosmos are contained an infinitude of infinities of universes,[46] of suns, and planets. Space itself must be exhausted before the universes are exhausted. Number itself must be exhausted, before their number is exhausted. Remember, they are the products of Infinity, and consequently their number, degrees, and variety is infinite in extent and possibility.

Nor should you think of the Cosmos as limited in time. Conceptions of finite time or space have no place in the consideration of the Cosmos, for the mind is unable to think of a period of time sufficiently great to cover even one phase of the cosmic process. The Cosmic Day is unthinkable in figures. The highest figures possible to the mind of man would not represent the year-periods involved in a single second of the Cosmic Day. We are still in the dawn of the day, and yet that which men would call an eternity has passed in the present Cosmic Day. Thought fails us. We are dealing in terms of infinity.

TRIAD VII.

Three voices of Nwyfre in living things: desire, will, and contemplation.

TRIAD VIII.

Three stages in the unfolding of Nwyfre: matter, life, and spirit.

TRIAD IX.

Three relations of Nwyfre to the individual soul: as the whole to the part, as the essence to the manifestation, as the master to the workman.

---

46. At the time this was written, the word "universe" was used for what we now call a galaxy.

Triad VII.

Three voices of Nwyfre in living things: desire, will, and contemplation.

In the Druid conception of the Cosmos as a World-Mind embodied in a World-Brain, we have a valuable truth stated in simple terms, and expressed by a familiar symbol. The human brain has its analogy in the World-Brain. In this teaching we may understand the principles of the embodiment of mind in matter, and the action of mind upon matter by means of motion. Compare this teaching with the teachings of science, in its phases of inorganic evolution, and organic evolution, and see how the teaching throws light on the whole process. See how there is ever a mental action preceding the physical manifestation.

Mind is always embodied in substance. Substance always contains mind. The building of the crystal; the growth of the animal form from the single cell; the evolution of the chicken from the creative cell in the egg; all these are manifestations of physical action, structural change, and substance moving in response to mental inner causes. From one, you may know all, for the Law of Unity is ever manifest in the Cosmos.

The conception of the cosmic World-Brain also throws much light upon many phases of mental, psychic, and occult phenomena. If thoughts become things in the cosmic brain, then following the Law of Unity it is possible for thoughts to materialize in things on all other planes of activity. The same principle is involved—the principle of mental creative activity. This is the secret of mentalism, the key to psychic phenomena, and the explanation of occultism. With a Cosmos that is mental in its nature, with energy and substance, matter and motion, all receptive, responsive, and plastic and obedient to mind, what cannot be accomplished by those who understand the laws of contemplation? Will is the great creative power in the Cosmos, and so what is not possible to him who understands the art of willing? With desire as the great creative energy, can we not see why desire may be harnessed, controlled, directed, guided, mastered and employed in our lives, careers and destinies?

Yet these three—contemplation, will, and desire—one in essence, are distinct in manifestation, because expressed in differing degrees of consciousness. To understand the distinction, it is necessary to follow the progress of the One Life up the ladder of being.

The very simplest forms of life have merely a dim consciousness of something outside themselves. This is built on foundations reaching even deeper, into the very origins of matter. Even atoms manifest reactions to the presence of other atoms, as evidenced by attraction and repulsion, the first adumbrations of desire. The chemical affinity of molecules shows a higher degree of this faint consciousness. Crystals manifest a still higher degree of it as they build up their forms. The cell-forms of the simplest kinds of life exhibit the simplest form that can properly be called mind; they are aware of food, and of other living things which seek them for food; consequently, driven by desire, they move toward the first, and away from the second.

This is the elementary form of "simple consciousness," that is, an awareness of outside objects and a response to them motivated by desire. Other living things demonstrate this form of consciousness, and not all human beings surpass it. Simple consciousness may be described as a state of knowing, but not knowing that one knows. Simple consciousness focuses primarily on perceptions of outside things received through the senses, and secondarily on physical sensations arising in one's own body, without any sense of an inner life apart from these things.

As simple consciousness matures and develops over many lives and degrees of complexity, it gradually evolves into the degree of consciousness which is known as "personal consciousness." At this point the sense of identity begins to awaken. Beings possessing personal consciousness perceive a mental life within themselves, and make connections between the inner and outer worlds: that is, they think. They not only know, but they know that they know, and this second level of knowledge gives them capacities of which simple consciousness is wholly destitute. Those capacities may be summed up in the word "will," for beings with personal consciousness do not simply react to desire; they possess some degree of inner freedom, and may to some extent choose the objects of their will.

Personal consciousness, like simple consciousness, has many degrees on its scale. We cannot pause here to consider this stage in detail, for our concern is with still higher degrees of consciousness. Still, in a general way, and in order that you may distinguish between simple consciousness and personal consciousness, think of the former as an awareness of material conditions, and of the latter as an awareness of mental conditions. Simple consciousness is entirely focused on the world of objects and perceptions outside the self. Personal consciousness moves one step inward to consider the world of thoughts and feelings inside the self. In neither of these modes of consciousness, however, is the self, itself, an object of experience.

Yet among the multitude of humanity, some few in each generation evolve the capacity to know not only their material surroundings and their mental activities, but themselves. This ability marks the coming of a higher stage of consciousness which surpasses the simple consciousness and personal consciousness just alluded to, and which may be called individual consciousness. Individual consciousness may be thought of as the consciousness of Spirit, in an elementary degree—there are many other and higher degrees.

Individual consciousness is more than an awareness of the outside world, or of one's own body as distinct from the bodies of others and other things. It is more than the awareness of one's own mind, even when this awareness is carried to a high degree of development. It is the awareness of the One Life. Where simple consciousness knows, and personal consciousness knows that it knows, individual consciousness knows who it is that knows.

Personality is but the character in which the One Life is playing a certain part. The very word "person" is derived from the Latin word *persona*, meaning "a mask used by actors." Your personality is merely the part in life you are playing—"the John Smith part of you." And, consequently, consciousness of personality is merely a knowledge of your own character, just as an actor is aware and conscious of the character of the play he is enacting. If you can imagine an actor forgetting his real identity, and becoming so rapt in the play that he imagines that he really is Hamlet or Richard III, you may gain a clearer idea of personal consciousness. When the actor shakes off the illusion, and realizes that he is something more than the assumed character—when you awaken to the fact that you are something more than "John Smith"—then the personality is seen to be in reality but an assumed character, or "mask used by actors."

The consciousness of individuality is an awareness that you are above the limits and character of personality—that you are a center of consciousness and force in the One Life. This awareness must, however, be more than a mere intellectual acquiescence in the teaching to that effect, or an agreement with some teacher or study course. These can be useful steps along the journey, but they are not the journey's goal. That goal is the direct personal knowledge that you are part of the One Life. It is the direct personal experience of your oneness with all things in the Cosmos, and it expresses itself in contemplation, the power of reflective consciousness to shape the world through consciousness itself.

Triad VIII.

Three stages in the unfolding of Nwyfre: matter, life, and spirit.

In previous triads we have seen that Nwyfre is the essence of all life, and consciousness is its highest manifestation. Back of every living thing, there is always the One Life. But the One Life precedes the particular manifestation that we call organic life, for it existed before organic life appeared in the Cosmos. The great cosmic energies and activities which manifested in world-building in all its phases, were but manifestations of the One Life bestirring itself. These fundamental activities show but little evidence of what we call life, but still the Will is seen in operation in the mineral kingdom, the realm of inorganic being, building up and tearing down, arranging and rearranging, combining and recombining. The attraction and repulsion of the atoms, and of the particles composing them, shows us that the One Life is present and in operation in these most basic manifestations. In gravitation, chemical affinity, and molecular cohesion, we see a wonderful evidence of the operation of the One Life. In all the great natural laws in evidence throughout the Cosmos, we may see the operation of the One Life. The laws of physics demonstrate clearly the existence of some great conative power, animating, energizing, and manifesting in every part and particle of creation. One must indeed be a blind materialist to fail to see ever at work that "something within" manifesting as the "something without." The building up of the crystal, from liquid to regular and exact geometrical form, should be sufficient to convince anyone that there is a "something at work" in it. Even the materialist is forced to recognize these facts—and he does recognize it, and calls that something by the name of "Nature." The Druids have used this same word for the same power. But if you think clearly, you must recognize that "Nature" is conative, and acts and manifests as a living will.

These fundamental activities and manifestations of the One Life are akin to the activities and manifestations of our own lives. Stop to consider that your body was built up from a single cell by the One Life in you—not only your fleshy parts, but your hair, nails, teeth, and even the hardest bones which form your framework. And, likewise, the flint-like shell of the clam, oyster, and other hard-shell animals were so built up; not to speak of the harder geometrical crystal forms of the diamond and other minerals. The hard ivory of the elephant's tusk was built up from cells, by the One Life at work within the animal itself. So you see that life can build up hard substances as well as soft ones. And the same force that builds up these hard substances, builds up the rocks and hills, and mountains, and minerals that form the body of Nature, just as certain functions of the animal or human brain manifest in building up the body of the Cosmos.

The One Life from the beginning of the Cosmic Day has sought to embody itself in objective form in order to manifest consciousness. As in the creation of any being, it first concerned itself in providing a body for itself, in order that it would have a substantial foundation for higher manifestation. In the Cosmos the material plane of activity is the one first operated upon. Then comes the slowing down of the vibrations of motion, and the principle of substance produces the elementary particles which, combining, form matter. Then matter begins to evolve into higher forms, until at last there is produced the combination in which is possible the manifestation that we call organic life. From the lowly living cell-like creatures in the slimy depths of the primeval ocean-beds, arise step by step, slowly, tediously, painfully, arduously, and haltingly, but surely and steadily, the vast diversity of living organisms. The modern scientific theory of evolution tells us a true tale of the slow rise and development of life forms.

Perhaps a million years ago, humanity, a poor, weak, brutal creature with wonderful possibilities, was evolved by the One Life in this world as one expression of its urge toward consciousness. This poor creature has accomplished much, and still has much to accomplish. Nor does evolution stop here, for humankind is but one manifestation, on one world, of one intermediate stage of being. On other worlds in the Cosmos, there are beings as much more complex and conscious than humanity, as humanity is more complex and conscious than the infusorium.[47] Our planet is but one of millions upon millions of millions of worlds, in which evolution is at work. We are away down low in the scale of worlds and being. There are beings as great as man's conceptions of the gods, dwelling on some of these worlds. Some of us have dwelt on these brighter spheres, but have been sent back a grade or two in order to complete tasks left undone; or to gain experiences necessary; or because certain desires had not yet died out in us, and we needed to "get enough of it" once more, in order to be free of the attraction to the lower and open to the attraction of the Higher. There are planes of life so transcendentally grand and exalted, that our wildest imaginations cannot conceive of them. On the other hand, there are worlds so much lower in the scale, that the hell of orthodox religion·would be less terrible to experience. Each of us goes where our desires take us. We travel the road of

---

47. *infusorium*: The old word for what scientists now call single-celled organisms, such as blue-green algae.

our desires and thoughts. We make our own route and guide our own vessel. The individual soul is its own destiny.

TRIAD IX.

Three relations of Nwyfre to the individual soul: as the whole to the part, as the essence to the manifestation, as the master to the workman.

The many lives we witness around us in the Cosmos are but centers of life in the One Life. Separate existence is but the creative fiction of the Cosmos—it is a relative truth, not an absolute one. All life is one, in its fundamental nature. The entire Cosmos shares One Life, in which we are parts or centers—in its being we "live and move and have our being." The One Life is not far away; it is all around us, and immanent within us. While the first part of this triad shows the individual to be but an infinitesimal unit in a stupendous whole, the second shows the individual to be inseparable from the whole, connected with all by spiritual bonds and links, and sharing the infinite possibilities of the All. The life of the individual is not bounded by his personal limitations, but includes the life of the All. In this understanding and recognition there is found the reconciliation, unity and agreement between the contradictory phases of life and the universe. True spiritual advancement depends upon the increasing recognition and identification of the individual with the All.

The third phrase of the triad teaches, however, that the One Life can fulfill its purpose only by means of the various centers of consciousness within itself. Without these centers of consciousness within itself—the consciousness of You and I and all the rest, from divine beings to infusoria—the One Life would be unconscious and inactive. Just as the individual can be conscious only through his stream of units of consciousness, so can the One Life be conscious only through its stream of centers of consciousness. Let these centers of consciousness disappear, and the Cosmos once more is resolved into Annwn. Moreover, the One Life lives only through its centers of life—the centers called You and I, and the rest. As the Cosmos advances in the Cosmic Day, there is manifested a constantly increasing blending or unification of the various centers of Life—a constantly increasing identification of the individual with the All. And, thus is accomplished the fulfillment of the Cosmic Day, when the One Life lives, wills and is conscious as One. Before that time comes, the illusion of Separateness is manifested—the "creative fiction" of the Cosmos operates in working out the approach to Cosmic Consciousness.

Thus it is seen that the One Life manifests through the centers, because it must do so in order to live and be conscious. Creation and the Universe is not a matter of whim, unreasoning desire, or arbitrary fiat of the One Life. Just as you find the imperative demand for life within yourself, so does the One Life find the imperative demand for life within itself. It is not free; the urge of "Must" is ever impelling it forward. The One Life is not a cruel or arbitrary ruler. It is the greater self of the Cosmos, and subject to the same laws which govern you. It is doing the best it can, for itself, and therefore for you. When the individual realizes that the One Life is doing the best it can, and is bound by cosmic law as much as is the individual; that there is no arbitrary desire or unreasoning whim in the Cosmic machinery; that One is All, and All is One; then there appears an explanation for much in life that finds no explanation from within the teachings of the popular theologies and philosophies of past and present.

Many daring thinkers who have set aside "the bribe of heaven and threat of hell" and dared to look Life in the face, have been overcome by a sense of impotent subjection to an arbitrary Being who, being able to remedy conditions, and knowing of the pains of mortal life in the universe, nevertheless has deliberately imposed such conditions upon living things. Such thinkers find it impossible to reconcile the claim that such a being is good, with the manifestations of apparent injustice, inequity, pain and suffering which made pessimists of so many great souls.

But with the dawning knowledge that the One Life, or World-Spirit, is not the Absolute, but is subject to cosmic law along with its manifestations, then we have a picture of a Being which suffers with us and through us; rises with us and through us; strives with us and through us; attains with us and through us; rejoices with us and through us; conquers with us and through us—and whose Life is composed of our lives; whose consciousness is composed of our consciousness. Such a Being is seen to be, at the last, one with ourselves, instead of an outside power—and consequently, such a Being is seen to be eternally making for Good—making for our good, for we are one with itself. Such a Being is seen to be the True Self of all the individual selves of the Cosmos. And in the recognition of all this, our bitterness must die away, and a great feeling of compassion, sympathy, understanding and love must be manifested by us—and felt by us. Then must come that sense of Oneness with the All which is the great reconciler—which harmonizes the opposites, and establishes the cosmic balance.

This One Life is YOU, and you are it. As centers of life within the One Life, we are steadily growing toward that state of cosmic consciousness, in which the All shall know itself as One, and the One know itself as All. As each soul proceeds through the stages of spiritual evolution, its consciousness enlarges, identifying more and more of the Cosmos as itself, until the stage of cosmic consciousness is reached in which the individual is one with the whole, and the whole awakens in the individual.

Nwyfre, the One Life, is the great universal spirit or life principle of the Cosmos, that in which "we live, and move, and have our being." This is the great being which begins to awaken in the dawn of the Cosmic Day, and thence evolves into the Cosmic Consciousness of the close of that day, when All is One and consciousness is resolved into unity; thence to pass into the blissful slumber of the Cosmic Night, when all is resolved into the infinite possibility of Annwn, until the first stirrings of the dawn of the new Cosmic Day.

This is the Great Cycle of the Cosmos. Awen abides in infinite peace, Annwn abides in infinite potentiality; between these two, the One Life that is Nwyfre emerges, strives, fulfills itself, and rests, in cycles beyond the reach of our present imaginative powers.

THE MAGICAL MEMORY:
ACQUIRING IMPRESSIONS

A S WAS EXPLAINED in the lessons appropriate to the Novitiate Grade, the subconscious function of the mind receives every impression presented to it, and stores it away in its enormous storehouse. There is, however, a very great difference in the nature of the impressions received. Some are vivid and strong; others less so; and still others faint and indistinct. The strength of the impression depends upon the involuntary interest and voluntary attention bestowed upon it by the mind at the time of its occurrence. A thing of interest, or a thing to which one has given attention, registers an impression much stronger than one exciting little or no interest or attention, and the record is much more easily recalled when it is needed.

To extend our metaphor of the subconscious storehouse, we may say that the attention given to a thing reaching the mind through the medium of the senses determines the size and shape of the thing to be stored away, while the interest awakened at the time of the impression gives the color to the impression. This may be taken as a rule: The attention determines the size; the interest determines the color.

When one wishes to bring to light an article stored away in the storehouse, he finds it much easier to find a large article than a small one—much easier to locate one of a fiery, red color than one of a neutral tint. This is true whether the goods are stored away carefully and systematically, or carelessly and without order. The careful and orderly keeping of stock greatly facilitates the finding of a desired article, but size and color make the thing itself more conspicuous.

Frequent recalling or handling the article not only tends to acquaint the storekeeper with the location of the article, but also adds to its size and color, as each time it is brought out, a certain amount of attention and interest is bestowed upon it. Attention has been defined as "the focusing of consciousness." Consciousness may spread itself over a number of objects, just as the sun spreads its rays over countless things, or it may be focused upon a particular object, just as the rays of the sun may be concentrated, by the means of a glass, upon a single point. The degree of attention is thus the measure of the impression made upon our subconscious mentality.

Attention may be divided into two classes, that is, involuntary and voluntary. The involuntary attention is that which is attracted by the interest inherent in the object, while voluntary attention is focused by an effort of the will. The undeveloped person has little or no voluntary attention, but involuntary attention is there in full force. The developed person manifests a high degree of voluntary attention, the degree of voluntary attention indicating the stage of development of the person. Many people scarcely progress further than the borderline of voluntary attention.

Put another way, involuntary attention is the birthright of the animal consciousness, while voluntary attention is the result of development of the will. In young children and undeveloped adults, an object must be interesting to hold the attention for more than a moment. The developed person is able by an effort of the will to direct attention to an uninteresting object, and hold it there until he has conveyed to his mind the desired information regarding it. Likewise, he is able to turn his attention from a most interesting object to one that is dull and uninteresting, all by the power of will.

It is true that the developed person finds something of interest in nearly every object or subject, which renders it far easier to focus the attention than it would be in the case of the undeveloped person, who sees nothing of interest in the same object or subject. The developed person also has the faculty of shutting out unwelcome subjects and objects from his attention. He uses will to accomplish this result, the process being similar to that by which he focuses his attention upon an uninteresting object or subject. The undeveloped person, having scarcely any voluntary attention, is almost at the mercy of outside impressions, and is practically in the position of the child who, viewing the passing circus parade, forgets himself, his home and his parents for the time being, and follows the procession until he is lost.

Impressions are received primarily through the five senses. The impressions conveyed by touching, tasting, or smelling are more difficult to recall by the memory without training and intelligent practice, while those obtained by the sight and sound are readily recalled. Most people find it difficult to recall the precise taste, smell, or feel of an object, even when they distinctly recall the act and time of the tasting, smelling and touching, and all the circumstances connected with it. But the mind indelibly registers the impression of the tasting, smelling and touching so that it may be recognized when it again occurs. This distinction between recall and recognition is of great importance in memory training, since much that is hidden from recall is still available to recognition, and if some single detail can be recalled, much else can be recollected along with it.

Memory for touch, taste, and smell may be deliberately cultivated, as in the cases of tea-tasters, wine experts, wool sorters, and the like, in whom the senses of tasting, smelling and touching are highly developed, and the memory of previous impressions readily recalled in its most minute details the instant the new impression reaches the brain. It is harder to recall the former impression of tasting, smelling or touching by an effort of the imagination. Exceptions are quoted by some writers who speak of certain gourmands and epicures, who can by an effort of the imagination and memory bring to their minds the distinct impression of the taste of their favorite dish. Hypnotic subjects also seem to get such impressions by suggestion. Generally speaking, however, it is harder to gain this facility with touch, taste, or smell than with sight or sound.

In the case of impressions received through the senses of seeing or hearing, most people can not only recall the occurrences but can also readily picture the sight or hear the sound, by means of the imagination aided by the memory. Some have this faculty largely developed, and can in the mind picture a sight or hear sounds almost as distinctly as in the original instance; many artists and musicians are examples of this fact.

It will readily be seen that in memory training the acquiring of clear and distinct impressions is a most important feature. Unless there is something to recollect, there is no use for the memory. Recall our illustration of the mental storehouse, with its varied and assorted stock, and you will readily see the importance of having your mental packages and parcels of such size, shape and color as to be easily seen and located when you need them.

Attention and Interest

Not only must the senses be trained to quickly and clearly record the impressions from outside so that they may be readily recalled, but the mind must be trained to direct its attention and interest to its own workings, to the end that thoughts and mental processes may be remembered when needed. Acquirement of impressions is often along two or more lines. For instance, in reading a printed page the eye records the impression of the words, sentences, paragraphs and page, while at the same time the other faculties of the mind receive the impression of the thought and meaning of the author, the impression of the thought and ideas of the reader, the conclusion arrived at by the reader after digesting and assimilating the reasoning of the author, mingling the same with the knowledge, information and opinions already stored away in his own mind. All these impressions may be recalled by means of the memory, according to the measure of the development of memory in the individual.

Cultivation of attention and interest has produced almost marvelous results in many well-known cases, and anyone may with a little practice acquire proficiency along these lines that will be as surprising to himself as amazing to his friends. Robert-Houdin, the celebrated French conjurer, whose best tricks depended materially upon his quick and correct observation and his wonderful memory, had developed his faculty of rapid observation and attention as well as his memory, by years of careful practice. It is related of him that in his earlier days he would pass rapidly by a Paris shop, giving one sharp, quick glance at the window, then turning his eyes in another direction. After walking along for a few minutes he would stop and, with pencil and paper, endeavor to recall and describe as many articles as possible.

He found that steady practice so sharpened his faculty of attention and observation that each day he would recollect a greater number of objects displayed in the windows, the explanation being that he was steadily developing the faculties which received and stored away impressions, as well as those which recalled them. It is said that in time he was able to rush past a large store window, filled with small wares, and receive such a full, clear and sharp impression of the objects displayed that he could, hours afterward, recall and describe every article with scarcely a mistake. This development made Houdin what he was, and helped him to amass a fortune. His mind apparently became like a camera, and registered everything in range, and all he had to do was to recall the impression and name the objects as he saw them with his mind's eye.

Rudyard Kipling, in his delightful story *Kim*, describes a similar proceeding. The old teacher Lurgan Sahib was training the boy for a career in espionage, in which the quick and clear seeing of things meant success, and perhaps even life itself. The old man took from a drawer a handful of jewels, and bade Kim to gaze upon them as long as he desired, and then see what he could remember of what he had seen. A native boy, who had been trained in this way for some time, was also there. Kim bent over the tray and gazed at the fifteen jewels upon it. He thought it was an easy game. The tray was then covered, and the native boy hastily scribbled his recollection on a sheet of paper.

'There are under that paper five blue stones—one big, one smaller, and three small,' said Kim, all in haste. 'There are four green stones, and one with a hole in it; there is one yellow stone that I can see through, and one like a pipe-stem. There are two red stones, and—and—I made the count fifteen, but two I have forgotten. No! Give me time. One was of ivory, little and brownish, and—and—give me time...'

But Kim could do no better.

'Hear my count!' the child burst in, trilling with laughter. 'First, are two flawed sapphires—one of two ruttees and one of four, as I should judge. The four-ruttee sapphire is chipped at the edge. There is one Turkestan turquoise, plain with black veins, and there are two inscribed—one with a name of God in gilt, and the other being cracked across, for it came out of an old ring, I cannot read. We have now all five blue stones. Four flawed emeralds there are, but one is drilled in two places, and one is a little carven—'

'Their weights?' said Lurgan Sahib, impassively.

'Three—five—five—and four ruttees, as I judge it. There is one piece of old greenish pipe amber, and a cut topaz from Europe. There is one ruby of Burma, of two ruttees, without a flaw, and there is a balas-ruby, flawed, of two ruttees. There is a carved ivory from China representing a rat sucking an egg; and there is last—ah ha!—a ball of crystal as big as a bean set on a gold leaf!'

He clapped his hands at the close.

Kim feels much mortified at the superiority of the native boy.

'But how is it done?' asked Kim.

'By doing it many times over till it is done perfectly—for it is worth doing.'

This game so graphically portrayed by Kipling is a favorite with the Orientals, many of whom attain a great proficiency in it as did Houdin in his form of the same game. You may do the same, if you will take the time and trouble to acquire the "knack."

It is related of a well-known artist that at a first sitting of a patron he would often sit gazing at his sitter for an hour at a time, and would then dismiss him, telling him that he need not return. He would then work at the portrait for months without another sitting, gazing from time to time at the empty chair of his late sitter, and then reproducing his features on the canvas. He said that he could actually see his model in the chair, the impression having apparently been indelibly impressed upon his memory. This, of course, is an extreme example, but other artists have developed the same faculty to a scarcely less wonderful degree.

The Chinese have a different character for every word, and the Chinese scholar carries thousands of these character in his mind, without any trouble. Similar results are recorded of musicians, many of whom have been able to reproduce page after page of music they had heard but once or twice. A celebrated composer, while but a boy, is said to have listened to a celebrated Mass sung at a monastery, the score of which was religiously guarded by the monks. Upon his return to his room he reproduced the entire Mass on paper, without the mistake of a single note. The monks forgave the theft in their admiration of the remarkable feat. Lesser feats of memorizing music are not uncommon. And mind you, it is not alone the faculty of memory that renders these things possible, but the developed faculty of seeing and hearing things clearly and distinctly.

There are Jews living today who can repeat by heart, from any given word, the whole of the Talmud. Similarly, the capacity to recite the entire Koran from beginning to end, without a flaw, is an ordinary attainment of educated persons in Muslim countries. Greater feats than these may be found in India, where it is far from rare to find storytellers who have committed to memory every line of the *Mahabharata,* the grandest of the old Indian epics, which is some six times as long as the Christian Bible. Ask such a storyteller to recount any episode from that stupendous work, and he will oblige at once, and recite hundreds of verses in their correct order without a single mistake. The ancient Druids, finally, were well known never to permit the writing of any of their sacred lore, and communicated the whole of it in the form of verses, which their students committed to memory.

Such abilities draw partly on practice, and partly on method. In earlier times, when books were costly, men were dependent upon their memories, and many developed memories which would now be regarded as marvelous, but which were then quite the ordinary thing, possessed by all who made any pretense to study. In the thirteenth and fourteenth centuries, students flocked to the universities in thousands. Books were scarce and costly, and the ancient custom of committing whole works to memory still prevailed. The methods used at that time descended from those of the ancient Grecians and Romans, among whom great masters of memory were commonplace.

The Roman philosopher Seneca, who was not considered unusually proficient at memory by his countrymen, was able to repeat two thousand disconnected words after having heard them once, in the same order as they were given. His friend, Porteus Latio, never forgot any of the speeches he had ever delivered, and never found his memory fail for a single word. Cyneas, an ambassador to the Romans from King Pyrrhus, learned in a single day the names of the assembled people so well that the next day he was able to salute the senators and the populace, each by his own name. Pliny says that Cyrus knew the name of every soldier in his army. Themistocles could call by their names the 20,000 citizens of Athens.

Nor have these methods failed to endure to our time. Muretus tells of a young Corsican pupil who was so practiced that he could repeat backward and forward 36,000 unconnected words, after having heard them but once. He said that he could do better, but the men who were reading to him became exhausted. There came to this Corsican a young man whose memory was wretched. The Corsican instructed him with such success that in a week or two the pupil could repeat five hundred words, backwards and forwards. This may appear a useless feat; just so, it is a useless feat to lift an iron bar to which great weights have been attached, but the strength gained in practicing that feat may be applied to many other things.

The methods used to develop such feats of memory may be compared to the filing system by which the owner of a storehouse keeps the goods stored therein in proper order, so that they may be found at once. Before such methods may usefully be applied, however, the power of concentration and attention must be developed and strengthened. The exercises already done in the previous grade will help lay the foundation for this development, and the second of them—the habit of recollecting each day at its end—should be made permanent.The following exercises will help you proceed further in this work.

Exercise 1

We have mentioned the exercise whereby "Kim" was trained. This same course of training may be followed by the student with great profit. Collect a large number—say, a hundred—small items of many different kinds, and keep them in a bag. Take at least seven of them at random from the bag and put them on a table, covering them at once with a cloth. Remove the cloth and count to ten slowly, then replace the cloth, and describe the articles as fully as possible, writing down their descriptions. The number of articles on the table may be increased in time to fifty small articles. It is wonderful what a degree of proficiency in observation may be attained in this manner.

The tale of "Kim" and his task, while fiction, is certainly based upon actual experiences known to Kipling, for such practices are quite common in India, a similar exercise being taught by certain of the Yogis. By it the students' powers of observation become so sharpened that without effort they may see many things in their everyday life that others would not notice, and thus become quite valuable to the business with which they are connected.

In this same class of exercises may be placed the method of Houdin, who walked past the store windows and then recalled the articles displayed in them. This exercise may be practiced alongside the one just mentioned. It adds variety, and also tends to develop the powers of observation and concentration while the observer is surrounded with noises and sights. Many other exercises of this sort will suggest themselves to the student as he progresses, and he will find the subject fascinating, after he once masters the trick of doing the thing.

Exercise 2

A valuable exercise is that of taking mental stock of a room and its contents. Go into a room and take a rapid survey of it and its contents, trying to get a good mental photograph of as many articles as possible—the size of the room, the height of the ceiling, the color of the paper, the number of doors and windows, the chairs, tables, carpet, pictures, etc. Then go out of the room and mark down what you have seen. Then compare with the room itself. Repeat until you have mastered the exercise. You will, by practice, be able to correctly describe any place you have visited, almost without effort, your powers of observation having automatically registered impressions, after you have trained them for a while.

Both these exercises may be performed during time that would otherwise be wasted—while waiting for an appointment, for example, or traveling by some public conveyance. Begin making a habit of turning such times to your benefit.

COMPLETION EXERCISES: FOCUSING THE SELF

HESE COMPLETION EXERCISES are meant to assist in the transition from the present grade of the Dolmen Arch study course to the next, the *Gradd yr Ymarferiwr* (Grade of the Practitioner). You should begin them when you have finished the other work of this grade.

The practice of the completion exercises included in the preceding lesson packet, if carefully and faithfully practiced, will begin to transform your sense of existence. You will have begun to realize by direct experience that you are an entity that is by no means limited to the physical body and the material plane.

You will also begin to experience your capacity to work with the physical body with the tools of consciousness. The physical body is a most responsive instrument of the mind and will, and may be healed and strengthened by the power of thought. This power, developed further in lessons to come, will also enable you to treat the physical bodies of others to excellent advantage. As the realization grows that your essential self is independent of, and on a higher plane than, the physical body, you will awaken into the power to guide and direct your physical functions, and those of others who have not attained the realization.

Still, this is only the beginning of a long journey. It is a natural mistake for students at this point to think that they have escaped the limits of personality and achieved the awakening of individuality, but this is far from the case. To rise above the trammels imposed by a too-great identification with the physical body, and in thus doing, awaken a sense of the possibilities of the self, is a first step only.

Later steps lead to the emergence of yet higher and clearer perceptions, of which the awakening of the individuality is the final term. But the step of building up the incorporeal personality must be attained before the next higher is possible. Thus be not in too much haste to pass on to the next step. Master each step as you proceed—thus do you rise naturally and easily on the Ladder of Attainment.

Once you have worked your way through the other practices in this grade, and gained a reasonable proficiency therein, you may proceed with the Completion Exercises of focusing the self, as follows:

Completion Exercise 1

Place yourself in the posture of meditation and perform the usual preliminaries of relaxation and breathing. When these are completed, meditate on incorporeality—that is, life independent of the physical body. Thinking of oneself as a physical being, one naturally and properly takes into account the incidents of corporeality or life in the body. For instance, you are always aware that you may be hurt by fire, water, earth, air or spirit. You may be burned by fire, drowned by water, smothered or bruised by earth, or swept away by air. And, again, you may be wounded by violence, meet with physical accidents, laid low by sickness, etc. These are the incidents that attend corporeal or embodied life.

In meditation, using the imagination intelligently to explore a mode of existence that may not yet be open to your perception, strive to realize that none of these incidents have any effect upon the plane of the essence of yourself. Imagine yourself stepping outside of your body in an incorporeal form, clothed only in Mind. In that condition you would readily pass through fire unscathed—through water untouched—through earth without hurt or interference—through air without being swept off your feet. These things of the physical plane have effect only upon the physical body; they cannot touch the self.

In some of the initiatory rites of the ancient Druids, it is said that the postulant was taken out of his physical body, and in an incorporeal form was bidden to plunge himself in the flames of the hottest bonfire, to throw himself from the highest mountain peak, and to plunge into a bottomless lake. Not realizing that these things could not affect him, and being bound up with the memory of the corporeal life, the postulant would often shrink from these tests. But after being encouraged by example and precept he would submit to the test, joyfully, with a laugh on his lips, as he realized that in the incorporeal state these corporeal things were mere dreams of the physical plane.

Of course the actual experience of temporary departure from the physical body is far more convincing than is the mere realization of the truth in meditation. Still, the latter must not be despised, for it gives one an intuitive realization of the truth, which, once attained, tends to destroy fear and to impart a new sense of courage, invincibility and invulnerability and mastery, which permeates the entire being and causes one to radiate power and strength. Likewise will come the realization that the self is incapable of hurt, harm, wounds, or sickness. These things belong to the corporeal life, and have naught to do with the inner self.

Persevere in this practice until you feel intensely that your innermost self is superior to all the incidents and accidents of the corporeal life, and whatever may happen to your physical covering you yourself will remain unhurt, whole, untouched, undisturbed.

The ancient British and Gaulish peoples are said to have cultivated this sense to a high degree. It is said that a Christian missionary in the days of King Arthur announced to a British Druid that the Second Coming of Christ was imminent and the world would end. "Well, what is that to me?" the Druid replied, and returned to his studies. He realized fully his spiritual invincibility. A similar tale is told of Ralph Waldo Emerson, who was halted in the street by an excited Millerite,[48] who informed him in strained tones: "Mr. Emerson, the world will be destroyed in ten days!" "Well, what of it?" replied Emerson, calmly, "I don't see but what we shall get along just as well without it." The nineteenth century Transcendentalist voiced the truth as clearly as did his predecessor in ancient Britain. This same poise may be cultivated by the practices here given.

Along with this sense of personal invulnerability comes a sense, even more reassuring to the sensitive mind, of the eternal and invincible nature of all other beings and things. Just as the body is simply a temporary expression and vehicle of the self, every physical thing without exception is a temporary expression and vehicle of some other center of consciousness and force, and the whole physical world together is a temporary and constantly changing expression and vehicle of the One Life. The beauty of the rose lasts but a few days, but the force that creates the rose and gives it its beauty is eternal—invincible—everlasting. So it is with every physical thing whatsoever; the form must inevitably be cut down by the scythe of time; the essence abides unharmed and untroubled forever.

---

48. The Millerites were a sect of Christian enthusiasts who, like many of more recent vintage, convinced themselves that the end of the world was imminent.

Completion Exercise 2

The next step in the process, which may be undertaken once a reasonable competence has been acquired in the preceding exercise, is the focusing of the self—the cultivation of an acute realization of one's existence as a center of consciousness and force. The goal of this stage is to gather up the dissipated sense of personal existence, and bringing it to a focal point, into vivid and actual conscious realization, preparatory to it being transmuted into the higher sense of individual existence. The following exercise will tend to bring about the desired realization:

Once again, take the posture of meditation and pass through the usual preliminaries. Meditate then upon the great ocean of the One Life, in which all individual entities are but focal centers of consciousness and force. Picture yourself, in imagination, as being the actual center of all things, with all the universe revolving around you. See yourself as the pivot around which the universe moves—the Central Sun around which the infinite worlds circle in their cosmic flight. Feel yourself to be the focal center of the Cosmos. This is indeed the case, in accordance with the ancient occult axiom which informs us that "The Cosmos is infinite; its circumference is nowhere and its center is everywhere." Strive to lose all thought of the outside world in this meditation—regard it as having been dissolved back into the unmanifest in Annwn—and allow your own body to share in that dissolution. See yourself as a disembodied center of consciousness and power. Repeat a few times the phrase "I am," and strive to realize the truth of it to the fullest extent of your power of imagination and conception.

Remain in this state for a time, and then close the meditation. Repeat it frequently, until the habit of experiencing yourself as a center of pure consciousness and energy becomes deeply rooted in your being.

GRADD YR YMARFERIWR

THE GRADE OF THE PRACTITIONER

INTRODUCTION
TO THE GRADE

WELCOME TO THE THIRD STAGE of the Dolmen Arch study course, the Grade of the Practitioner! You have now reached the halfway point in your journey through the lesser mysteries. Since a central theme of these lessons is the awakening of individuality, it is appropriate here to discuss in a little more detail exactly what individuality is, and why it is so rarely found among humanity.

Most people, were they to be told that they are not yet individuals, would likely be surprised and even indignant. They might well insist with some heat that they think and act for themselves, making their own decisions and choosing their own beliefs, and they cannot imagine that anyone would have the audacity to disagree with truths so self-evident. Yet a rich irony lies here, for it is very often the case that the more forcefully someone insists on their own originality and independence, the less of both that person actually has. The situation is all too often reminiscent of the scene from a well-known movie in which the lead character tells a crowd, "You are all individuals," and the crowd shouts back, in perfect unison, "Yes, we are all individuals!"

A little self-examination is a useful exercise here. Consider, let us say, your own opinions and beliefs about the world. How many of them did you adopt because you craved the good opinion of others who hold the same opinions and beliefs, or because those beliefs embody favorable judgments of you and the people you like and unfavorable ones of people you dislike, or because those opinions are the common property of the circles in which you were raised or the one in which you now spend your time? For most people, opinions motivated by causes such as these far outnumber those that are held on the basis of clear thought and personal experience.

Reflecting in this way, it becomes possible to see the meaning hidden within the irony. As long as we assume unthinkingly that we are free to think and act for ourselves, we very often fail to notice the ways in which we fail to think and act for ourselves. When we accept that many of our thoughts and actions are conditioned by outside forces, we begin to understand the role these forces play in our lives, and this opens a window of opportunity through which we can become something more than the automatic product of our heredity and our environment. On a deeper level, it is when we recognize that we are not isolated separate lives, but manifestations of One Life, that we can grasp the unique aspect of Awen that each of us comes into the world to manifest.

The state of humanity has been compared to a bridge with one end firmly planted in the world of animal existence and the other reaching up to potentials hidden in mist. While we are crossing that bridge—which is to say, while we are embodied as human beings, living human lives on this world—much of what passes in our minds differs only in minor ways from what passes in the minds of the more intelligent animals. Like our animal brothers and sisters, we are powerfully influenced by our own unthinking passions and biological drives, and by the collective consciousness of family and herd. Problematic though these conditioning factors on our mind and thought may sometimes seem, they are the foundation on which all higher thought rises. It is as much a mistake to despise or condemn them as it is to ignore their power.

It is only when the mind turns inward and reflects upon itself, rather than upon the objects of its thought or perception, that it becomes possible for it to complete the crossing of the bridge and enter into full possession of all its possiblities. It is the task of the mystery schools, of which this course is one manifestation, to lead you across that bridge toward a realm of possibility and promise of which the ordinary person can scarcely dream.

This lesson packet, like the first two, contains seven instructional papers:

Like the lessons of the two grades you have already completed, these papers are to be worked through at your own pace, with the Completion exercises reserved for last. The practical work given in this lesson packet builds on that of the previous grade, and a similar length of time, i.e., at least three months and possibly more, should be allotted to their completion. Once again, remember that rushing through the exercises benefits no one, least of all yourself. A few extra weeks, or even a few extra months, devoted to mastering some exercise that seems more than usually challenging, will pay substantial dividends further along the path.

Wishing you all the best in your journey on the Path of the Druid Mysteries,

 *John Michael Greer*

THREE CURRENTS AND
THREE CAULDRONS

NWYFRE, THE ONE LIFE, is the foundation of all work in the Druid Mysteries, as it is in every other mystery tradition. It is present in all things, but not in all in the same degree or in the same manner. Just as a ray of light is divided into rays of many different colors by a prism, nwyfre is divided into many different rays by material things. Each of the Seven Cantrefs is a primary ray issuing from the One Life, and every material thing participates in one of the Cantrefs more than the others; thus an herb or a stone, for example, corresponds to one Cantref, the ray and energy whereof is more potent therein than those of the other Cantrefs. From this unfold secrets of healing and enchantment, which are taught in later grades of this study course.

Eliphas Levi, the great renovator of occult philosophy in the West, had this to say about nwyfre:

> There exists in nature a force that is immeasurably more powerful than steam, and a single man, who is able to adapt and direct it, might change thereby the face of the whole world. This force was known to the ancients; it consists in a Universal Agent having equilibrium for its supreme law, while its direction is concerned immediately with the Great Arcanum of Transcendental Magic.

Three manifestations of the One Life have so great a power that they are to be considered apart from all others. These are the Sun, the Earth, and the human soul. From these extend the three primary currents of power worked in the Druid mysteries. These are the solar and telluric currents, which flow from Sun and Earth, and the lunar current, which is born of the union of Sun and Earth in the human soul. About these Levi says further:

> The Great Magical Agent is the fourth emanation of the life-principle, of which the Sun is the third form. In this way, the eye of the world, as the ancients called it, is the mirage of the reflection of God, and the soul of the earth is a permanent glance of the sun which the earth conceives and guards by impregnation. The moon concurs in this impregnation of the earth by reflecting a solar image during the night, so that Hermes was right when he says, "The sun is its father, the moon its mother."

Then he adds:

> "The wind has borne it in the belly thereof," because the atmosphere is the recipient and, as it were, the crucible of the solar rays, by means of which there forms that living image of the sun which penetrates the whole earth, fructifies it and determines all that is produced on its surface by its emanations and permanent currents, analogous to the sun itself.

The solar current emerges from the heart of the Sun, flows through space to the Earth's upper atmosphere, and cascades from there down to the surface. It waxes and wanes according to the position of the Sun in the sky, reaching maximum strength at dawn and noon, but it is present even at midnight; it flows wherever light from the sky can reach, and even penetrates a short distance down into the soil. Its energies also wax and wane over the longer cycle of the year, and their changes at the solstices and equinoxes are of special importance in Druid ritual. In myth and legend, the solar current is represented by such birds as the eagle, hawk, and heron. It is the *aud* or *od* of the magicians, and the Sun, the Red King, and the eagle of the alchemists. Its primary symbol in Druid lore is the circle, representing the sun's orb, and it is the primary expression of Spirit Above.

The telluric current rises up from the heart of the Earth and passes through the crust to the surface, and takes its form and character from the landscape the way the solar current takes its character from the turning day and year; what time is to the solar current, place is to the telluric current. Just as certain days and seasons manifest particular expressions of the solar current, certain places and regions manifest particular expressions of the telluric current. Underground water affects it powerfully, and springs and wells where water comes to the surface are afire with it, as witnessed by the traditions of sacred wells through the ages. In myth and legend, the telluric current is represented by the serpent and the dragon. It is the *aub* or *ob* of the magicians, and the Mercury, the White Queen, and the dragon or serpent of the alchemists. Its primary symbol in Druid lore is the triangle, representing its fiery and transforming nature, and it is the primary expression of Spirit Below.

Popular religion, here as so often, takes a partial view of the world, and calls one of these currents good and the other evil; thus the solar current is often equated with God, and the telluric current with Satan. The reality is less simplistic. The telluric current corresponds to what may be called the animal self, the dimension of the self that has been built up in previous cycles of evolution and incarnation; in the Welsh terms used in the Druid mysteries, it governs the *corff* or physical self (body), the *bywyd* or biological self, and the the *nwyd* or passionate self. The solar current corresponds to the *hunan* or personal self, with its three powers of thought, will, and memory. Neither of these is evil in itself; both are good when in harmony with the other and with the higher self, the *enaid*; and both can be productive of various kinds of evil when out of balance with each other or the enaid. Even the passions and appetites, so often blamed for the world's evils, are only harmful when unbalanced or wrongly directed; while the reasoning mind, so often considered the source of all virtue, can be productive of many vices destructive of self and others when it strays from its proper sphere.

Like their reflections in the self, the two currents balance and complete one another. They also can fuse, or in the language of mythology, mate with each other, and by this means they give rise to a third current that is the central secret of the Druid mysteries. This third current has many names, but the name that will be used here is the lunar current. Unlike the solar and telluric currents, the lunar current does not exist naturally in the individual or the world. It must be made by the balanced fusion of the solar and telluric currents.

The lunar current is the *aur* or *or* of the magicians and the stone, the elixir, and the magical child of the alchemists. Its mythic symbols include the egg, the jewel, the sacred cup, and the child. In Druid lore, its primary symbol is the crescent moon, because it mediates between solar and telluric currents in the same way that the moon mediates between sun and earth; it is the primary expression of Spirit Within. As such, within us, it functions on a higher level than do the solar and telluric currents, since it is still evolving in human beings and must be created consciously. Where the telluric current works through the body and its passions, and the solar current acts through the mind and its perceptions, the lunar current appears through the soul and its powers. When the lunar current awakens in an individual person, it awakens the inner senses and unfolds into enlightenment. When it awakens in the land, it brings healing, fertility, and plenty.

Each of these three currents corresponds to a center or Cauldron of energies in the body. The telluric current's center, the Cauldron of the Earth, may be found in the belly just below the navel, in the area of the womb. The solar current's center, the Cauldron of the Sun, may be found in the chest, behind the breastbone at the level of the heart. The lunar current's center, the Cauldron of the Moon, may be found in the center of the head, directly behind a point between the two eyebrows.

To awaken these cauldrons, you must first build up their images in your imagination. First, picture the Cauldron of the Earth in the middle of your belly, about two inches below the level of your navel. Make it four inches or so across, the color of dark bronze, with a triangle on its side to represent the secret fire. This cauldron corresponds to the passions, vitality, and the material body, and forms your link with the telluric current.

Once you have this image firmly in place, picture the Cauldron of the Sun in the middle of your chest at the level of your heart. Make it the same size as the Cauldron of the Earth but the color of red gold, with a sunburst on its side. It corresponds to thought, will, and memory, and connects you with the solar current.

After getting this image firmly in place, picture the third cauldron, the Cauldron of the Moon, in the middle of your head. Imagine it the size of the others but made of crystal, with a crescent moon on its side. It corresponds to intuition, inspiration, and enlightenment, and forms the vessel where the lunar current will manifest once you create it.

Once you have practiced formulating the three cauldrons in your imagination, and can build up clear images of all three without difficulty, you may proceed to begin filling them with nwyfre. This is done in the Sphere of Protection ritual, in place of the invocations of Spirit Below, Spirit Above, and Spirit Within that you learned in the last grade. Perform this expanded Sphere of Protection ritual as follows. It should be done every day while you are working on this grade of the Dolmen Arch.

THE THREE CAULDRONS WORKING

First, perform the Elemental Cross as usual, then invoke and banish with the elements of Air, Fire, Water, and Earth in the usual way. When you begin the invocation of Spirit Below, trace the orange circle as usual and say this: "By the bright heart of the Earth Mother, and in the great name Cêd, I invoke Spirit Below, its gods, its spirits, and its powers. May a ray of the telluric current ascend into me this day and always. May the cauldron of the earth be filled within me." Breathe in, and as you do so, imagine yourself drawing the telluric current up through the soles of both feet, imagining it as a light from within the earth the

Fig. 23. The Lunar, Solar, & Telluric Cauldrons

pale bright green of sunlight through new spring leaves. Lead it up through your legs, and into the lowest of the three cauldrons. As you breathe out, imagine the cauldron filled and surrounded with green light that ripples like water. Repeat this process, drawing the telluric current into the cauldron on the inbreath and letting it radiate there on the outbreath, nine times in all. Then say, "I thank Spirit Below for its gifts."

Go on to the invocation of Spirit Above in the usual way. Trace the purple circle and say this: "By the sun in its glory, the father of light, and in the great name Cêli, I invoke Spirit Above, its gods, its spirits, and its powers. May a ray of the solar current descend into me this day and always. May the cauldron of the sun be filled within me." Breathe in, and as you do so, imagine yourself drawing the solar current in through your solar plexus and up to the middle cauldron at the level of your heart. As you breathe out, imagine the cauldron filled and surrounded by golden sunlight. Repeat this process, drawing the solar current into the cauldron on the inbreath and letting it radiate there on the out-breath, nine times in all. Then say, "I thank Spirit Above for its gifts."

Go on next to the invocation of Spirit Within, and say this: "By the six pow-ers here invoked and here present, and in the grand word Awen, I invoke Spirit Within. May the lunar current be born in me this day and always. May the cauldron of the moon be filled within me." Breathe in, and imagine silvery light rising straight up the midline of your body from the cauldron of the earth. As it reaches the cauldron of the sun, it blends with the golden light there, and a stream of mixed silver-gold light rises the rest of the way to the cauldron of the moon and flows into it. On the outbreath, the light in the cauldron of the moon turns into pure white radiance, filling and surrounding the cauldron. Repeat this process, drawing light up from the two lower cauldrons on the inbreath and converting it to white radiance on the outbreath, nine times in all. Then imag-ine a drop of pure white light falling from the cauldron of the moon all the way to your solar plexus, halfway between the two lower cauldrons. Once there, it expands out in all directions to become the sphere of light used in the Circula-tion of Light, and proceed with the Circulation as before.

Perform this ritual daily along with the Sphere of Protection during the time you spend in this grade, and keep a record of the results in your practice journal.

THE AWAKENING OF THE SOLAR PLEXUS

HE SOLAR PLEXUS or, as it was often called a century ago, the "abdominal brain," is a large plexus (cluster) of nerve cells located below the place where the sides of the ribcage divide, or roughly halfway between the center of the breastbone and the navel. Many mystery schools treat it as one of the most important centers of subtle energy in the human body. In the tradition of the Druid mysteries communicated in these lessons, the solar plexus is understood to be the link between the enaid, the subtle body or atmosphere of nwyfre surrounding the individual, and the great ocean of nwyfre that surrounds and permeates all things. It is thus an energy center, like the three cauldrons in the exercise just given, but it operates on a different plane; where they develop the flow of nwyfre within the self, it connects the nwyfre in the self to the nwyfre of the universe around the self.

The solar plexus center is one of the two points energized in the Elemental Cross ceremony, and your regular practice of that exercise will have begun the process of awakening it. In addition, the solar plexus lies halfway between the Cauldrons of Sun and Earth, and your practice of the ritual work given in this grade, by awakening the two currents associated with these energy centers, will also assist the further development of the solar plexus center.

The further exercises taught in the present grade will carry forward that awakening, and begin the work of tapping into subconsciousness—the storehouse of the mind, as was explained in an earlier lecture, but also the aspect of the mind by which the consciousness of the individual blends into the One Life that surrounds and sustains us all. The solar plexus is the focal point of subconsciousness, and it is thus through the gate of the solar plexus that the Druid initiate is able to draw on knowledge and power from beyond himself or herself.

The lecture that follows was adapted from a popular early twentieth century text on the subject, with the addition of exercises and applications from within the tradition of Druidry presented in these lessons. It presents the theory and practice of working with nwyfre through the solar plexus. It should be carefully studied, and the practices it presents should then be made part of your daily routine.

The Four Brains

Each human being has four brains, and not merely one as commonly believed. These four brains, each having its separate characteristics and distinctive functions, are (1) the cerebrum; (2) the cerebellum; (3) the medulla oblongata; and (4) the solar plexus, or abdominal brain. The structure and the respective functions of each of these four brains are as follows:

1. The Cerebrum. The cerebrum is the higher and front portion of "the brains" located in the cranium or skull. It consists of two symmetrical halves, which are connected by a broad band of white substance. Each hemisphere is composed of a center of white substance, surrounded by a gray border, following the convolutions which constitute its external form. The functions of the cerebrum are as follows: the forward portions of the cerebral hemispheres are the chief centers of voluntary motion, and of the active outward manifestations of intelligence; the individual convolutions constitute separate and distinct centers, and in certain groups of convolutions are localized the centers for various physical movements, such as the motions of the eyelids, face, mouth, tongue, ear, neck, hand, foot, etc.

2. The Cerebellum. The cerebellum is the hinder and lower part of "the brains" located in the cranium of skull; it is situated beneath the posterior lobes of the cerebrum, and is about one-seventh the size of the latter. It is composed of white matter in the interior, and of gray matter on the surface. It is divided into two hemispheres, separated on the upper surface by an anatomical process, and on the lower surface by a deep fissure corresponding in form to the medulla oblongata. The white center of the cerebellum takes on the form of a miniature tree, with trunk, branches, twigs, and leaves—this is known as the "Tree of Life." The offices and functions of the cerebellum are as follows: it is concerned with the powers of motion in various ways and forms, in various degrees; and it performs

certain important offices in connection with the physical phase of the sexual functions.

3. The Medulla Oblongata. The medulla oblongata is the upper and enlarged end of the spinal cord—the extension and prolongation of the latter into the cranium or skull. Its substance resembles that of the spinal cord in its structure of gray and white matter; but it possesses a peculiar and different arrangement of the strands of the cord before it enters into and forms a connection with the brain. In the substance of the medulla oblongata are situated the great ganglionic centers which control respiration, swallowing, vomiting, etc. Pressure on the medulla oblongata, and not simple strangulation, is held to be the actual cause of death in the process of judicial hanging. From the interior portion of the medulla oblongata, and the under surface of the cerebrum, arise the cranial nerves, which emerge from the cranial cavity through openings in the base of the skull; these are distributed to various parts of the head and neck; to the organs of special sense; and to some of the thoracic and abdominal organs. In the posterior and lowermost portion of the substance of the medulla oblongata, are located the original sources of certain nerves which indirectly control the organs and functions of respiration.

4. The Solar Plexus, or Abdominal Brain. The solar plexus, or abdominal brain, the functions and offices, powers and activities of which constitute the chief subject matter of this lecture, is, as the name indicates, situated in the abdomen. Some of its filaments, however, accompany the branches of the aorta (the great artery) which are distributed to the stomach, intestines, spleen, pancreas, liver, and certain other organs, but not to the lungs. It is situated in the upper part of the abdomen, behind the stomach, in front of the aorta or great artery, and in front of the pillars of the diaphragm. Its place is popularly known as "the pit of the stomach," or back of the point where the ribs begin to separate and spread to each side.

The solar plexus is the great plexus or network of nerve-fibers and nerve-substance of the great sympathetic nervous system. It is composed of both gray and white nervous substance, or brain-matter, similar to that of the other three brains. It receives and distributes nerve-impulses and currents to all of the abdominal organs, and supplies the main organs of nutrition and digestion with their nervous energy. It performs most important offices in the so-called "vegetative life" of the body, supplying the nerve-energy which is required for the processes of nutrition and growth. In fact, it is the great powerhouse of physical life-energy. The bodily functions cannot be performed without it; when it is injured the entire physical well-being is at once seriously affected; and when it receives a severe shock, death often ensues, a fact which the history of prizefighting amply illustrates.

Its name, "solar," was bestowed upon it by reason of its central position; the fact that its filaments extend in all directions to the important abdominal organs, like the rays of the sun; and the fact that it is recognized as being the powerhouse and great reservoir of nwyfre, the life force, just as the sun is the great powerhouse and reservoir of material energy of our solar system.

The sympathetic nervous system, over which it presides, is that great division of the nervous system which regulates and energizes the important functions of the organs upon which physical life depends, and by which it is sustained. The solar plexus both receives and transmits nerve impulses, just as do the better-known brains. Its distributed filaments contain both afferent (inward-conducting) and efferent (outward-conducting) nerve-fibres, just as is the case with the other three brains. Its ganglia are true nerve-centers, and from them emerge and pass the filaments of nerve-force distribution to the involuntary muscles of the organs under its control, and to the secreting-cells of the various glands which depend upon it for their nerve supply.

It is easily seen why an injury to the solar plexus seriously disturbs the life-processes, and why a severe blow so paralyzes the vital organs that death ensues almost immediately. A man may survive a serious injury to any one of his other three brains; but a serious injury to the solar plexus, or abdominal brain, strikes right to his seat of life—and that life ceases to manifest itself further. If we may properly say of any portion of our physical being, "Here is the seat of my life; here is where I live!" the solar plexus, or abdominal brain, surely is that portion.

As an additional illustration of the essential part played by the solar plexus in the processes of physical life, we have the well-known fact that it is found fully formed and perfect, and even then performing some important functioning, in the human embryo or fetus at a very early stage—at a stage in which the "skull brain" of the developing unborn creature is a merely pulpy mass of substance, incapable of performing any function whatsoever. Moreover, in those cases of the birth of abnormal infants—babies born without a "skull brain" or perfected spinal cord—the solar plexus has been found to be perfectly developed, and to perform its full functions; and under such circumstances the child has lived for months before delivery, and in some cases for some time afterward.

So much for the offices and functions which orthodox physiologists freely ascribe to the solar plexus. Other careful investigators take up the inquiry at this point, but carry the story much further. These are not alone modern scientific investigators, but also many very ancient investigators, such as the ancient Druids, who many centuries ago recognized certain subtle functions and offices of this "fourth brain" of humanity, and taught their students many valuable methods of effectively employing its finer forces and hidden energies. In this lecture, we shall try to convey to you the essence and fundamental substance of these higher teachings concerning the solar plexus, or abdominal brain.

The Emotional Center

One of the great facts concerning the solar plexus which is not as yet generally recognized by modern psychology and physiology, but which has been known for centuries by occultists, and which is now becoming recognized by the advanced minds of modern science, is the fact that the solar plexus is the seat of the passions and the emotional nature, and the center of the intuition. In short, the part popularly held to be played by "the heart," is in reality performed by the solar plexus, the great center of the sympathetic nervous system.

That there is an important relation between emotional states and the physical organism, everyone knows. We know that fear, dread, and suspense are accompanied by a sinking or even a "sick" feeling at the pit of the stomach. We know that the heart beats rapidly when we are excited, angry, or in love. We know, particularly of later years, that emotional states react upon the physical organs, working physiological changes in them, and often exercising a decided influence upon the health or lack of health in the organs affected. You have had presented to your attention hundreds of books discussing "the effect of mind upon body."

Likewise, the condition of certain physical organs has much to do with our "state of feeling." Many people know from experience the state of "blues" and emotional depression caused by the failure of the liver to function properly. They may know also the lack of energy, and the feeling of heaviness caused by the constipated condition of the bowels. They may know the generally "crabbed" feeling caused by indigestion and dyspepsia; the heavy, sluggish feeling caused by breathing the heavy air of an ill-ventilated room, and the nervous, excitable, hysterical emotional states arising from an ill-managed sexual life.

One should not overlook the fact that the lower animals in whom reasoning and intellectual faculties are comparatively quite undeveloped, nevertheless experience and express feelings as strong and passionate as any human emotion. Moreover, in the human race, strong feelings and emotions are experienced and manifested by those of comparatively undeveloped thinking powers. Feeling, in short, is far more basic than is thought—far more primitive and fundamental in nature—and is evidently seated in far more primitive and fundamental nervous centers than the "thinking brain." It evidently belongs to "brains" and great nervous centers which were produced in the evolution of life long before the development of ideative thought. This insight is embodied in the Druid teaching that the nwyd or passionate self is more ancient and more basic than the hunan or conscious self. That feeling is found in all living things is a teaching of all the ancient nature religions, and here, too, the teachings of modern science are tending more each day to support the ancient wisdom of bygone days.[1]

Moreover, the close relationship of the passions and the great physical organs regulated and supplied with energy by the sympathetic nervous system, and not by the cerebro-spinal system, clearly indicates that the seat of the passions must be looked for in the great nervous energy-center of the sympathetic nervous system. That great nervous center, as you have seen, is the solar plexus—the center of life, of the life force or nwyfre, and of the fundamental activities and processes of life.

Thus the advanced thought of modern science is fast approaching the position of the ancient occultists, and is adding modern testimony to the teachings of these great ancient teachers that the solar plexus is the great center and seat of the feelings, the source and origin from which all of our strong and elemental passions and intuitions flow.

The passionate nature may be a great source of strength or a great source of weakness. Brought into harmony with the thinking self, it becomes a fount of power, and also a source of subtle perceptions of great value—for it is by emotion that we feel the movements of the One Life, perceive the positive or negative conditions of places and people, and note our harmony or disharmony with our surroundings. Out of balance, it too often brings its great power to bear in harmful ways: now confounding the mind with appealing falsehoods, now overcoming the will with emotional outbursts, and too often oversetting the whole of the personality with those mental ailments which modern psychologists term "neuroses" and "psychoses."

---

1. Experiments have shown, for example, that living plants register fear and shock on an electro-encephalograph when the leaf of a nearby plant is burnt. See *The Secret Life of Plants* by Peter Tompkins and Christopher Bird.

The thought of an earlier generation held that the hunan or conscious self had to domineer over the passions and biological processes of the nwyd and bywyd by a sheer effort of will—this effort tending to hold back, restrain or control the action naturally tending to follow the rise of the emotional feeling. More recent psychologists have found that the passions respond more effectively to subtler guidance than to the old and heavy-handed rule of will. Two new methods have become common in recent years.[2] The first is the method of "holding the thought" of the opposite emotion, thus neutralizing the passion sought to be controlled; the second is the method of deliberately assuming the physical motions associated with the passion directly opposed to the ones sought to be overcome. By these same methods, desirable emotions may be cultivated, encouraged, stimulated, and developed, by "holding the thought" of them, and by deliberately assuming their associated physical actions.

These two above stated methods are quite scientific, and have been employed by many with excellent results. We encourage you to use these methods, should you already practice them, and to add the additional method which is presented in this lecture. This third method has the same underlying principle, but it enters into the center of that principle, while the others work upon its surface.

Here is the mechanism employed in this third system. In the first place, the cerebrospinal nervous system, controlled by the cerebrum—the seat of thoughts and ideas—is directly connected with the sympathetic nervous system, controlled by the solar plexus, or abdominal brain—the seat of feelings and vital processes. They are connected by means of many delicate nervous filaments, or "connective nerves," which are both efferent and afferent—that is, both sending and receiving. They are like telephone wires, connecting the two great systems and their respective centers. Over them pass the messages which, on the one hand, cause physical states to arouse mental states; and, on the other hand, cause mental states to arouse physical states.

By means of this intercommunication between the two systems and their respective brains, we have on the one hand the phenomenon of the disturbed liver, stomach, bowels, spleen, glands, sexual organism, etc., arousing corresponding ideas in the mind—which we know to be of common occurrence; and, on the other hand, we have the phenomenon of ideas held in the mind arousing the activity of the physical organs—which we also know to be of com-

---

2. These methods were central to the New Thought movement of the early twentieth century, and were still new when the original version of this lecture was written.

mon occurrence, and which gives us the key to "mind over body" methods of mental healing. If there were no such connecting links, or nerves, between the two systems and their respective brains, none of the above phenomena would be manifested, and body and mind would act independently of each other—though in such case there would be a speedy dissolution of living partnership, and death would come in due course.

In ordinary cases, this interchange of messages and orders, from one system to the other, is performed unconsciously and instinctively by the nervous mechanism of the individual—he is neither aware of the process, nor does he consciously will its performance. But the ancient Druids, like other sages of the past, discovered many centuries ago that the individual could deliberately send messages from the cerebrum to the solar plexus. Modern psychologists are now making the same discovery, though they give to the old occultists no credit, but bestow new names upon the process—the facts remain the same, however.

The two brains are far more influenced by each other than most persons realize, even without the conscious use of the will and attention. When the individual, however, deliberately turns his conscious attention to the matter, and uses his will in connection with the process, then the cerebrum exerts a tremendously increased power and influence over the solar plexus, and likewise becomes much more receptive to intuitions proceeding from the latter.

Vitality and Health

That the solar plexus, or abdominal brain, should be able to exercise an important influence and power over the health and vitality of the individual is perceived immediately when we realize its relation to the organs performing the important functions of life. The solar plexus, as you have seen, is the great central storehouse of nwyfre in the physical body. It sends to the organs and glands the supply of vital force which is necessary to animate and energize those parts of the body, and the other parts adjacent thereto.

To understand the importance of this vital force which is controlled and dispensed by the solar plexus, it is necessary only to consider the activities performed by means of its power. For instance, we find that the processes of digestion, assimilation, nutrition and elimination are possible only when the supply of vital force is sufficient. Likewise, we find that the processes of the circulation of the blood are dependent upon the supply of the vital force.

Our food is digested and transformed into the nourishing substances of the blood; then carried through the arteries to all parts of the body, where it is absorbed by the cells and used to replace the worn-out material, the latter then being carried back through the veins to the lungs, where the waste-matter is burned up, and the balance again sent on its journey through the arteries re-charged with the life-giving oxygen. All of these processes are performed by the power of the life force which is sent to the organs by the solar plexus, and which serves to energize and to animate them; and by means of which the organs are enabled to perform their functions.

Moreover, the solar plexus not only sends the vital force to the physical organs, but it also exercises a control over them in a way so closely resembling a mental control that many writers have spoken of the presence of "something like intelligence" being manifested in the performance and direction of the vital processes. This "something like intelligence" is identical to the "subconscious-ness" which is central to the theories of the most advanced modern psycholo-gists. The subconscious mind, in fact, employs the sympathetic nervous system as its mechanism—and the solar plexus, or abdominal brain, is "the brains" of that system, just as the cerebrum is "the brains" of the cerebro-spinal system. So we must always come back to the solar plexus when we wish to see how that "other mind," the subconsciousness, works.

The great regulative, directive, and therapeutic activities of Nature, which are manifested in the human physical body, are mental or quasi-mental in their essential nature—mind of some degree is perceived to be at work there. The life-processes are seen to be mind-processes. There is no life-activity without mind activity—the two are inextricably combined and correlated. This fact is thoroughly recognized by the practitioners and students of mental healing, and their efforts are accordingly directed to "reach the mind" of the individual, in order to "set the mind to work" in the direction of restoration of normal healthy functioning and activity. But what "mind" should be reached for this purpose? In what brain does that "mind" function and have its seat? Not in the ordinary "thinking mind," to be sure—for the vital processes are not under the control of that mind and its brains, though its thoughts and beliefs reflect upon the mind which really is concerned, as we know.

No, the only logical conclusion is that the vital processes and physical organs are under the direction and control of that "mind" which may be called the "instinctive mind" (because it is possessed by the lower animals as well as by man)—which mind has control of the instinctive activities of the physical body, such as we have mentioned. And as every "mind" must have a brain through which to function and manifest itself, we naturally look for the brain or brains of this "instinctive mind." Where? Nowhere else than in that great center of physical life and organic control—the solar plexus, or abdominal brain.

The importance of the above discovery lies in the fact that just as the minds of all living things can be developed through appropriate exercise and directed through appropriate communication and instruction, so can the "mind" of the solar plexus be developed and directed, if one proceeds properly. In the following sections of this lecture, you will be given detailed particulars concerning methods of this kind. First of all, you must thoroughly grasp the fundamental principle involved: that the physical organs and activities are controlled by subconsciousness; that subconsciousness has its seat in the solar plexus; and that subconsciousness may be reached and appealed to, when the solar plexus—its "brains"—is awakened into a state of conscious attention. This is the whole matter in a nutshell—the rest is merely finding effective methods of manifesting the principle.

Awakening the Solar Plexus

In most people, the "mind" of the solar plexus—that subconscious mind which is to the latter what the conscious mind is to the Cerebrum—exists in what may be called a state of sleep. In cases of great need, or of threatened danger to the organism, the "instinctive mind" of the Solar Plexus does wake up; and in such cases manifests a far greater degree of consciousness than normally expressed by it.

From this, however, it must not be understood that subconsciousness is ever "asleep" in the sense of not being able to attend to its offices and directive functions. On the contrary, its state of consciousness really arises by reason of its close concentration upon its work. Its state of consciousness is very similar to that of the workman who has so closely concentrated upon the work at hand that he has become practically unconscious of the things of the outside world. You, yourself, have often manifested a similar state when you were reading an interesting book, when you were "buried in your newspaper," or when you were engrossed in the performance of some task to which you have devoted your entire and undivided attention—to which you have given your whole mind for the time being.

The subconscious mind of the solar plexus is not asleep in the sense of "being asleep at the switch," as the current phrase expresses the idea. On the contrary it is "on the job" to such an extent that it perceives nothing else. It is a most faithful and tireless worker, never sleeping in the usual sense of the term, and always concerned with the great work under its direction and charge. Were it to "go to sleep," actually—were it to take a rest, or "go on strike"—the vital processes would cease, and death would speedily result. For all that, so far as the outside world is concerned, it may be considered as asleep, or at least wrapped in revery to such an extent that it must be awakened in order to turn its attention to the channels of communication linking it to the other three brains of the organism.

This awakening is done in the following way:

First, sit in a comfortable chair or lie on a couch or bed, on your back. Your clothing should be loose and comfortable, particularly about your chest and abdomen. Relax your body in the ordinary way. Take a few deep, regular breaths; and then finally, after you have established a regular breathing rhythm, hold the inhaled breath instead of exhaling it. Do this without shutting the throat—the muscles of the trunk, rather than those of the throat, must hold the breath in.

While still holding the breath, employ your abdominal muscles to press downward and outward upon the "pit of the stomach", as though you were pushing the air in your lungs down into the lowest part of your abdomen; and then draw in the same muscles so as to reverse the preceding motion, as though shifting the air in your lungs back up into your chest. This outward and inward motion is to be performed three times, while holding the breath. Once this is done, allow the breath to flow out slowly and gently—do not let it go all in a rush. Then breathe normally for a few minutes, resting yourself. When your breathing has returned to normal, repeat the entire process; spend several minutes breathing normally; then repeat the whole sequence one more time.

Each time you hold your breath, while doing this exercise, imagine a ball of many-colored light at your solar plexus. Seven rays of light, one of each of the seven colors of the Cantrefs, stream out from it. Keep your attention on this image while you hold your breath, and then release the image as you release your breath.

Perform this exercise once each day during the time you spend in this grade. It may be done before or after your ritual and meditation, or at any other convenient time during the course of the day.

Using the Solar Plexus

After you have performed the practice given above daily for at least two weeks, you may proceed to work with the solar plexus to attain spiritual and practical ends. In doing this, however, always keep in mind that the nerves that communicate between your conscious mind or cerebrum and your subconscious mind or solar plexus operate and must operate in both directions. If you approach subconsciousness in the right way, it will obey your commands, but it can and should also guide your actions, for on its own plane it is wiser as well as more knowledgeable than you.

An additional source of complication is the fact that subconsciousness does not think or speak in words, which belong entirely to the cerebrum and the thinking mind. To address the solar plexus, then, you must use such wordless means as will best convey your intention; to listen to it, you must be prepared to interpret the wordless messages it sends you. There is no single rule here—each person will find some means of communication better suited to the task than others. Some find that visual imagery is the most effective way to address the solar plexus, while others find that emotional states evoked with the aid of the imagination and memory are better suited to their needs. Examples of these and other methods will be given below.

You will find it valuable as well as interesting, during the time you spend in this grade, to experiment with using the solar plexus in the following ways:

Your Emotional Life. As the emotional center of the body, the solar plexus may be called upon to aid you whenever you need to act upon your emotional life, either by controlling the expression of emotions or by attending to the messages they have to communicate to you. By exerting a control upon the physical organs concerned with the passions—by controlling the glands and their secretions—the solar plexus is able either to weaken the current of a hurtful feeling, or else to initiate and strengthen the current of a helpful one.

As an example, should an enemy attempt to provoke you to anger at a time when a display of anger would be to your disadvantage, you can quell your rising temper by imagining a state of calm and imperturbability and, focusing this state at the solar plexus, feel that emotion spread through the whole of yourself.

You may also use your knowledge of the Cantrefs to your advantage in this context. Know that there are seven basic negative emotional states, and each of them may be attributed to one of the Cantrefs. These states are counteracted by seven basic positive attitudes, which may also be attributed to the Cantrefs, in the following manner:[3]

Awyr, the First Cantref: negative state, pride;
positive attitude, justice.

---

3. Note that these seven positive and negative states are based on the seven virtues and seven vices of traditional morality, but with certain deliberate changes. Meditation on the changes will reveal much.

Dŵr, the Second Cantref:	negative state, greed;
	positive attitude, temperance.
Ufel, the Third Cantref:	negative state, anger;
	positive attitude, courage.
Daear, the Fourth Cantref:	negative state, fear;
	positive attitude, wisdom.
Maen, the Fifth Cantref:	negative state, grief;
	positive attitude, faith.
Nef, the Sixth Cantref:	negative state, envy;
	positive attitude, hope.
Byw, the Seventh Cantref:	negative state, sloth;
	positive attitude, love.

The rule here is that the negative state of each of the first six Cantrefs is countered by the positive attitude of the Cantref opposite to it; the negative state of the Seventh Cantref may be countered by any of the seven positive states, "but the greatest of these is love." Thus anger, as in the example just given, can be countered by imagining the green energy of the Fourth Cantref concentrated in your solar plexus, and spreading through your body, bringing with it the calming and steadying influence of wisdom to overcome the anger. The relation between each negative state and its opposing positive attitude is a worthwhile subject for meditation.

Your Health. The solar plexus, as the center of the One Life in your physical body, may be called upon to help you treat your entire system or any organ which may have become inactive or unhealthy, restoring it to normal and healthy functioning. The solar plexus normally attempts to do this, but when it does not receive the proper cooperation from the thinking mind, it cannot always achieve its ends. By giving it the conscious attention it needs, you can readily enable it to do its job.

That attention, like communication with the solar plexus generally, moves in both directions. On the one hand, with the use of imagination you may direct the attention of subconsciousness to any part of your body that is not functioning as it should. This may be done by concentrating on the solar plexus, and imagining a ray of light or current of energy moving from there to the organ or body part desired.

On the other, it is wise to listen to the solar plexus and make use of its peerless perception of the interior state of your organism. This will particularly be useful when deciding whether a food, for example, is suited to the needs of your body. Smell the aroma of the food or, should you not have it present, imagine yourself eating some of it, while your attention rests on your solar plexus. Note the feeling that arises in response, and take it into consideration.

In working with the solar plexus in the matter of restoring physical health and proper functioning of the organs, you should always bear in mind the fact that the solar plexus "understands its business"—you do not have to tell it how to proceed to secure the results from the organs in its care, for it understands this far better than can you. It has its own chemical laboratories; its machine-shops; its repair shops; and in fact a most wonderful establishment under its direction and care—and it knows how to run this, and it does run it right, provided that it is not hampered by conditions which it is unable to overcome.

Remember, always, that it represents the *vis vitæ*,[4] the *vis medicatrix naturæ*,[5] or in short, Nature itself within you, which cures diseases and strives to establish, maintain, and re-establish normal physical functioning. You do not need to tell it how to go about its work—that would be an impertinence. All that you need to do is to alert it to the fact that you are experiencing physical difficulties or weaknesses of such-and-such a nature or kind, and that such-and-such an organ does not seem to be functioning normally—in short that you are not obtaining normal results from certain organs or sets of organs.

Furthermore, you must remember to do your part in the work of establishing and maintaining the normal physical conditions. If you expect the solar plexus to do its share of the work, you must be prepared to do yours. You cannot expect to neglect your end of the job, and have the solar plexus take up the slack. You must see that the body gets sufficient exercise, rest, fresh air, water, and food of the right kind. Your solar plexus cannot do this for you; that is the job of the thinking mind, which has been created to cope with the demands of the world outside you, as the solar plexus has been created to cope with the demands of the world inside you.

Your Vital Force. The solar plexus is the source of nwyfre—the great storehouse of the life force, as well as its generator. You may call upon it for an increased supply thereof, and the solar plexus will respond. The solar plexus may be called upon by you for an abundant supply of Vital Force or Physical Energy—and it will respond. The practice of imagining the solar plexus as a

---

4. Latin for "Power of life."

5. Latin for "Healing power of nature."

radiant ball of brilliant light, shining with the rays of the Seven Cantrefs, is a fundamental practice in this regard. Build upon it by maintaining the vigorous, vital mental attitude—by seeing and thinking of yourself as filled with vital force—by confidently expecting the flow thereof into your nervous system from the solar plexus, and, in short by being a "positive pole," instead of a "negative pole," in the scale of mental life.

Your Magical Force. There is another phase of power inherent in the solar plexus, which we shall merely mention here, for it concerns a subject central to later lessons in this course. This additional phase of power is that which underlies the legends of magic. By it is meant that peculiar force, power, or energy which when manifested by human beings is called "Odic Force," "Human Magnetism," "Vril," "Prana," "Ga-Lama," etc.[6] It is the force which underlies every form of magical and psychic activity, and all forms of manifestations in which the will and imagination of the individual take up a physical form, and act with a subtle physical energy, when it flows from one mind to others. Its vibrations constitute the body of the mental currents used in this work, while other of its qualities constitute the vitality thereof; the conception that sets the currents into motion may be said to be the soul thereof.

The practical application of this side of the power of the solar plexus will be discussed in later lessons, but it may be said here that magical power may be obtained from the solar plexus in precisely the same way in which one obtains vital force from it, or as one causes it to act in the direction of the control of the emotions, or in the restoration and preservation of physical health and normal functioning of the physical organs. The general principle of awakening the solar plexus, and of then inducing it to send forth its latent and inherent powers in the direction indicated by you, is the same in all of the cases. Understand the principle, and acquire the knack of setting the subtle forces into operation, and you have the whole principle at your command.

---

6. Each of these is a term used for the life force in the occult traditions or popular culture of the late nineteenth and early twentieth century. Had this lecture been written more recently, the author could have added a great many more terms to this list; "The Force," the life-energy used by George Lucas' fictional Jedi Knights, comes to mind.

MEDITATION:
THE SEVENFOLD
WHEEL OF THOUGHT

HE ART OF MEDITATION that has been presented in these lessons has many applications not easily grasped from within the meditative traditions of the Eastern Schools—though those, to be sure, also have their distinctive applications difficult to grasp from within the way of the West. The choice of methods that distinguishes the Western from the Eastern Schools—the decision to use discursive thought, on the one hand, or to eschew it on the other—is a parting of the ways with sweeping implications; though both paths lead eventually to the same goal, not merely the scenery along the route but many of the things to be achieved on the way to that final goal are different.

The meditation of the Western Schools being a way of Mind, many—though by no means all—of its immediate benefits are mental in nature, and many of its applications likewise fall into the mental sphere of life. The following practice belongs to these mental applications. It will be found valuable in many of the activities of everyday life, as well as in the study of the Druid Mysteries. It begins, like so much in these lessons, from the Seven Cantrefs.

Among the attributes of each Cantref is a basic conception or condition of existence present in each existing thing. Collectively, these are called the Seven Conceptions. They are:

Being: corresponding to Awyr, the First Cantref

Becoming: corresponding to Dŵr, the Second Cantref.

Source: corresponding to Ufel, the Third Cantref.

Substance:	corresponding to Daear, the Fourth Cantref.
Power:	corresponding to Maen, the Fifth Cantref.
Purpose:	corresponding to Nef, the Sixth Cantref.
Value:	corresponding to Byw, the Seventh Cantref.

Each Cantref also corresponds to a fundamental question, and so the Seven Questions are paired with the Seven Conceptions.

Whether?	corresponding to Awyr, the First Cantref
What?	corresponding to Dŵr, the Second Cantref.
How?	corresponding to Ufel, the Third Cantref.
Who?	corresponding to Daear, the Fourth Cantref.
Where?	corresponding to Maen, the Fifth Cantref.
When?	corresponding to Nef, the Sixth Cantref.
Why?	corresponding to Byw, the Seventh Cantref.

The relationship between each Conception or Question and its corresponding Cantref is worth exploring in meditation. The practical application of the Conceptions and Questions, though, may be explored before this work is completed. Here is the key to the Sevenfold Wheel of Thought, which is born of the union between the Questions and Conceptions:

Each of the Questions may be applied to each of the Conceptions in relation to any theme of meditation or subject of thought.

Let us suppose that you are considering the Mabinogion, either in meditation or in ordinary focused thought. All that you might need to know about it can be summed up in the varying combinations of the Conceptions and Questions.

Take the first Conception, Being, and apply each Question to it, and you may ask the following: Whether it is (that is, whether it has being); What it is; How (in what form or manner) it is; Who or Whose it is; Where it is; When it is; and Why it is.

Take the second Conception and do the same, and the following questions might result: Whether it changed over time (that is, whether it became); What changed over time; How it changed over time; Who changed it; Where it changed; When it changed; and Why it changed.

The third Conception might yield the following questions: Whether it had a source, or sources; What those sources were; How it drew on those sources; Who made use of those sources; Where it drew on those sources; When it drew on those sources; and Why it drew on those sources.

The remaining Conceptions may be combined with the Questions in exactly the same way, to produce twenty-eight more questions. Ask those questions and then answer them to the best of your ability, and you will have a much more thorough knowledge of the Mabinogion than you had before you started. The same is true of any other topic of meditation or thought.

This exercise may seem at first glance like pointless drudgery, or at best a sort of calisthenics of thought, worthwhile only as a way to build mental strength through systematic exertion. Yet the greatest weakness of most thinking, and the source of most of life's failures, is the inability to distinguish between what one knows and what one does not know. In every walk of life, what separates the genius from the ordinary practitioner is the ability to ask the right questions.

Think of the famous Sherlock Holmes, or his equivalents in real life, whose attention to minute details and ability to pose the right questions quickly unraveled the most complicated criminal case; or the famous scientists whose achievements are a matter of asking Nature herself a question no one else thought to ask; or in literature, those authors whose stories are most delightful, because they open up vistas on life from a direction the reader has never anticipated. These individuals have developed, often in an unsystematic and idiosyncratic way, the same habit of repeated questioning that the Sevenfold Wheel of Thought is meant to develop in a more structured way.

The following exercises should be used to explore the possibilities of the Sevenfold Wheel of Thought. Before beginning either one, you will find it helpful to learn the Seven Conceptions and Seven Questions by heart, relating them in your mind to the Cantrefs.

Exercise 1

As you pursue the meditations assigned in this and subsequent lesson packets, apply the Sevenfold Wheel of Thought any time you find yourself stymied by a theme. Start with the first Question of the first Conception—"Whether it is?" That is, does the thing about which you are thinking exist at all, or is it a figment of language, such as "a four-cornered triangle"? Think through what the question implies when applied to the theme. When you have finished considering this, go on to apply the second Question to the same Conception—"What is it?" Consider this in its turn, in every sense of the question—for example, you might ask yourself what kind of thing it is, what its definition is, and so on. Proceed through as many Conceptions and Questions as needed to make sense of the theme. It can be a worthwhile experience, though one best pursued over multiple sessions of meditation, to take a single theme and approach it through all seven Questions applied to all seven Conceptions, for a total of forty-nine queries.

Exercise 2

The same thing may be done with good effect outside the confines of meditation. In dealing with any subject of study or any of the events of daily life, when you encounter any puzzle or any cause of confusion, make use of the Sevenfold Wheel of Thought. In every field of learning or of business, countless opportunities are lost because no one thinks to ask the right question concerning the right topic. While it must be admitted that the Sevenfold Wheel of Thought cannot contain every question that may be useful or necessary to ask in the course of study or of life, the habit of orderly thinking it imparts will be found useful in the highest degree in every calling and every circumstance of earthly existence.

THE MABINOGION:
MANAWYDDAN SON OF LLYR

HE THIRD BRANCH of the Mabinogion follows directly on the end of the Second, but returns to the scene and the characters of the First. Once again Dyfed in the south of Wales is the setting of the story, and several of the crucial events take place upon the mound of Gorsedd Arberth, where Pwyll first met Rhiannon. The story, in turn, turns away from the tragic and heroic themes of the Second Branch and reverts to the same pattern of repeated trials and ultimate success that characterizes the First.

This is the simplest of the Branches, and follows a pattern of narrative that has many equivalents both in the literature of the Middle Ages and in more recent fiction. Beneath the apparent simplicity of the story, however, much is concealed. Tradition has it that this Branch, like the First, deals with the events upon the earth rather than those in the heavens, or of the sun by day rather than by night; here, though, the sequence of time represented by the symbolism extends from *Calan Haf* (Bealteinne, May 1) to *Calan Gaeaf* (Samhuinn, November 1), completing the cycle of the year begun in the First Branch. On another level, the journey of Pryderi the Mabon through the process of Druid initiation and attainment moves toward its conclusion in this Branch, though that conclusion can only be understood in the context of the Fourth Branch that is yet to come.

It may not be out of place to point out here that the characters of the story are, in a sense, parts or manifestations of the central character of the Four Branches, and their interactions trace changes within that character. It may already have occurred to you that the name of Pryderi's bride Cigfa, which literally means "house of flesh," might be seen as an indication that she may be identified with Pryderi's material or fleshly body; the identities of the other characters in the story, and the implications of their various experiences, should be studied with care. The story itself, of course, may and should also be enjoyed for its own sake.

Manawyddan Son of Llyr

When the seven men of whom we spoke above[7] had buried the head of Bran the Blessed in the White Mount in London, with its face towards France; Manawyddan gazed upon the town of London, and upon his companions, and heaved a great sigh; and much grief and heaviness came upon him.

"Alas, Almighty Heaven, woe is me," he exclaimed, "there is none save myself without a resting-place this night."

"Lord," said Pryderi, "be not so sorrowful. Thy cousin is king of the Island of the Mighty,[8] and though he should do thee wrong, thou hast never been a claimant of land or possessions. Thou art the third disinherited prince."[9]

"Yea," answered he, "but although this man is my cousin, it grieveth me to see any one in the place of my brother Bran the Blessed, neither can I be happy in the same dwelling with him."

"Wilt thou follow the counsel of another?" said Pryderi.

"I stand in need of counsel," he answered, "and what may that counsel be?"

"Seven Cantrefs remain unto me," said Pryderi, "wherein Rhiannon my mother dwells. I will bestow her upon thee and the seven Cantrefs with her, and though thou hadst no possessions but those Cantrefs only, thou couldst not have seven Cantrefs fairer than they. Cigfa, the daughter of Gwynn Gloyw, is my wife, and since the inheritance of the Cantrefs belongs to me, do thou and Rhiannon enjoy them, and if thou ever desire any possessions thou wilt take these."

"I do not, Chieftain," said he; "Heaven reward thee for thy friendship."

"I would show thee the best friendship in the world if thou wouldst let me."

"I will, my friend," said he, "and Heaven reward thee. I will go with thee to seek Rhiannon and to look at thy possessions."

---

7. That is, at the end of the Second Branch of the Mabinogion.

8. A traditional name for Britain in Celtic times.

9. This is a reference to one of the Welsh bardic triads.

"Thou wilt do well," he answered. "And I believe that thou didst never hear a lady discourse better than she, and when she was in her prime none was ever fairer. Even now her aspect is not uncomely."

They set forth, and, however long the journey, they came at length to Dyfed, and a feast was prepared for them against their coming to Narberth, which Rhiannon and Cigfa had provided. Then began Manawyddan and Rhiannon to sit and to talk together, and from their discourse his mind and his thoughts became warmed towards her, and he thought in his heart he had never beheld any lady more fulfilled of grace and beauty than she.

"Pryderi," said he, "I will that it be as thou didst say."

"What saying was that?" asked Rhiannon.

"Lady," said Pryderi, "I did offer thee as a wife to Manawyddan the son of Llyr."

"By that will I gladly abide," said Rhiannon.

"Right glad am I also," said Manawyddan; "may Heaven reward him who hath shown unto me friendship so perfect as this." And before the feast was over she became his bride.

Said Pryderi, "Tarry ye here the rest of the feast, and I will go into Lloegyr[10] to tender my homage unto Caswallawn the son of Beli."[11]

"Lord," said Rhiannon, "Caswallawn is in Kent, thou mayest therefore tarry at the feast, and wait until he shall be nearer."

"We will wait," he answered. So they finished the feast. And they began to make the circuit of Dyfed, and to hunt, and to take their pleasure. And as they went through the country, they had never seen lands more pleasant to live in, nor better hunting grounds, nor greater plenty of honey and fish. And such was the friendship between those four, that they would not be parted from each other by night nor by day.[12]

And in the midst of all this he went to Caswallawn at Oxford, and tendered his homage; and honourable was his reception there, and highly was he praised for offering his homage.

---

10. *Lloegyr*: the ancient name of the part of Britain now called England.

11. *Caswallawn son of Beli*: "Foe-scatterer son of Light," a traditional name for the Sun's dawn ray. Notice that Caswallawn is in the easternmost province of southern Britain, another reference to the First Cantref.

12. Not inappropriately, since they are four parts of one person.

And after his return, Pryderi and Manawyddan feasted and took their ease and pleasure. And they began a feast at Narberth, for it was the chief palace; and there originated all honour. And when they had ended the first meal that night, while those who served them ate, they arose and went forth, and proceeded all four to the Gorsedd of Narberth, and their retinue with them. And as they sat thus, behold, a peal of thunder, and with the violence of the thunderstorm, lo there came a fall of mist, so thick that not one of them could see the other. And after the mist it became light all around. And when they looked towards the place where they were wont to see cattle, and herds, and dwellings, they saw nothing now, neither house, nor beast, nor smoke, nor fire, nor man, nor dwelling; but the houses of the Court empty, and desert, and uninhabited, without either man or beast within them. And truly all their companions were lost to them, without their knowing aught of what had befallen them, save those four only.

"In the name of Heaven," cried Manawyddan, "where are they of the Court, and all my host beside these? Let us go and see." So they came into the hall, and there was no man; and they went on to the castle and to the sleeping-place, and they saw none; and in the mead-cellar and in the kitchen there was nought but desolation. So they four feasted, and hunted, and took their pleasure. Then they began to go through the land and all the possessions that they had, and they visited the houses and dwellings, and found nothing but wild beasts. And when they had consumed their feast and all their provisions, they fed upon the prey they killed in hunting, and the honey of the wild swarms. And thus they passed the first year pleasantly, and the second; but at the last they began to be weary.

"Verily," said Manawyddan, "we must not bide thus. Let us go into Lloegyr, and seek some craft whereby we may gain our support." So they went into Lloegyr, and came as far as Hereford. And they betook themselves to making saddles. And Manawyddan began to make housings, and he gilded and colored them with blue enamel, in the manner that he had seen it done by Llassar Llaesgyfnewid.[13] And he made the blue enamel as it was made by the other man. And therefore is it still called Calch Lasar,[14] because Llassar Llaesgyfnewid had wrought it.

And as long as that workmanship could be had of Manawyddan, neither saddle nor housing was bought of a saddler throughout all Hereford; till at length every one of the saddlers perceived that they were losing much of their gain,

---

13. This is the giant who brought the Cauldron of Rebirth to Bran, as described in the Second Branch.

14. *Calch Lasar*: a pun, meaning both "blue enamel" and "Llassar's enamel."

and that no man bought of them, but him who could not get what he sought from Manawyddan. Then they assembled together, and agreed to slay him and his companions. Now they received warning of this, and took counsel whether they should leave the city.

"By Heaven," said Pryderi, "it is not my counsel that we should quit the town, but that we should slay these boors."

"Not so," said Manawyddan, "for if we fight with them, we shall have evil fame, and shall be put in prison. It were better for us to go to another town to maintain ourselves." So they four went to another city.

"What craft shall we take?" said Pryderi.

"We will make shields," said Manawyddan.

"Do we know anything about that craft?" said Pryderi.

"We will try," answered he. There they began to make shields, and fashioned them after the shape of the good shields they had seen; and they enamelled them, as they had done the saddles. And they prospered in that place, so that not a shield was asked for in the whole town, but such as was had of them. Rapid therefore was their work, and numberless were the shields they made. But at last they were marked by the craftsmen, who came together in haste, and their fellow-townsmen with them, and agreed that they should seek to slay them. But they received warning, and heard how the men had resolved on their destruction.

"Pryderi," said Manawyddan, "these men desire to slay us."

"Let us not endure this from these boors, but let us rather fall upon them and slay them."

"Not so," he answered; "Caswallawn and his men will hear of it, and we shall be undone. Let us go to another town." So to another town they went.

"What craft shall we take?" said Manawyddan.

"Whatsoever thou wilt that we know," said Pryderi.

"Not so," he replied, "but let us take to making shoes, for there is not courage enough among cordwainers either to fight with us or to molest us."

"I know nothing thereof," said Pryderi.

"But I know," answered Manawyddan; "and I will teach thee to stitch. We will not attempt to dress the leather, but we will buy it ready dressed and will make the shoes from it."

So he began by buying the best cordwal[15] that could be had in the town, and none other would he buy except the leather for the soles; and he associated him-

---

15. *Cordwal*: shoe leather.

self with the best goldsmith in the town, and caused him to make clasps for the shoes, and to gild the clasps, and he marked how it was done until he learnt the method. And therefore was he called one of the three makers of Gold Shoes;[16] and, when they could be had from him, not a shoe nor hose was bought of any of the cordwainers in the town. But when the cordwainers perceived that their gains were failing (for as Manawyddan shaped the work, so Pryderi stitched it), they came together and took counsel, and agreed that they would slay them.

"Pryderi," said Manawyddan, "these men are minded to slay us."

"Wherefore should we bear this from the boorish thieves?" said Pryderi. "Rather let us slay them all."

"Not so," said Manawyddan, "we will not slay them, neither will we remain in Lloegyr any longer. Let us set forth to Dyfed and go to see it."

So they journeyed along until they came to Dyfed, and they went forward to Narberth. And there they kindled fire and supported themselves by hunting. And thus they spent a month. And they gathered their dogs around them, and tarried there one year.

And one morning Pryderi and Manawyddan rose up to hunt, and they ranged their dogs and went forth from the palace. And some of the dogs ran before them and came to a small bush which was near at hand; but as soon as they were come to the bush, they hastily drew back and returned to the men, their hair bristling up greatly.

"Let us go near to the bush," said Pryderi, "and see what is in it." And as they came near, behold, a wild boar of a pure white color rose up from the bush. Then the dogs, being set on by the men, rushed towards him; but he left the bush and fell back a little way from the men, and made a stand against the dogs without retreating from them, until the men had come near. And when the men came up, he fell back a second time, and betook him to flight. Then they pursued the boar until they beheld a vast and lofty castle, all newly built, in a place where they had never before seen either stone or building. And the boar ran swiftly into the castle and the dogs after him. Now when the boar and the dogs had gone into the castle, they began to wonder at finding a castle in a place where they had never before seen any building whatsoever. And from the top of the Gorsedd they looked and listened for the dogs. But so long as they were there they heard not one of the dogs nor aught concerning them.

"Lord," said Pryderi, "I will go into the castle to get tidings of the dogs."

---

16. Another reference to a Welsh bardic triad.

"Truly," he replied, "thou wouldst be unwise to go into this castle, which thou hast never seen till now. If thou wouldst follow my counsel, thou wouldst not enter therein. Whosoever has cast a spell over this land has caused this castle to be here."

"Of a truth," answered Pryderi, "I cannot thus give up my dogs." And for all the counsel that Manawyddan gave him, yet to the castle he went.

When he came within the castle, neither man nor beast, nor boar nor dogs, nor house nor dwelling saw he within it. But in the center of the castle floor he beheld a fountain with marble work around it, and on the margin of the fountain a golden bowl upon a marble slab, and chains hanging from the air, to which he saw no end.

And he was greatly pleased with the beauty of the gold, and with the rich workmanship of the bowl, and he went up to the bowl and laid hold of it. And when he had taken hold of it his hands stuck to the bowl, and his feet to the slab on which the bowl was placed, and all his joyousness forsook him, so that he could not utter a word. And thus he stood.

And Manawyddan waited for him till near the close of the day. And late in the evening, being certain that he should have no tidings of Pryderi or of the dogs, he went back to the palace. And as he entered, Rhiannon looked at him.

"Where," said she, "are thy companion and thy dogs?"

"Behold," he answered, "the adventure that has befallen me." And he related it all unto her.

"An evil companion hast thou been," said Rhiannon, "and a good companion hast thou lost." And with that word she went out, and proceeded towards the castle according to the direction which he gave her. The gate of the castle she found open. She was nothing daunted, and she went in. And as she went in, she perceived Pryderi laying hold of the bowl, and she went towards him.

"Oh, my lord," said she, "what dost thou do here?" And she took hold of the bowl with him; and as she did so her hands became fast to the bowl, and her feet to the slab, and she was not able to utter a word. And with that, as it became night, lo, there came thunder upon them, and a fall of mist, and thereupon the castle vanished, and they with it.

When Cigfa the daughter of Gwynn Gloyw saw that there was no one in the palace but herself and Manawyddan, she sorrowed so that she cared not whether she lived or died. And Manawyddan saw this.

"Thou art in the wrong," said he, "if through fear of me thou grievest thus. I call Heaven to witness that thou hast never seen friendship more pure than that which I will bear thee, as long as Heaven will that thou shouldst be thus. I declare to thee that were I in the dawn of youth I would keep my faith unto Pryderi, and unto thee also will I keep it. Be there no fear upon thee, therefore," said he, "for Heaven is my witness that thou shalt meet with all the friendship thou canst wish, and that it is in my power to show thee, as long as it shall please Heaven to continue us in this grief and woe."

"Heaven reward thee," she said, "and that is what I deemed of thee." And the damsel thereupon took courage and was glad.

"Truly, lady," said Manawyddan, "it is not fitting for us to stay here, we have lost our dogs, and we cannot get food. Let us go into Lloegyr; it is easiest for us to find support there."

"Gladly, lord," said she, "we will do so." And they set forth together to Lloegyr.

"Lord," said she, "what craft wilt thou follow? Take up one that is seemly."

"None other will I take," answered he, "save that of making shoes, as I did formerly."[17]

"Lord," said she, "such a craft becomes not a man so nobly born as thou."

"By that however will I abide," said he.

So he began his craft, and he made all his work of the finest leather he could get in the town, and, as he had done at the other place, he caused gilded clasps to be made for the shoes. And except himself all the cordwainers in the town were idle, and without work. For as long as they could be had from him, neither shoes nor hose were bought elsewhere. And thus they tarried there a year, until the cordwainers became envious, and took counsel concerning him. And he had warning thereof, and it was told him how the cordwainers had agreed together to slay him.

"Lord," said Cigfa, "wherefore should this be borne from these boors?"

"Nay," said he, "we will go back unto Dyfed." So towards Dyfed they set forth.

Now Manawyddan, when he set out to return to Dyfed, took with him a burden of wheat. And he proceeded towards Narberth, and there he dwelt. And never was he better pleased than when he saw Narberth again, and the lands where he had been wont to hunt with Pryderi and with Rhiannon. And he accustomed himself to fish, and to hunt the deer in their covert. And then he

17. Manawyddan's skill as a leatherworker conceals a pun on his name; in Welsh, the word for "awl"—the tool used by leatherworkers—is *mynawyd*.

began to prepare some ground, and he sowed a croft, and a second, and a third. And no wheat in the world ever sprung up better. And the three crofts prospered with perfect growth, and no man ever saw fairer wheat than it.

And thus passed the seasons of the year until the harvest came. And he went to look at one of his crofts, and behold it was ripe. "I will reap this to-morrow," said he. And that night he went back to Narberth, and on the morrow in the grey dawn he went to reap the croft, and when he came there he found nothing but the bare straw. Every one of the ears of the wheat was cut from off the stalk, and all the ears carried entirely away, and nothing but the straw left. And at this he marvelled greatly.

Then he went to look at another croft, and behold that also was ripe. "Verily," said he, "this will I reap to-morrow." And on the morrow he came with the intent to reap it, and when he came there he found nothing but the bare straw. "Oh, gracious Heaven," he exclaimed, "I know that whosoever has begun my ruin is completing it, and has also destroyed the country with me."

Then he went to look at the third croft, and when he came there, finer wheat had there never been seen, and this also was ripe. "Evil betide me," said he, "if I watch not here to-night. Whoever carried off the other corn will come in like manner to take this. And I will know who it is." So he took his arms, and began to watch the croft. And he told Cigfa all that had befallen.

"Verily," said she, "what thinkest thou to do?"

"I will watch the croft to-night," said he.

And he went to watch the croft. And at midnight, lo, there arose the loudest tumult in the world. And he looked, and behold the mightiest host of mice in the world, which could neither be numbered nor measured. And he knew not what it was until the mice had made their way into the croft, and each of them climbing up the straw and bending it down with its weight, had cut off one of the ears of wheat, and had carried it away, leaving there the stalk, and he saw not a single stalk there that had not a mouse to it. And they all took their way, carrying the ears with them.

In wrath and anger did he rush upon the mice, but he could no more come up with them than if they had been gnats, or birds in the air, except one only, which though it was but sluggish, went so fast that a man on foot could scarce overtake it. And after this one he went, and he caught it and put it in his glove, and tied up the opening of the glove with a string, and kept it with him, and returned to the palace. Then he came to the hall where Cigfa was, and he lighted a fire, and hung the glove by the string upon a peg.

"What hast thou there, lord?" said Cigfa.

"A thief," said he, "that I found robbing me."

"What kind of thief may it be, lord, that thou couldst put into thy glove?" said she.

"Behold I will tell thee," he answered. Then he showed her how his fields had been wasted and destroyed, and how the mice came to the last of the fields in his sight. "And one of them was less nimble than the rest, and is now in my glove; to-morrow I will hang it, and before Heaven, if I had them, I would hang them all."

"My lord," said she, "this is marvellous; but yet it would be unseemly for a man of dignity like thee to be hanging such a reptile[18] as this. And if thou doest right, thou wilt not meddle with the creature, but wilt let it go."

"Woe betide me," said he, "if I would not hang them all could I catch them, and such as I have I will hang."

"Verily, lord," said she, "there is no reason that I should succour this reptile, except to prevent discredit unto thee. Do therefore, lord, as thou wilt."

"If I knew of any cause in the world wherefore thou shouldst succour it, I would take thy counsel concerning it," said Manawyddan, "but as I know of none, lady, I am minded to destroy it."

"Do so willingly then," said she.

And then he went to the Gorsedd of Narberth, taking the mouse with him. And he set up two forks on the highest part of the Gorsedd. And while he was doing this, behold he saw a scholar coming towards him, in old and poor and tattered garments. And it was now seven years since he had seen in that place either man or beast, except those four persons who had remained together until two of them were lost.

"My lord," said the scholar, "good day to thee."

"Heaven prosper thee, and my greeting be unto thee. And whence dost thou come, scholar?" asked he.

"I come, lord, from singing in Lloegyr;[19] and wherefore dost thou inquire?"

"Because for the last seven years," answered he, "I have seen no man here save four secluded persons, and thyself this moment."

---

18. The word "reptile" originally meant any animal that creeps on the ground, and only gained its more restricted modern meaning in the nineteenth century.

19. The "scholar" was thus a bard in the original version of the story, since scholars are not known for their singing! The priest who follows later will originally have been an Ovate, and the bishop a Druid.

"Truly, lord," said he, "I go through this land unto mine own. And what work art thou upon, lord?"

"I am hanging a thief that I caught robbing me," said he.

"What manner of thief is that?" asked the scholar. "I see a creature in thy hand like unto a mouse, and ill does it become a man of rank equal to thine to touch a reptile such as this. Let it go forth free."

"I will not let it go free, by Heaven," said he; "I caught it robbing me, and the doom of a thief will I inflict upon it, and I will hang it."

"Lord," said he, "rather than see a man of rank equal to thine at such a work as this, I would give thee a pound which I have received as alms, to let the reptile go forth free."

"I will not let it go free," said he, "by Heaven, neither will I sell it."

"As thou wilt, lord," he answered; "except that I would not see a man of rank equal to thine touching such a reptile, I care nought." And the scholar went his way.

And as he was placing the crossbeam upon the two forks, behold a priest came towards him upon a horse covered with trappings.

"Good day to thee, lord," said he.

"Heaven prosper thee," said Manawyddan; "thy blessing."

"The blessing of Heaven be upon thee. And what, lord, art thou doing?"

"I am hanging a thief that I caught robbing me," said he.

"What manner of thief, lord?" asked he.

"A creature," he answered, "in form of a mouse. It has been robbing me, and I am inflicting upon it the doom of a thief."

"Lord," said he, "rather than see thee touch this reptile, I would purchase its freedom."

"By my confession to Heaven, neither will I sell it nor set it free."

"It is true, lord, that it is worth nothing to buy; but rather than see thee defile thyself by touching such a reptile as this, I will give thee three pounds to let it go."

"I will not, by Heaven," said he, "take any price for at. As it ought, so shall it be hanged."

"Willingly, lord, do thy good pleasure." And the priest went his way.

Then he noosed the string around the mouse's neck, and as he was about to draw it up, behold, he saw a bishop's retinue with his sumpter-horses, and his attendants. And the bishop himself came towards him. And he stayed his work.

"Lord bishop," said he, "thy blessing."

"Heaven's blessing be unto thee," said he; "what work art thou upon?"

"Hanging a thief that I caught robbing me," said he.

"Is not that a mouse that I see in thy hand?"

"Yes," answered he. "And she has robbed me."

"Aye," said he, "since I have come at the doom of this reptile, I will ransom it of thee. I will give thee seven pounds for it, and that rather than see a man of rank equal to thine destroying so vile a reptile as this. Let it loose and thou shalt have the money."

"I declare to Heaven that I will not set it loose."

"If thou wilt not loose it for this, I will give thee four-and-twenty pounds of ready money to set it free."

"I will not set it free, by Heaven, for as much again," said he.

"If thou wilt not set it free for this, I will give thee all the horses that thou seest in this plain, and the seven loads of baggage, and the seven horses that they are upon."

"By Heaven, I will not," he replied.

"Since for this thou wilt not, do so at what price soever thou wilt."

"I will do so," said he. "I will that Rhiannon and Pryderi be free," said he.

"That thou shalt have," he answered.

"Not yet will I loose the mouse, by Heaven."

"What then wouldst thou?"

"That the charm and the illusion be removed from the seven Cantrefs of Dyfed."

"This shalt thou have also; set therefore the mouse free."

"I will not set it free, by Heaven," said he. "I will know who the mouse may be."

"She is my wife."

"Even though she be, I will not set her free. Wherefore came she to me?"

"To despoil thee," he answered. "I am Llwyd the son of Cilcoed,[20] and I cast the charm over the seven Cantrefs of Dyfed. And it was to avenge Gwawl the son of Clud,[21] from the friendship I had towards him, that I cast the charm. And upon Pryderi did I revenge Gwawl the son of Clud, for the game of Badger in the Bag that Pwyll Pen Annwn played upon him, which he did unadvisedly in the Court of Heveydd Hên. And when it was known that thou wast come to dwell in the land, my household came and besought me to transform them into mice, that they might destroy thy corn. And it was my own household that

---

20. *Llwyd son of Cilcoed*: "Gray son of Corner of the Forest."

21. *Gwawl son of Clud*: "Radiance son of Burden."

went the first night. And the second night also they went, and they destroyed thy two crofts. And the third night came unto me my wife and the ladies of the Court, and besought me to transform them. And I transformed them. Now she is pregnant. And had she not been pregnant thou wouldst not have been able to overtake her; but since this has taken place, and she has been caught, I will restore thee Pryderi and Rhiannon; and I will take the charm and illusion from off Dyfed. I have now told thee who she is. Set her therefore free."

"I will not set her free, by Heaven," said he.

"What wilt thou more?" he asked.

"I will that there be no more charm upon the seven Cantrefs of Dyfed, and that none shall be put upon it henceforth."

"This thou shalt have," said he. "Now set her free."

"I will not, by my faith," he answered.

"What wilt thou furthermore?" asked he.

"Behold," said he, "this will I have; that vengeance be never taken for this, either upon Pryderi or Rhiannon, or upon me."

"All this shalt thou have. And truly thou hast done wisely in asking this. Upon thy head would have lighted all this trouble."

"Yea," said he, "for fear thereof was it, that I required this."

"Set now my wife at liberty."

"I will not, by Heaven," said he, "until I see Pryderi and Rhiannon with me free."

"Behold, here they come," he answered.

And thereupon behold Pryderi and Rhiannon. And he rose up to meet them, and greeted them, and sat down beside them.

"Ah, Chieftain, set now my wife at liberty," said the bishop. "Hast thou not received all thou didst ask?"

"I will release her gladly," said he. And thereupon he set her free. Then Llwyd struck her with a magic wand, and she was changed back into a young woman, the fairest ever seen.

"Look around upon thy land," said he, "and then thou wilt see it all tilled and peopled, as it was in its best state."

And he rose up and looked forth. And when he looked he saw all the lands tilled, and full of herds and dwellings.

"What bondage," he inquired, "has there been upon Pryderi and Rhiannon?"

Fig. 24. The Mabinogion • The Restoration of the Wife of Llwyd son of Cilcoed

"Pryderi has had the knockers of the gate of my palace about his neck, and Rhiannon has had the collars of the asses, after they have been carrying hay, about her neck."

And such had been their bondage. And by reason of this bondage is this story called the Mabinogi of Mynweir and Mynord.[22] And thus ends this portion of the Mabinogi.

22. *Mynweir and Mynord*: these words mean "by hay" and "by hammer" respectively, and have meanings that go a good deal beyond the deliberately facile interpretation provided in the story.

DRUID PHILOSOPHY: THE WAY OF EVOLUTION

HIS THIRD LECTURE on Druid philosophy, like the two already presented, presents ideas for meditation and study in the form of triads and commentaries. The subject of this lecture, however, may seem slightly less abstract than those that you have studied in earlier grades, for it deals with the origin, history, and destiny of the human soul—a subject of understandable interest to most students.

Because of the natural attractiveness of these teachings to many, it is all the more important to remember that the ideas and imagery presented here are meant to be understood and used rather than believed. It is entirely up to the individual student to decide whether the vision of the Way of Evolution presented in these pages is a literal description of the course of the soul from its source to its grand destiny, or whether the teachings have a symbolic meaning entirely, to be interpreted in some other sense. What is crucial is that each student familiarize himself or herself with these teachings, think through their meaning and implications, and explore them in meditation and thought.

All that we know of the ancient Druids teaches us that, like all the sages of the past, they taught the world-old and world-wide doctrine of metempsychosis or reincarnation. This lecture shall not attempt to prove the doctrine of metempsychosis. The Druid wisdom has it that every soul which has experienced even the first stirrings of individuality has an intuitional knowledge of having lived before, sometime, somewhere—a knowledge perhaps dim, but persistent, and impossible to gainsay. Those who have not this inner knowledge in some degree have not yet awakened into individuality, though such an awakening may come to them in their present life. To them, it is folly to attempt to prove metempsychosis—at most they will receive it merely as an idle speculation on the hereafter. To those who have the inner knowledge, no other proof is necessary, although explanation and teaching regarding the same is often eagerly sought after.

The following three triads explain the nature of the greater Cosmos in which the soul's evolution unfolds.

Triad I.

Three circles of manifestation: the Circle of Abred, the Circle of Gwynfydd, and the Circle of Ceugant.

Triad II.

Three conditions of all created beings: their origin from Annwn, their travail through Abred, and their rejoicing in Gwynfydd.

Triad III.

Three embodiments of all created beings: the material body in Annwn, the personality in Abred, and the individuality in Gwynfydd.

Triad I.

Three circles of manifestation: the Circle of Abred, the Circle of Gwynfydd, and the Circle of Ceugant.

Nwyfre, the One Life, possesses two complementary aspects, which we may describe as the One and the Many. As the One, it forms, fills, and vitalizes all things and beings throughout the Cosmos without any division or separation. As the Many, it condenses into individual things and beings—those same things and beings which, as the One, it surrounds and sustains.

These expressions of the One Life therefore have one common source but differ in kind, or, as the Druid teachings express it, in manifestation. There is an infinite diversity in manifestation, from the simplest particle of cosmic dust to the vast centers of intelligence and will which humanity terms gods, and which the children of humanity will one day joyously acknowledge for their elder brothers and sisters. For the sake of understanding, the Druid teachings divide this infinite diversity into the three great circles of Abred, Gwynfydd, and Ceugant.

The Circle of Abred is the realm of corporeal manifestation. Here all beings that exist are bound to material bodies, from the simplest forms of life to the most complex and elegant living organisms. Being bound to the realities of matter, those expressions of the One Life that dwell in Abred know suffering, limitation, and death. These things are essential to their further progress, and may not be dispensed with until their lessons have been learnt. This is the origin of the word *abred*, which means "release," for it is by learning the lessons of matter that we are released from its burdens and its sufferings.

The Circle of Gwynfydd is the realm of spiritual manifestation. Here all beings that exist may take on material bodies at will, but are not bound to the world of matter; centers of consciousness and life, they may participate in any material form that will further their own attainment and the work they pursue. Gwynfydd is thus not a static perfection, as heaven has been said to be in some religions, but a realm of further learning and development for those beings that exist in it. The word *gwynfydd* means "the white or luminous life."

The Circle of Ceugant, finally, is the realm beyond all manifestation where Nwyfre, the One Life, is One rather than Many. As the lore of the Druid mysteries has it, Ceugant "may not be traversed by any created being," for to enter into Ceugant is to pass out of manifestation and return to the One. The word *ceugant* accordingly means "the empty circle."

Triad II.

Three conditions of all created beings: their origin from Annwn, their travail through Abred, and their rejoicing in Gwynfydd.

Annwn, as explained in a previous lesson, is the realm of pure possibility, the primal abyss out of which all things emerge. It is in Annwn that the One Life begins its work of evolution, first developing those basic materials from which all the rest would be built: the atoms and molecules, and the aggregates formed of them, such as air, water, stone, and the like. These aggregates had no individual lives of their own until a later period in the great unfolding, when they were ensouled by spiritual beings of a kind appropriate to them, a theme which will be developed in detail in another lecture.

From combinations of these aggregates, in turn, the One Life shaped the first and simplest living beings, such as the infusoria,[23] composed of merely a single cell and capable only of the most rudimentary consciousness and will. Here the Many first takes shape from the One—the first individual beings are born. Thereafter, working from these lowly forms, the One Life shapes more complex beings, the benefits of acquired conscious experience being transmitted through the laws of heredity, which are manifestations of the Law of Sequence. In this way the bodies were shaped through which the Many advanced in the scale of evolution.

The bodies inhabited by the Many are the lessons by which each soul learns and grows, and the framework that gives structure to its future powers. They shape the evolving soul, forcing its innate powers into manifestation by means of the constraints of material form and the challenges of suffering and death. But there comes a point upon the scale of evolution at which the soul has learnt those lessons that matter teaches, and its further evolution requires that it learn to shape matter, instead of being shaped by matter. The souls who pass this point enter into bliss in the Circle of Gwynfydd, the realm of spiritual manifestation.

Of Gwynfydd little may be said by, or to, those still in Abred except by way of oppositions. Where Abred is constraint, Gwynfydd is freedom; where Abred is suffering, Gwynfydd is joy; where Abred presupposes death, Gwynfydd is limitless life. In Gwynfydd the soul works out its own evolution by the free and conscious use of its own powers. The Druid teachings state that there are as many steps in the scale of evolution in Gwynfydd as there are in Abred, and that therefore, those souls who have attained the heights of Gwynfydd stand as far above humanity as does humanity above the infusorium.

At the summit of Gwynfydd, the upper end of the scale of evolution, comes that point at which the evolving soul has become one with the whole universe and is therefore identical with the One Life. Here the Many becomes One; the rivulet of water that flowed out from the earth in a tiny spring among the rocks, now become a mighty river, flows at last into the sea. That sea is the Circle of Ceugant, where no individual being exists, and only the One Life is present.

---

23. *infusoria*: An old word for single-celled organisms of the sort that can be seen with a microscope in water.

TRIAD III.

Three embodiments of all created beings: the material body in An-nwn, the personality in Abred, and the individuality in Gwynfydd.

The aspects of the self discussed earlier in this course may be assigned to the stages in the evolutionary process just outlined. The material body, *corff* in Welsh, is composed of the aggregates first formed by the One Life out of the void of Annwn, and retains the trace of this origin; it is for this reason that it so readily decays and disintegrates, returning to the No-thing from which it was created. The *bywyd, nwyd,* and *hunan,* the three parts of the personality—the basic biological drives, the passions and irrational life, and the self composed of thought, will, and memory—are evolved step by step and stage by stage. The *elaeth* or individuality, however, is the distinctive embodiment of Gwynfydd, and those who have begun to evolve their own individuality have risen to the brink of the Luminous Life that knows no death.

TRIAD IV.

Three levels of human existence: the lower, which falls back into Abred; the middle, which returns to human life; and the higher, which proceeds to Gwynfydd.

TRIAD V.

Three falls from the human level: from cruelty and passion, to the animal kingdom; from indolence and passivity, to the vegetable kingdom; from pride and despair, to the Cauldron of Annwn itself.

TRIAD VI.

Three fates for the human soul: in Gwynfydd, remembrance; in Abred, forgetfulness; in Annwn, annihiliation.

TRIAD IV.

Three levels of human existence: the lower, which falls back into Abred; the middle, which returns to human life; and the higher, which proceeds to Gwynfydd.

The Druid teaching does not hold that rebirth is imposed arbitrarily upon the soul, or by reason of punishment or reward for good or evil deeds in life. On the contrary, it proceeds in accordance with the order of the Cosmos, following the general path of the desire and character of the Individual. In other words, character becomes fate; the sum of the individual's experience and his desires determines his future embodiment and life.

The desires predominating in life reveal the character of the soul, and the urges of character toward expression, lead the soul into certain channels of rebirth. Those whose desires focus primarily on the experiences of the lower circles of Abred will be drawn to repeat those experiences, and take shape in bodies appropriate to them: the bodies of other living things, less intellectual than man, more suited to a life consisting solely of eating, mating, and the like. Those whose desires focus primarily on the experiences of the human level will be drawn to repeat those experiences in another human body. Those whose desires focus primarily on the experiences possible to the individuality will be drawn to attain those experiences, in a body appropriate to them: the Body of Light, the vesture of the dwellers in Gwynfydd.

Nor does the Druid teaching hold that rebirth need always be an unconscious and automatic process, though it is this for most beings. By understanding and regulating the growth of one's character, one may thus shape future lives in advance. With the practice of certain spiritual disciplines, the soul becomes able to direct its destiny, and accompanying this comes the memory of past lives, so that life becomes continuous in consciousness and memory. Throughout the world in the distant past, it has been the duty of some who attained this state to choose deliberately to return over and over again to the same family or the same nation, to offer guidance and direction to less evolved souls; in some few countries this continues to this day.[24]

It must be remembered that the mental state of the average man of today, in relation to the wider perspectives of the elaeth, is akin to the mental state of a child of a few years of age in relation to the things of this life. The child remembers but little of its past—the happenings of a few months ago are forgotten—even the affairs of yesterday seem dim today. But as the child advances in years it has a better and still better remembrance of the past. In the same way the soul develops a clearer and still clearer recollection of its past lives. The dim

---

24. This is probably a reference to the Tibetan belief that some lamas, such as the Dalai Lama, reincarnate repeatedly for the benefit of Tibet's Buddhists.

memories and feelings of familiarity which many of us now have, will be succeeded eventually by a full remembrance of the details of our past lives. This will certainly happen to each of us when we attain Gwynfydd; it may also happen before that stage.

TRIAD V.

Three falls from the human level: from cruelty and passion, to the animal kingdom; from indolence and passivity, to the vegetable kingdom; from pride and despair, to the Cauldron of Annwn itself.

It must be understood that the descent of the soul from the human level into some less developed stage among the realms of Abred is not a punishment; nor, seen in the broader light of the Druid wisdom, is it even a failure. The soul goes forth from each life to that next life best suited to its needs and potentials. If it has risen prematurely to the human level, it may yearn for some other form of manifestation and find its fulfillment in a descent to that form.

Thus the soul that has not yet outworn the delights of the animal passions is drawn to lives and forms where those passions may be enjoyed freely, with an intensity that cannot be matched by thinking and reasoning beings. The animal passions are, in their proper places, holy and mighty shapers of the evolving soul; the wolf as it chases the stag, the stag as it battles another stag for the attentions of the does, the fawn as it hides trembling from the wolf, are building up patterns of reaction in their souls that will blossom in future lives as great powers and potentialities of being. It is only when these reactions are out of place and out of balance that they become destructive of higher values.

In the same way, the properties of the vegetable life are essential to the growth and evolution of the soul. The human soul that has not yet completed the process of absorbing these lessons, and is drawn to the indolence and passivity that are the reflections of the vegetable life on the human plane, is following its proper course to return to the vegetable level for one or more lives. Every descent thus prepares the ground for a new uprising, until the soul has learned all that it needs to learn from the Circle of Abred, and is ready to embrace its proper freedom in Gwynfydd.

Yet the transition from Abred to Gwynfydd is not without its dangers. With the first stirrings of the individuality at the human level comes the awakening of the will and the beginnings of the capacity for free choice. The soul becoming conscious of its powers and its destiny must choose to enter into Gwynfydd, and it is possible, though it is fortunately not common, for a soul in this position to refuse Gwynfydd and turn away from its own individuality. Its refusal of its destiny sets terrible consequences in train.

TRIAD VI.

Three fates for the human soul: in Gwynfydd, remembrance; in Abred, forgetfulness; in Annwn, annihiliation.

The Druid teachings hold that each individual may be thought of as an "I" and a "Me." The Me is the personality which is shaped by heredity, environment, habit, and the like. The I is the real self, the first stirrings of the individuality. The character of the individual arises from the balance struck between the two. The soul still mired in Abred allows the Me, the personality, to bear down the balance in its own direction; while the soul ready for Gwynfydd asserts the I, and begins to waken to the wonder of its own individuality.

The existence of such a struggle between the Me and the I shows that there must be something in the self in a measure independent of the inherited and acquired Me. When the individual experiences this inner conflict, this is the sign that he has attained at least the first stirrings of individuality, for those human souls whose individuality has not yet begun to stir from sleep simply follow the promptings of heredity and environment. The only conflict in the minds of those still bound by Abred is conflict between competing desires—there is no I to set aside desire and master it by will. The awakening self is able to master desire by will—able not only to desire to will, but to will to will. Desire and will are the two poles of the manifestation of one force, one unconscious, the other conscious. Desire rules the individual, unless he awakens to the potentials of will. It is through will that the individuality asserts its prerogatives over the personality and its unthinking and unconscious desires.

Personality is ultimately rooted in the physical body, its inherited mental and emotional properties, and the tendencies it acquires over the course of a single life. Individuality is the expression of the One Life within the self, and transcends personality and the things of personality. Personality is bound to one's personal present incarnation. Individuality embraces that incarnation and rises above it. Personality says "I am John Smith, of Chicago, clerk, aged 28"; or "Mary Jones, of New York, schoolteacher, aged 45"; as the case may be. Individuality says "I am that I am"—above names, and forms, and personal sheaths or vehicles.

This distinction applies as well to the memory. The memories of the personality endure with the personality, and die with it. Thus each life in Abred begins with a clean slate of memory. The character built up laboriously over countless lives and forms does not depart, for it is woven into the core of the being, but the newborn infant normally recalls no more of its prior existence than does the newborn fawn, or the newborn infusorium. Only when the individuality has begun to awaken does the first dim recollection of the soul's long past begin to awaken as well, and in such cases it happens betimes that a child will recall some glimpse of a previous life, or display some talent that bears the fruit of exertions in some past existence.

But when it first awakens, the individuality is little more than a dim sense of identity, and the recollection of past lives little more than a dim sense of familiarity of things not before seen in the present life. The personality remains the dominant part of the self; and it must choose, of its own free will, whether to explore these first dim promptings of the individuality. If it does so, well and good; it begins to rise up toward Gwynfydd. If it fails to do so, because the time is not yet ripe for its full awakening, it is free to wander further in human, animal, or vegetable bodies to fulfill its desires and complete its education.

The danger comes if it attempts to harness the individuality to the purposes of the personality, to make will the slave of desire and wisdom subject to the animal passions. Many souls that take the upward path dabble in this, and learn from the consequences; some few persist in it for a time, until the conflict between the individuality and the personality rises to such a pitch of intensity that they are perforce either driven to recognize the claims of the individuality or flung back down the scale of being to some animal or vegetable form, there to revisit the lessons they have not learned well enough. A very few persevere in this path of reverse evolution. No power in the universe can make the will choose what it will not choose, and a soul that repeatedly turns its back on the One Life and seeks to harness the potentials of the awakening self to the service of selfish cravings cannot be forced to do otherwise.

Yet the soul that turns its back on the One Life turns its back on its own existence. When the soul realizes its individuality, then the things of personality are left behind in their proper time, and the desire and will is simply to be. The soul in the bonds of personality, however, desires to be and remain what he was—his personality of "John Smith, of Chicago, clerk, aged 28," is his idea of his self. If this idea of the self is all that remains, the individuality having been rejected, such a soul has nothing in itself with the capacity to persist as an I independent of the personality. There is no I in such a person—it is all Me, the Me of the personality.

There is no "future life" awaiting such people, after they have passed out of the physical body. They may, if they have the necessary skills and training, endure for a time out of the physical body, but rebirth is abhorrent to them; they cannot conceive of it for they would in that case "be some other person," or more properly some other personality, and their love of their own personality shivers and shrinks at the thought of losing the only self they know. Thus they refuse the choice of rebirth. As they are all Me, with no I, and the Me always perishes sooner or later, they endure for a time and then are not. Of them it is said that they have returned to the Cauldron of Annwn and do not come forth again.

Still, this is no more a punishment than is any other destiny open to the soul. There is "no bribe of heaven or threat of hell" to those who know the nature of birth and rebirth. All is cause and effect—each gets that for which he pays—each pays his price. Finally, to all who seek it, comes that peace which passeth all understanding. Even among those who return to the Cauldron, there are none outside of the One Life. There is no Outside. All are included, for there is but One!

Triad VII.

Three powers shaping the life of every being: destiny, will, and fate.

Triad VIII.

Three worlds present in every choice: Ceugant in the form of destiny, Gwynfydd in the form of will, and Abred in the form of fate.

Triad IX.

Three things that release beings from the power of fate: suffering, understanding, and the right use of will.

Triad VII.

Three powers shaping the life of every being: destiny, will, and fate.

From the earliest days of philosophical reasoning, the great questions regarding the relationship of fate and freedom have formed an important subject of speculation and debate. In many forms, and in manifold guises, has this great question presented itself for consideration by the human mind: is the course of human life subject to the choice of the individual, or is it determined by some outside power? Backward and forward has this tennis-ball of thought been tossed, victory being claimed by all parties engaging in the game of discussion. Early philosophy was concerned with the concepts of fate, destiny and freedom, and able thinkers arrayed themselves on various sides of the question. Metaphysics joined in the controversy with subtle and hair-splitting definitions, theories, explanations, and conceptions. Theology took an active interest in the fray, its particular sides of the tennis court being named Predestination and Free Will. Modern Science has now entered the field and many of her advanced thinkers insist upon the principle of determinism by natural laws in all the fields of human and nonhuman activity.

The Druid teachings take it as a basic axiom that everything and all things—every event and all events—are governed by law; every thing and every event is subject to its proper order and sequence, and there is in reality no such thing as chance. Every event is thus a link in the cosmic sequence of events, for everything is a part of, and not apart from, the One Life. Nothing "just happens" without its precedent causes proceeding regularly and in their proper sequence; there are no "accidents," or events outside of the natural order.

Hearing these statements, the student will likely feel impelled to ask the inevitable question: "Is the reign of law and orderly sequence but another name for the old fetish of fate, destiny, or predestination? Are we ruled by arbitrary fate—governed by the decree of destiny? Are all events predetermined?" This question must be met, not ignored and evaded as is customary in too many teachings.

One of the main points of difference between the Druid conceptions of law and orderly sequence, and the common conceptions of fate and predestination, is the assumption in the case of the latter of divine foreknowledge and decree. The tradition of fatalism holds that some supernatural being, having foreknowledge of all events, exercises arbitrary decrees determining all events, including the fate or destiny of mankind, collectively and individually. The teaching of law and orderly sequence, on the contrary, does not require the idea of foreknowledge or the notion of an arbitrary divine will. Instead, it holds that all activities in the Cosmos, down to the most incidental events, proceed regularly and in their proper sequence by the action of natural laws. These laws, in turn, are superimposed by, and are reflections of, Awen—the efficient reason of the Cosmos. The modern scientific schools of determinism parallel this Druid teaching so far as the idea of determination by natural laws is concerned, but differ from it by failing to recognize the role of a timeless reality, Awen, from which natural laws unfold.

Another great point of difference between fatalism and the Druid teaching is that fatalism insists upon arbitrary happenings and events unrelated to natural law. The common idea of fate denies that preceding events have any relation to the "fated happening," and holds that the latter would have happened in spite of any combination of preceding events. In short, fatalism makes the "fated happening" a thing standing apart from the chain of sequence—something resulting from an arbitrary and independent decree. Thus, fatalism holds that one's death, for instance, is "fated" (decreed) to happen in a certain way, at a certain time, and at a certain place, irrespective of the order of the Cosmos.

The Druid teachings, by contrast, use the term "fate" to represent the sum total of the effects of past causes, unfolding according to law and orderly sequence. Those effects are determined, but they are not predetermined, and as new causes are set in motion by every action, new effects are added to the total at every moment, and may change the shape of an individual's fate, at least in part. What binds the individual to his fate is not the arbitrary decree of an outside power, but the effect of character and habit, which leads each soul to reinforce whatever chains of cause and effect have been most strongly established by past action.

The Druid teachings also differentiate between fate and destiny. Where fate is the effect of the past, destiny is the call of the future: the specific potential for attainment within each individual, which differs from soul to soul and, to some extent, from life to life. Observe a child with musical talent, and compare him with a child whose gifts lie in the fields of thought and learning rather than music. One, given appropriate circumstances, will grow up to be a musician; the other, given a different set of appropriate circumstances, will grow up to be a philosopher. Put either child in the other's place, and you will have an unhappy and unsuccessful child and, should the experiment be continued, the very real risk of a failed life. Give both of them an identical education with no relevance to either set of talents, and both children will struggle to achieve their respective destinies against longer odds.

According to Druid teachings, every soul at every point along the long course of evolution has its distinctive destiny. In the lower reaches of Abred, it may be impossible to tell that destiny apart from those of a million other lives of the same kind, but the further the soul ascends and the more possibilities its form of incarnation open before it, the more distinctive its destiny will be. In the heights of Gwynfydd, the destiny of each soul will be totally unique, the full expression of that distinctive facet of the One Life that it expresses. That is the bliss of Gwynfydd, for the destiny of each soul is the form in which its highest bliss comes into manifestation.

Between the pressures of fate and destiny, holding the balance of both, is will. The evolution of the soul is in large part the evolution of will—the development of the capacity to choose—to choose firmly, and wisely, and with full awareness of the context and the consequences. It is by the development and the right use of will that each soul becomes able to alter its fate, to pursue its destiny, and to move from being subject to the effects of causes outside itself, to becoming a cause of the effects it desires to experience in this and subsequent lives.

Triad VIII.

Three worlds present in every choice: Ceugant in the form of destiny, Gwynfydd in the form of will, and Abred in the form of fate.

This Triad expresses the points already made in another way. Fate represents the legacy of Abred in the soul. Each of us still bears with us the legacies of the long journey up through the circles of Abred, from the infusorium through all the forms of plant and animal existence, and finally to the level where choice and will become fully active and Gwynfydd becomes a possibility. These legacies take the form of fate: all the consequences of past actions and experiences, taking the form of character and, through character, affecting the events of the present moment.

Will represents the possibility of Gwynfydd in the soul. The nature of Gwynfydd is freedom, and in the long ascent up the circles of Gwynfydd, the will becomes increasingly free to make its own choices. The will as it is manifest in today's humanity, even among those who have developed it to a very great extent, is scarcely a shadow of the will as it is manifest in those great beings who are the elder brethren of humanity, and as it will be manifest in time in each of us when we have risen to the same high estate. Yet the simplest act of free choice offers a first faint adumbration of the freedom of Gwynfydd.

Destiny represents the presence of Ceugant in the soul. Each soul, as it takes shape as an individual reality out of the One Life at the lowest point of Abred, is in potential a manifestation of one aspect, one set of possibilities, or one energy that inheres eternally in the One Life. The unfolding of those possibilities is the expression in time, in Abred or Gwynfydd, of what is manifest in eternity in Ceugant.

Each of these, as the Triad so well expresses it, is present in every choice. Consider a decision that you have made, or are in the process of making, or expect to make: you will find that three forces are in play. One of these forces consists of the external circumstances that have entered your life as a result of your past choices, and of the internal habits and tendencies that have become part of your character, equally as a result of your past choices. All these will push you in one or several directions, and these directions normally amount to the repetition of existing habits and the continuation of the state internal to yourself that is most customary for you. All this is of the nature of fate.

A second force consists of your own freedom to decide. While the pressure exerted by fate may seem overwhelming, this perception is as much a product of your habits and character as it is a reflection of the real nature of the forces acting upon you. You always have the power to choose otherwise, and though there will be consequences proceeding from that choice, there will equally be consequences that proceed from your failure to choose, or your decision to allow the pressure of fate to have its way with you. In most of life's decisions, many options stand open, though most people perceive only a few of them, or only one.

A third force, finally, consists of the inner prompting that may at times be called conscience, or intuition, or the voice of the inner or higher self: a prompting that makes no arguments and exerts no pressure, but shows the right way forward. This is the voice of destiny in the self. Following its promptings is no guarantee of comfort or convenience or, in the short term, of happiness; it judges all things from the point of view of eternity rather than that of the present moment. Still, cultivating the habit of listening to that inner prompting, and following its guidance, is among the surest paths to the fulfillment of the soul's destiny.

Triad IX.

Three things that release beings from the power of fate: suffering, understanding, and the right use of will.

One great difference between the teaching of fatalism, on the one hand, and that of the Druid wisdom on the other, lies in the latter's recognition of the soul's capacity to overcome its fate. This may seem like a contradiction of points already made—we have already affirmed the power of cause and effect in the Cosmos, and if fate is the working out of the effects of past causes, it may seem impossible that the impulses of fate may be changed or altered.

But it must be remembered here that fate, as the Druid teachings understand it, is not set in stone—it has not been established from the beginning of time, as fatalism avers. Instead, it is constantly being made by the choices, actions, and experiences of the self. Since fate is thus made, it can be remade, and even unmade.

The Triad names three things that remake and unmake fate. The first of these, by far the most common, is suffering. When the pressures of fate expressed in character and circumstance move out of harmony with the destiny of the soul, the result is suffering, and in the experience of suffering the force of fate is absorbed and used up. Should the soul continue to make the same fate by its choices, new sufferings of the same kind take the place of old, until finally the soul can no longer bear the cost of its own choices and begins to choose differently. For this reason it has been said by the Druids that suffering is a mercy provided by the Cosmos for the healing of all souls within it.

The second, and much more difficult, is understanding. When the soul confronts suffering, if it refuses the easy path of blaming itself or others and strives to understand the causes of its suffering, it may grasp the nature of the choices that are creating its fate anew, and grasp also the lesson that its suffering is meant to teach. In this act of understanding the causes of suffering can be dissolved. This way of dealing with fate is not often mentioned outside of the circles of students of the Mysteries, for nothing is easier than to pretend to oneself that one has understood the nature of one's mistakes and the causes of one's sufferings. The test for all such perceptions is twofold. The first part of the test is whether one's actions and choices change significantly and lastingly thereafter; the second part is whether one's sufferings depart and the events that cause them are no longer repeated.

The third, which is present in the first two as well, is the right use of will. Faced with a choice between an action that will follow the pressures of fate, and an action that will overcome those pressures, the soul always has the choice to do the latter. Done in a small way, here and there, in the midst of a life otherwise dominated by fate, such choices will begin weakening the grip of fate on the soul, and lay the foundation for future achievements. Done with strength and continued resolve, such choices can overthrow the grip of fate completely. The effects of past causes must still be experienced, and when fate is confronted all at once, those effects are commonly encountered all at once, leading to suffering; they may also be cognized all at once, leading to understanding; yet the strong will, focused on the promptings of destiny and guided by a recognition of the nature of fate, can overcome all this within the course of a single life, and often in a portion of one life.

In the place of fatalism, therefore, the Druid teachings offer the natural unfolding of laws inherent within the Cosmos, proceeding in an orderly sequence of cause and effect. Not the result of arbitrary fiat or decree, but the result of natural laws proceeding in regular order, as the Cosmos evolves from the One to the Many and back again to the One. When the Cosmos is resolved into Infinite Nothingness, then we find naught existent but Awen. And Awen is the only thing left upon which to fix the final blame, if blame there be. Fix it so, if you will. If it belong to Awen—give to It Its own. But Awen is no person—no being—It is the Absolute—constant, unchanging, invariable, eternal. In Awen we find the only refuge in our highest flights of thought, reason, or imagination. It is not a lawgiver—It is Law in itself.

THE MAGICAL MEMORY:
MEMORY OF SIGHT

I T HAS BEEN WELL SAID that "the eyes are the windows of the soul," and it is indeed true that through these windows, in most of us, the mind receives the greatest number of impressions, and those impressions of the very finest quality. It will be found by experience that in most cases, training of the mind to correctly register the impressions received through the medium of the eye will have more immediate effect on the development of memory than the cultivation of any other of the senses.

We cannot too strongly urge upon our readers the vital importance of the training of the eyes to receive correct impressions clearly and distinctly. Such training, and the consequent development, will result to the benefit of the man or woman in any walk of life, and in any profession. It is not merely the artist or sculptor who needs the aid of the trained eye, but every artisan, businessperson, or professional who has not developed along these lines suffers every day for his negligence.

The artist cannot reproduce unless he observes correctly; the writer cannot describe scenes, persons or character unless he has the sharpened faculty of observation; the artisan needs no one to tell him of the importance of seeing things. There is no occupation the followers of which are not benefited by trained power of observation.

One adds very materially to his fund of information, and to his pleasure, by cultivating the art of perception. In traveling, for instance, many persons miss much of the best scenery—many objects of the greatest interest—by failing to perceive them. They return and read works of travel describing the same location, and are astonished at the wealth of description while they saw so little. Many miss the best parts of a book, by reason of careless reading. The Indian and the backwoodsman will notice the broken twig, the turned leaf, the foot-print, where the untrained observer sees nothing uncommon.

We remember reading somewhere of a merchant who was laughed at for having an ignorant man in his employ as buyer. He replied that it was true that the employee could not spell a word or form a grammatical sentence, and had never read the works of a standard author, but he knew how to SEE things—he bought thousands of dollars' worth of goods every year for the merchant and had never been known to make a mistake, or to fail to note a defect, or any ob-jectionable feature in the goods. This man had cultivated the faculty of percep-tion, and was turning it to account.

Very few of us notice the details of the most common objects. How many of you know whether a cow's ears are above, below, behind or in front of her horns? How many can tell whether a cat descends from a tree head or tail first? How many know whether cows and horses rise with their fore or hind feet first, or whether both animals have the same habit of rising? How many know how the number "four" appears on a watch dial?—most of you will say IV—look at your watch.[25]

The eminent scientist Louis Agassiz[26] had a wonderful success in training his pupils to observe. The highly trained powers of perception which he developed in them undoubtedly contributed largely to the success of the large number of his pupils who made names and places for themselves in after years. It is related of him that one day a favorite pupil asked for additional training along these lines. Agassiz handed him a jar containing a fish, and told him to examine it carefully and report to him later what he had noticed about the fish. The pu-pil had seen the same kind of fish before, and could not understand why the professor had given him so trifling a task. He looked at the specimen but saw nothing of interest. He was unable to find the professor, and was compelled to remain with the tiresome fish for several hours, much to his disgust. After a bit, to relieve the monotony, he took the fish out of the jar and began to draw its figure. This was easy enough until he began to fill in the details. Then he made the interesting discovery that the fish had no eyelids, also several little points of interest that were new to him.

---

25. These examples are admittedly somewhat outdated.

26. A leading biologist of the nineteenth century, Agassiz was also the first scientist to recognize, from its geological traces, the existence of the Ice Age.

When Agassiz returned he seemed disappointed that the student had found out so little about the fish, and told him to try for a few hours more. The student, finding that there was no escape, started to work in earnest, bearing in mind Agassiz's remark that "a pencil is the best of eyes." He began to see more and more of interest in that fish, and grew quite interested in the task. The professor would come in from time to time, and hear of the student's new discoveries, but would say little or nothing. He kept the student at work on that same fish for three long days, and the student wondered greatly that he had been able to see so little before, where there was so much to be seen and noted. The student, many years after, had made a name for himself, and was wont to tell this story, with the observation that the lesson gained by the study of that fish had extended to the details of every subsequent study, and that the experience thus gained was of inestimable value to him. It is said of Agassiz that he could deliver a popular lecture on an insect like the grasshopper, and make it so interesting that the audience became as intent as if they were witnessing a play.

In London there are said to be places where young thieves are instructed in the art of rapid and close observation. The "professor" instructing young rascals will place in his hand a number of small objects, such as a key, a button, a coin, a ring, etc. He will open his hand an instant before his class, who are required not only to name the objects seen but to describe them. Then changes will be made in the object and the boys must detect the article substituted at once. These students, after a course of training, are sent out as beggars. They endeavor to catch a glimpse into offices, rooms, houses, etc., and to note any article of value within range of their sight, its location, the doors, locks, etc., etc. They report to headquarters and if the prospects are good a burglary is forthcoming.

The above will be seen to resemble the method used to train "Kim," as related in the last lesson packet. Readers of Arthur Conan Doyle's fascinating "Sherlock Holmes" tales will remember the wonderful powers of perception possessed by that amateur detective, and the results accomplished because of same. Gamblers are close observers, and can often tell the hand held by their opponent, by the expression of his face, although the opponent may not be aware of betraying himself.

Coture, the great teacher of drawing, instructed his pupils to let their eyes rest for a moment on passers-by in the street, and then attempt to draw them. The plan met with perfect success, after practice. At first only a hat, or an arm or a leg would be distinctly registered, but in a short time the entire figure in all its details was recorded. In the School of Design in Saint Petersburg, Russia, the pupils are instructed to study an object for ten minutes, and then, the object being withdrawn, they proceed to draw it. Varney, the celebrated teacher, would place the object to be drawn in one room, and have his pupils at work in another room, allowing them to go from time to time to take a look at the object.

Gabrielli, a French artist, painted a most expressive portrait of James Gordon Bennett, whom he had only seen once as he went by rapidly in a carriage. One of the most speaking pictures of Lincoln we have ever seen was painted by a talented but practically unknown artist in New Jersey, who was a most ardent admirer of the great President, whom he had seen but once. The artist was so overcome with emotion at hearing of the assassination of his idol that he sought his easel for solace, and reproduced the murdered President's features entirely from memory.

Many years ago, about 1845, the old Academy of Fine Arts in Philadelphia was destroyed by fire, and among other valuable paintings there perished a picture by Murillo, entitled "The Roman Daughter." Nearly thirty-five years afterwards Sartain drew the picture from memory. In 1805 the French troops carried away a masterpiece of Rubens, which had formed the altar-piece in the Church of St. Peter, in Cologne. A local painter, a great admirer of the picture, made from memory a copy of the painting which seems to be absolutely perfect in drawing, detail and color. The original painting was afterwards restored and the copy compared with it, but the closest inspection fails to show any perceptible difference between them. There is a waiter in a leading hotel in a large city, who takes the hats from the guests as they enter the dining room. He can identify the owners of hundreds of hats, without a single mistake, by associating the face of the wearer with the hat, and recalling it by eye memory. "I see the face under the hat, and then I know whose hat it is," he says, and as each guest leaves the room he is handed his own hat.

The eye, of course, transmits to the brain every ray of light entering it, and it is believed that every impression as received is registered faintly. But the mind fails to store away and subsequently recall any impressions except those which are the result of more or less interest or attention. But we may so train the sense of seeing that the impressions are received so clearly and distinctly that the mind considers it worthwhile to store them away carefully that they may be recalled when needed, instead of dumping them in a pile in the waste heap where it is almost impossible to find them when one desires them. Very few people are close observers. The average person will remember a thing in a general way—will recall what it is like—but the details are missing. A thing of interest, however, receives a greater share of the attention, and a clear and full impression is registered.

An instance of the operation of interest in this connection is had in the example of an average man and woman walking leisurely along the street.[27] Another woman passes them, wearing a rather attractive gown. Both notice her. The man remembers only the fact that "she had on something blue" and that "her sleeves bulged out near the wrist and she had on rather a big hat." If he remembers that much he has done well—many men would not have seen the sleeves, and the rest of the impression would have been hazy. But the woman would be able to tell just what the other woman had on—the waist and how it was trimmed—the style in sleeves to a fine detail; the skirt, how it was cut and of what material composed; its quality and probable cost; the hat and its feathers, silk and velvet; all the little details of style, etc. She would be able to describe to a woman friend all that she had seen, and the friend would be able to see it all "in her mind's eye." Now, both the man and the woman had equally good eyes—both received a photographic impression of the passing woman and her finery, and yet notice what a difference in the respective observation of the two people. What caused the difference? Simply the fact that the woman's interest was along the lines of dress, and she had trained her attention to focus on such things. With the man there was no interest—no attention. And yet the man probably remembered that the woman had bright blue eyes and fluffy golden hair—that is, if he were a young man.

But the quality of interest may be trained and acquired, and the quality of attention will follow it.

You realize, of course, that it is not the eye that requires training, for every healthy eye does its work well. It is that part of the mind that "sees" through the eye that needs the lessons you are about to give it. The eye is the camera—the mind the sensitive plate.[28] You wish to develop the faculty of observation. Your desire gives you an interest in the subject, and in the details of the plan, and you devote your attention to it. Important factors these—Interest and Attention—don't forget them. But the mind has been lazy, and it will take time, patience and practice to get it down to work in earnest.

---

27. While the following example is outdated due to a century of changes in gender relationships and cultural attitudes, the principle can be applied equally well to other differences in attention and interest.

28. That is, the film—or as we would now say, the CCD chip.

In order to remember objects, it is first necessary to see them plainly—to have the mind register a clear impression of them and store them away carefully as things of value. And the only way to get the mind to do this is to train its powers of observation. Things to be impressed upon the mind must be observed carefully and thoughtfully. This training of the powers of observation will amply repay the student for the time and labor expended, and the task itself is not irksome or dull, as the progress of the task is attended with such marked improvement of so pleasant a character that the student almost forgets that it is a task rather than a pleasant series of experiments.

Following are a number of exercises calculated to develop your powers of observation—intended to help you to "see" things clearly and carefully. These exercises are useful not only in training your memory, but will give you such sharp powers of observation that you will be much more valuable to yourself and others than ever before. It will be a liberal education to you, along new lines.

Exercise 1

One of the simplest but best exercises in the training of the power of observation consists in the correct seeing of familiar objects. This may seem like a very easy thing, but after you have tried it a few times you will have more respect for it.

Begin by placing before you some familiar object; something of a bright color is preferable, as it is easier to remember bright objects. Suppose it is a book, an apple or inkstand. Look at it intently, calmly but deliberately, for a few moments, trying to get the picture impressed upon your mind. Then close your eyes, and try to remember as much as possible about the object. Try to remember its shape, its details. Fix these things in your mind. Then open your eyes and take another look, and see how many details you missed in your mental picture. Note these forgotten points carefully, then close the eyes again and endeavor to re-form the picture. Then open the eyes and take stock over again, repeating until you are able to form a perfect mental picture of the object in all its details. A little practice will give you a wonderful proficiency in this experiment which will prove quite gratifying to you. But it is not alone what you have gained in this experiment, but the preliminary training you have acquired for greater things, that renders it worthwhile.

Exercise 2

After you have mastered Exercise 1, take one of the same objects with which you have familiarized yourself, and, after getting a good mental impression of it, try to draw the general shape and such details as you remember, with a pencil upon a sheet of paper. Do not hesitate because you are not an artist. We are not trying to make an artist of you and wish but to develop your observation and the recalling of what you have observed. Take something easy for the first trial, and you will feel less discouraged. The success of your drawing will depend not upon its artistic merit, but upon the percentage of details, etc., you have been able to remember sufficiently well to indicate upon the paper. It is astonishing how these two exercises will develop your faculties of observation and recollection. After a bit you will be able to give one good look at a thing, and then make a rough drawing, showing all its principal points and details.

You, of course, understand that the drawing is not from the object itself, but from the mental picture of it. After you have noted all the details in your mental picture, take a look at the object and see what you have missed. Then repeat. In both of these exercises, change your objects frequently, thus gaining proficiency and giving the mind an agreeable change.

Exercise 3

Begin noticing the details of things, instead of observing only the thing in its general aspect. It has been said that intelligent observation is the most difficult of arts. Do not try to "take in" a complex object in its entirety at one look, at the start. This is something that is reserved for future practice when you have developed further. Take in the details of portions of the object; rivet these in your mind, and then proceed to the next portion, and so on.

Take faces for example. Nothing is more mortifying than to forget the faces of those whom we have met, and many a person's chances have been injured by a lack of correct observation in this direction. The trouble with most of us is that we have been endeavoring to remember faces by observing them as a whole, paying no attention to details. Begin practicing on your acquaintances, then proceeding to strangers, and in a short time you will be surprised at your proficiency in recalling details of countenances. Notice carefully the nose, eyes, mouth, chin, color of hair, general shape of head, etc. You will find that you will be able to recall the nose of Smith, or the eyes of Brown, or the chin of Tompkins, and so on.

Before doing this, sit down and try to describe the features of some of your most intimate friends. You will be surprised at the scantiness of your recollection of them. You have never taken a good look at them, in detail. If this is so, how can you expect to remember the faces of strangers? Begin noticing everyone you meet, and studying features carefully, and then later on taking a pencil and endeavoring to jot down a brief description of their features. This exercise will prove very interesting, and you will notice your rapid improvement from the start.

Another good exercise along this line is to observe the exterior of buildings, in detail. First try to describe some building you pass every day. You will be able to give a fair idea of its general aspect, its shape, color and so on. But how about the number of windows on each floor, the size and location of the doors, the shape of the roof, porch, chimneys, etc. How about the cornices, the trimmings, etc.? And the angles of the roof? You find that you have not really seen the house at all, do you not? You have merely looked at it. Begin now, noticing the buildings on your road, and then later in the day, endeavor to form a mental picture of the details, seeing how many you can remember of image correctly. Next day take the same building and look for new details (you'll find many of them) and keep this up until you know something about the building in question. This is a most valuable exercise for the training of the powers of observation.

Exercise 4

An interesting exercise is to acquire a set of dominoes, and put them all face down on a table in front of you. Turn one over, and attempt to name the sum total of the spots at once, instead of counting them in the ordinary way. Then try two dominos, then three, and so on. With a little practice one can give the sum total of the spots on several dominos almost instantaneously. A variation of this exercise, and one much easier to master, is to turn over a playing card and turn it back face down again, while in the interval naming the color, suit, and number of spots on the card. This may be done rather slowly at first, increasing the speed until you barely catch a glimpse of the card before naming it.

Exercise 5

Many persons are able to practically grasp the meaning of a paragraph of printed matter at a glance. Busy men who read newspapers have this faculty, and men and women employed in journalism are often able to grasp the sense of a page by apparently just glancing at it. Book reviewers also have this faculty. (In fact, judging from the character of some of the reviews in the daily press, the reviewer does not look at the book at all.)[29] Begin by trying to read several words at a glance; then sentences; then several sentences; then a group of sentences; then paragraphs, and so on. In all this work of developing mental faculties, one must proceed as he would were he developing a muscle or set of muscles—by degrees. It is all a matter of practice.

29. Clearly modern book reviewers are following in an old tradition.

COMPLETION EXERCISES:
LIBERATING THE SELF

HESE EXERCISES, like the completion exercises of the preceding grades, are intended to be performed during the transition between this grade and the next. You should begin them when you have finished the other work of this grade.

In the exercises of the preceding grades we have directed your attention to the process of mentally freeing oneself from the restrictions imposed by the illusory identification of the Self with the physical body. If the Practitioner has caught the spirit of these exercises, and has put the same into practice, he will have begun to grasp the reality of a self within him that is not bound to, or limited by, the body of flesh we inherit from our parents, our ancestors, and all the ancestors of humanity back down through the Circle of Abred.

Still, this recognition is only the first step toward freeing the self. Even with a clear awareness of the incorporeal nature of the self, when the awareness is still bound by the illusionary equation of the self with the personality, one fails to realize the truth. Only when the bonds of personality are loosened, does the student begin to realize his true nature.

The "I" recognized by the individual, even faintly, is the conscious recognition of the One Life which is our true and inmost nature. This recognition is mutual, for in it also is comprised the recognition of the individual by the One Life. When we know, recognize and realize the One within us, then the One recognizes us within itself. Thenceforth it remembers us, and the spiritual phase of our evolution begins. In the Circle of Abred, all the activities of the One Life are along subconscious lines. The Being in which we live and move and have our being, knows and is conscious of us, only when we are conscious of that Being within us. The recognition is mutual in consciousness. Correspondingly, as we advance in the great scale of consciousness, we come into a closer recognition and consciousness of the One, and the One comes into a closer recognition and consciousness of us. Finally, at the sunset of the day of manifestation, the Many come to know that they are the One, and the One comes to know itself through the Many.

Just as one is bound by the illusion of the corporeal nature of the "I," so is it further bound—and even more closely bound—by the illusion of the personal nature of the "I." The self is not only more, and greater, than the physical body it uses—but it is also more, and greater, than that part of the mind, consisting of a series of inherited or acquired impressions which constitutes the personality, which we have called the "Me." As already stated, there is a great difference between the Me and the I. The Me is the individual as he thinks he is—a bundle of prejudices, tastes, ties, etc. The I is the individual as he is in reality—a center of pure consciousness free from physical and mental ties of all kinds. The Me is the character being played by the self—the "John Smith" part of him. The "I" is the actor who plays the character. It is often very difficult for one to disentangle and free himself from the overwhelming force of personality, so completely is the average person self-hypnotized and socially hypnotized with the "John Smith" idea. Thoughtful and persistent practice is needed to pass beyond the Me to the I.

Completion Exercise 1

First take up the standard posture of meditation, and perform the usual preliminaries of relaxation and breathing. Then take mental stock of yourself. Ask yourself the question: "What am I?" You will find, upon self-examination, that you considers yourself to be a certain person—"John Smith," for instance, "aged 45, grocer, of Cincinnati, Ohio," or whatever it happens to be. This "John Smith" has a character of his own, which you suppose to be yourself. Laying aside the illusion of the appearance, shape, form, etc., of the body, you will still find that you have decided personal characteristics. You like certain things and hate certain others. Those likes and dislikes, loves and hates, tendencies, general "nature" and "characteristics" are bindings that tie you tightly to the personality. You may imagine that these things are yourself, and that if they were taken away from you, you would cease to exist.

Then proceed as you did when divorcing yourself from the illusion that the self is identical to the physical body. Set aside first one like, and then another—first one hate, and then another. In imagination, visualize yourself as being divested of first one "characteristic" and then another. As the process continues, you will find, possibly to your surprise, that notwithstanding that your most cherished and firmly rooted "characteristics" are sheared away from you, you yourself remain. When all your mental feelings, as well as the objects thereof, are removed from your mental vision, you yourself remain. You will find something remaining that is back of, underneath, and at the center of all these "feelings" and "characteristics," and which persists in full vigor when they have been stripped away from you.

Then, mentally, in imagination, see yourself as acting out other characters. You will find that you can play any number of other characters, as well as you have been playing the old "John Smith" part, which you have been imagining as yourself. You will then see that just as the body was but an instrument and covering, so is this habitual "character" but an instrument and mental covering—useful but not essential to your being—something that can be put on, and taken off—something that could be exchanged without affecting the "I." You will realize that this "character" is but your Me—and that you may have other Mes at will—but the "I" remains the same in each case.

Try as you may, you will never be able to shake off or discard the I. You will find that there is a core to the self that is unchangeable, and cannot be gotten rid of—for it is yourself, your real self—in the language of the Druid mysteries, your elaeth or individuality. You will find this same I always at the center of every "character" you assume—always behind every mask you choose to wear. You will find that it will always be the same I, of which you can always say "I AM." No one can truthfully assert of his real self, "I AM NOT." Such a statement is always a lie upon the face of Truth. One may say "I am not this, or I am not that"—but he can never say of that Central I, that it is not.

This I is always the Actor—the Doer—the Seer—the Thinker. It is always the Center. Divest it of every characteristic, and there will always remain that Something that IS.

This I is absolutely subjective, or inner—all else is objective, or outer, to it. It cannot be identified with any mental state, for all mental states are objective to it. We are each conscious of it, not through any channel of sense, or feeling; rather, its existence impresses itself upon us directly. We cannot separate ourselves from it, for it is the Self, itself. We cannot stand off and examine it, nor set it off for examination—for where it is so must we be, for the two are one. It is never objective to anything else in us, but everything else in us is objective to it. It may, in our ignorance, be mistaken for our feelings, thoughts, sensations, etc., but when we recognize it, it reveals itself as the unchanging witness of all these experiences.

Distinguish this I from all mental characteristics, all thoughts and feelings and sensations, and instead of seeming weakened, it is increased in strength. It then appears as untrammeled, and unrestricted will. It gives and can give, but two reports of itself: it must always, and does always say of itself: "I AM"; it must always say, and does always say, of itself: "I DO." This is all. This is what the I is—the Something that IS, and Something that DOES. All the rest of the mental furniture belongs to the Me, and is changeable, inconstant, and shifting. The I is always the same—there is nothing else for it to be.

By practicing this mental stock-taking, and self-examination, the student will soon be able to at least partially distinguish his I from his Me, at least in imagination, sufficiently to testify to the different nature of the two. Other exercises taught later on in this course will aid in this attainment. This is the foundation of all attainment; it is the one thing, which when found, gives us the key to all the rest.

The following exercise builds on this, and should be practiced once a certain degree of facility has been gained with the first Completion Exercise.

Completion Exercise 2

Once again, take up the standard posture of meditation, and perform the usual preliminaries of relaxation and breathing. Then meditate upon your own identity, as distinguished from the outside objective world. Reach mentally into the very center of your being, where Me gives way to I. In this meditation, repeat softly to yourself your own name—that is, the name which you apply to yourself at times when you think of yourself in the third person. Or else, your favorite "short name" or familiar "nickname," such as "Jim," or "Beth," or "Chris," etc.—in short, the name which you most familiarly identify with yourself.

Let the student repeat this name over and over again, softly, throwing into it his earnest attention as if in that name were contained the secret of his existence. In many cases the student will find that a significant shift of consciousness unfolds as this practice is pursued.

Rudyard Kipling, in his great story already referenced in these lessons, "Kim," speaks of this practice, which is familiar among the Oriental peoples. He describes his hero, Kim, attempting to gain this state of consciousness. We quote from this book, as follows:

A very few white people, but many Asiatics, can throw themselves unto amazement, as it were, by repeating their own names over and over again to themselves, letting the mind go free upon speculation as to what is called personal identity.

"Who is Kim—Kim—Kim?"

He squatted in a corner of the clanging waiting-room, rapt from all other thoughts, hands folded in lap, and pupils contracted to pin-points. In a moment—in another half-second—he felt that he would arrive at the solution of the tremendous puzzle, but here, as always happens, his mind dropped away from those heights with the rush of a wounded bird, and passing his hand before his eyes, he shook his head.

A long-haired Hindu bhairagi[30] who had just bought a ticket, halted before him at that moment, and stared intently. "I also have lost it," he said sadly. "It is one of the gates of the Way."

"What is thy talk?" said Kim, abashed.

"Thou wast wondering there in thy spirit what manner of thing thy soul might be...I know. Who should know but I?"

---

30. *Bhairagi*: holy man.

GRADD YR ATHRONIWR

THE GRADE OF THE PHILOSOPHIZER

INTRODUCTION
TO THE GRADE

WELCOME TO THE FOURTH STAGE of your journey through the Dolmen Arch study course, the Grade of the Philosophizer! This is the final grade of the Lesser Mysteries in this system, and finishes laying the foundations for the Greater Mysteries to come. Its title sounds odd in English, since we are used to the word "philosopher" instead; nonetheless a direct derivation from the verb "to philosophize" is required here, for the work of this grade requires the active application of the intellectual powers.

The mystery teachings of all lands and ages have had an attitude toward the intellect and its activities that may seem paradoxical or even inconsistent at first glance. On the one hand, they have taught that the balanced development of the mind's reasoning powers, and what could once, without fear of misunderstanding, be called a liberal education—that much-misused word "liberal" meaning, as it originally did, "that which is proper to a free person," as distinct from the purely practical training appropriate to the servile state—is an important preparation for the awakening of the higher potentials of the self. It is for this reason, to cite only a single example, that Plato's Academy famously had the words "Let no one ignorant of geometry enter here" above its door.

On the other hand, these same mystery teachings speak with a single voice in proclaiming that the mind's reasoning powers, and the benefits of a broad education, are in no way adequate to the work the mysteries exist to perform. One may possess a brilliant intellect and a familiarity with every branch of learning, without having taken the first step toward the awakening of the individuality, as that term has been defined in these lessons. It is even possible to study the teachings and symbolism of the mysteries for many years without passing beyond their purely intellectual dimensions and using them, as they are meant to be used, as tools for the transformation of personality into individuality.

Still, this apparent paradox is a reflection of the complex nature of human existence. If a man is in poor health as a result of improper diet and inadequate exercise, his capacity to pursue the mystery teachings may be limited by that fact. A change of diet and a habit of daily exercise may well offer him great benefit in his efforts, as well as in his daily life; nonetheless diet and exercise by themselves will not accomplish the work of the mysteries, and an obsessive attention to diet and exercise can be a barrier to attainment in the mysteries if it distracts the attention from the more important work to be done.

The intellectual powers are subject to similar considerations. Most of us provide our minds with only the most inadequate and unhealthy nourishment; to the sensationalistic journalism, cheap literature, and hackneyed and sentimental popular theater that made up the bulk of public entertainment when the materials in this course were originally composed, our age has added the even more dubious fare to be found in movies, television, video games and the internet. Most of us, in turn, too often forget that the mind as well as the body needs healthy exercise, and avoid the labor of sustained and serious thought by accepting opinions and beliefs in predigested form from the swarm of those who, in this age as in every other, have much to gain by encouraging others not to think.

The proper nourishment and exercise of the mind thus provides as many benefits to the student of the mysteries as the proper nourishment and exercise of the body. You are encouraged, as you pursue this and future lessons, to assess how well your current habits of diet and exercise—whether physical or intellectual—further your goals in everyday life as well as in your studies of the Dolmen Arch course. At the same time, these concerns must not distract you from the work of meditation, ceremony, and introspection that develop those potentials of the self that reach beyond mind and body alike.

This lesson packet, like the others you have received, contains seven instructional papers:

Like the lessons of the previous grades, these are to be worked through at your own pace, with the Completion exercises reserved for last. The practical work given in this lesson packet builds on that of the previous grade, and a similar length of time, three or more months, should be allotted to their completion. Once again, remember that rushing through the exercises benefits no one, least of all yourself. A few extra weeks, or even a few extra months, devoted to mastering some exercise that seems more than usually difficult, will pay substantial dividends further along the path.

Wishing you all the best in your journey on the Path of the Druid Mysteries,

 *John Michael Greer*

THE SEVEN COSMIC LAWS

HE FOLLOWING PRINCIPLES, under various expressions and forms, have been taught in the mystery schools of many lands and times. If you have studied other esoteric teachings you may be familiar with these same principles in a different order, or under different names. The expressions used in this course derive, as mentioned earlier, from teachings formulated in the early twentieth century, and those familiar with the esoteric literature of that time will find close parallels in other traditions, some of them apparently unrelated to Druidry. This is as it should be, for the Druid mysteries are not a thing apart, unrelated to other mystery schools; they are a particular expression, in the language of a given place and time, of insights that transcend place and time and are common to all of humanity.

It is worth repeating here what was said in an earlier lesson about the teachings of the Druid mysteries: they are not arbitrary statements meant to be believed, but rather practical tools that have been crafted so that they can be used. The seven cosmic laws or creative principles are not statements of fact about the universe. Rather, they are viewpoints from which the Cosmos can be experienced and understood, and they bring in their train practical applications of a myriad kinds. As you read each of them, take a moment to think about their implications. What would you become—what would the Cosmos around you be like—if you began to experience the Cosmos in terms of these seven principles?

THE SEVEN COSMIC LAWS OR CREATIVE PRINCIPLES

I. The Principle of Unity. This principle holds that all things in the Cosmos are fundamentally One Thing, for all that partakes of form, energy, and life is an expression of the One Life under Awen. Thus everything from galaxies to atoms partakes of a common unity, and shares in a common life. Nothing in the Cosmos has its own separate origin or destiny, nor is there any division or separation between one thing and any other thing, for all things are One. The right understanding of this principle is the key to the secret of creative force.

II. The Principle of Polarity. This principle holds that everything has its opposite; everything is, and is not, at the same time; everything has its other side; every thesis has its antithesis; every truth contains a bit of untruth, and every untruth a bit of truth; every male contains the female and every female contains the male. It also teaches that opposite things are alike in the end; that extremes meet; that all contradictions may be reconciled. In this great cosmic law is found the fact that what humanity perceives as diametrically opposite things in the planes of matter, life, and mind, are in reality but the different poles of the same thing. In this principle is found the mystery of sex and the hidden laws of generation and regeneration.

III. The Principle of Balance. This principle teaches that a universal equilibrium, compensation and balance exists throughout all of the manifestations of the Cosmos. One thing balances another throughout all the realms of matter, energy, and life. Everything has something set opposite it, to balance it. Everything has its compensation. Everything has its cosmic price. In an understanding of this principle is found the secret of power and poise.

IV. The Principle of Causation. This principle teaches that nothing anywhere in the Cosmos happens by chance. Nothing happens without a preceding manifestation, and a following manifestation. Everything comes from what is before it and creates what comes after. Nothing is independent of what has gone before, nor can it avoid acting upon that which comes after. Everything proceeds from something, and is succeeded by something. From mastery of the principle of Causality comes the knowledge of destiny and the proper guidance of power.

V. The Principle of Vibration. This principle reveals that everything is in constant vibration, and upon its rate or mode of vibration depends its relationships with everything else in the Cosmos. All is in vibration—matter, life, and mind all have their own rate of vibration, and each degree of manifestation within the three principles also has a unique rate of vibration by which it may be known, summoned, or banished. Vibration is the key of relative power, and relative activities. To rightly grasp this principle is to become the master of all the forces of the universe.

VI. The Principle of Correspondence. This principle reveals the analogy and agreement between all of the various forms of manifestation. What is true of the atom, is true of the sun. What is true of the amoeba is true of humanity, and of beings whose capabilities surpass those of humanity to the same degree that humanity surpasses the amoeba. What is true of matter, is likewise true of energy and life. To know one is to know all. By knowing one thing, the Druids teach, you may know all other things. This law is applied in studying the higher planes; they may be known by the lower, just as the substances that make up the Sun's physical body can be known by studying the behavior of matter here on Earth. In this principle is the secret of universal wisdom.

VII. The Principle of Circularity. This principle teaches that the essential shape of all motion and change, in the realms of matter, energy, and life, is circular. Everything moves in circles. Worlds and atoms, Cosmos and man, all are under this law, and move in accordance therewith. The wise and strong, however, convert their own circles into spirals; instead of traveling around in an eternal circle, they rise in spirals to attainment and advancement. To convert the circle into the spiral is one of the great secrets of Druidry, conveyed in the practical formulae of our mystery teachings.

The Meaning of the Principles

To many people, these principles seem like abstractions removed from the realities of daily life, but it is important to move beyond this misjudgment and grasp the principles as the tools they are. Each of the principles has direct practical application; any one of them, explored thoroughly in meditation and put to use in your life, will lead to remarkable transformations in you and the world as you experience it; all of them taken together, explored and then embraced by a mind trained according to the methods of the Druid wisdom, will throw open portal after portal, opening onto unimaginable vistas.

All seven of the principles are meant to be used, and used in the realm of ordinary life. By learning them, understanding them, and putting them to use, you can recognize your oneness with sources of power and life throughout the Cosmos; master the hidden energies and processes of generation and regeneration; balance opposing forces against one another to achieve inner and outer poise; take advantage of causality and thus become fate's master rather than her slave; learn to attune yourself to healing and empowering patterns of vibration, instead of those that bring frustration and unhappiness; read the language of correspondences written throughout the worlds of matter, life, and mind, and decode the messages they have for you; and convert circles in your life into rising spirals that will take you to places and experiences you can hardly dream of attaining today.

Do these promises sound extravagant? They are nothing of the kind. They are the gifts and the powers that occult and esoteric teachings have always offered freely to those willing to take up the work of the Mysteries.

Most people, today as in ancient times, believe that the world around them is the source of the limitations that restrict the attainments possible to them in this life. Under the spell of this belief, they direct all their efforts toward changing the world so that it will give them what they desire. Most of them fail, and even those that succeed in imposing their will on the world around them find themselves cheated by success. Think of the people who have won great wealth and power in their lives, those whose names and images fill the front pages of newspapers. How many of them have achieved happiness? How many, when they come to the end of their lives, are secure, beloved, and at peace?

All these efforts fail because they are misdirected. What keeps most people from achieving their goals and fulfilling their dreams is not somewhere out in the world around them, but within them. Misdirected and self-defeating patterns of perceiving, desiring, thinking, and remembering keep them trudging in unproductive circles. These patterns are not forced upon their victims, but embraced by them as truth. Very many people, indeed, will argue fiercely for the very habits that are frustrating their fondest hopes and crushing their most deeply held aspirations.

To those who are willing to make the effort to rise above these limits, come the teachings of the Mysteries of every land and age, and among these the Druid mysteries hold an honored place. The Mystery teachings seek to awaken the immense potentials for power and wisdom that lie slumbering within every human soul. They seek to inspire the soul with broader conceptions of human possibility; to educate desire, so that it aims at those things that conduce to happiness rather than suffering; to train the mind to achieve a far greater share of its capacity for understanding and knowledge; and, in sum, to provide tools and instructions whereby each initiate may craft his or her own future self.

THE AWAKENING OF
THE DRAGONS

HE WORK OF ESTABLISHING the three currents of the One Life in the three cauldrons or psychic centers in the body, as presented in the previous lesson of this course, has great value in its own right; practiced regularly, it benefits mental, emotional, and physical health, and brings the whole self into harmony with the flow of nwyfre through the Cosmos. Still, this work is also one step along a path begun with your first performance of the Elemental Cross—a path which leads to capacities of action and perception. The next step in that path calls upon manifestations of the One Life that have not yet been discussed in these lessons.

As they flow through the Cosmos, the two primary currents of nwyfre discussed in the previous lesson—the solar and telluric currents—set in motion secondary currents in all things. Examine anything on any plane of being and you will inevitably find two forces maintaining that thing in being; one of these forces has an affinity with the solar current, the other with the telluric current. Much of the traditional lore of magic and the mysteries has, at its root, the art of making use of these secondary or reflected currents on the three planes of being. Each mystery tradition has its own preferred medium or matrix in which these secondary currents are to be found; in this tradition of the Druid mysteries, these are the human body and the land itself.

The reflected currents are described in Druid lore as two dragons, a red dragon representing the reflected solar current and a white dragon representing the reflected telluric current. In the land, these two dragons follow the lines of hills, ridges and mountains, in the case of the red dragon, and valleys, lowlands and watercourses, in the case of the white; in the human body, they twine around the midline of the body, rising from the point of contact between the body and the earth to the Moon Cauldron or psychic center within the head.

When the dragons are properly awakened in the land, the threefold gifts of peace, equity and abundance result; when they are properly awakened in the individual, the threefold powers of healing, enchantment, and initiation come within reach. Most of the practical work of the Greater Mysteries depends on the regular practice of this and the preceding stages of the Sphere of Protection working. The following exercise will help you establish the two dragons or reflected currents in balanced disposition within your body. It should be performed in the Sphere of Protection ritual, immediately following the establishment of the three cauldrons as described in your previous grade, and is done as follows.

The Awakening of the Dragons

Begin by performing the Sphere of Protection as you did while working in the previous grade. When you reach the invocations of spirit, awaken the Three Cauldrons; now and in the future, it will be sufficient to breathe nwyfre into each cauldron three times, in place of nine.

When you finish this stage, turn your attention to the heavens high above you. Imagine the Sun at zenith far above your head. As you draw in a breath, imagine a ray of light streaming straight down from the Sun to you. It passes through the center of your head and through each of the cauldrons, and as you breathe out, it continues down to the center of the earth. Repeat this same image a total of nine times, on nine breaths.

Then clasp your hands over your cauldron of the earth, an inch below your navel, and hold your elbows a little out and rounded. Make sure your knees are slightly bent and your weight rests equally on both feet. These details of posture help guide the currents through your enaid and physical body along the proper paths.

Next, turn your attention to the earth below your feet. Reach deep into the earth with your imagination, and picture the heart of the earth ablaze with light. From that deep source of light, imagine two currents of nwyfre rising up, one red and one white, like twin serpents or dragons. The red one rises until its head is just below the sole of your right foot, and the white to just below the sole of your left foot.

Next, bring the red current up through your right leg and the white current through your left leg, and draw them into your cauldron of the earth. The two currents cross there, so that the white current flows to your right side and the red to your left. They flow into your arms, curve out and then back in, and flow into your cauldron of the sun. Here they cross again, so that the red is again on the right and the white on the left. The two currents arc up the sides of your head and neck and flow into your cauldron of the moon. Here they fuse in a blaze of pure light.

Repeat this upward motion of the two currents three times in all. It often works best to take two breaths in the course of each upward movement—breathing in as the currents flow up your legs to the cauldron of the earth; out as they flow out and back inwards to the cauldron of the sun; in again as they flow out and back inwards to the cauldron of the moon; out again as they fuse and fill the cauldron of the moon with blinding light. If you need to take more breaths, however, by all means do so. The goal of the ritual is to get the imagery and flow of the rising dragons firmly established, not to get it done quickly.

When the dragons have risen to your cauldron of the moon three times, allow the drop of light to fall from the moon cauldron to the solar plexus as before, then go on to the circulation of light and closing as usual. If you feel dizzy after the practice, as many students do the first few times they perform this practice, eat something as soon as possible to refocus your consciousness on the material world.

Perform this ritual daily as part of your Sphere of Protection during the time you spend on this grade, and keep detailed notes on your experiences in your practice journal.

AWAKENING THE
INNER POWER

T SEVERAL POINTS in these lessons, the arts of healing, enchantment, and initiation have been mentioned as the particular disciplines and practical arts exercised by an initiate of the Dolmen Arch. Much of the work you have done heretofore in these lessons has been concerned with laying the foundations and developing the inward capacities needed for these arts. The lessons of this grade are meant to conclude that work of preparation.

This paper therefore communicates several practices directed toward this end. The point of these practices, and their relationship to the purposes just mentioned, may not be immediately clear to you. Nonetheless, you are asked to work at them regularly during the time you spend in this grade. They form a valuable part of your preparation for the Greater Mysteries.

THE GRAND PSYCHIC BREATH

The following breathing exercise, known as "The Grand Psychic Breath," was once widely taught in mystery schools across much of the Western world. The details of the exercise are variously given by different writers, but the following form includes all of the important elements and movements, and is less technical than some other forms. In this exercise, the various parts of the body are charged with nwyfre by way of a special form of breathing, as you will see as you proceed. Its effect has been stated as "a general house-cleaning of the nervous system." Its relation to the solar plexus exercises given in the previous lesson of this course will be clear to you after a few repetitions, if not before.

The Grand Psychic Breath should not be done within an hour of eating a meal, and is best done either early in the morning or just before going to bed.

Begin by lying at ease in a relaxed position, your arms at your sides and your legs comfortably extended. No part of your body should lie across any other part; in particular, your arms and legs should not be crossed, as this interferes with the free flow of nwyfre. Your clothing should be loose and comfortable; tight belts and tight bras are particularly to be avoided.

Once you are comfortably settled in your position, breathe tranquilly, easily, and rhythmically through your nose for a few moments, leaving the mouth closed, until the breath rhythm is secured and becomes regular. Then as you inhale and exhale, imagine that the current of breath is being drawn in and then breathed out through various parts of your body, in the way you learned to imagine breath moving in and out of your solar plexus. Draw in and breathe out one breath each through the following parts of your body, in the following order:

(a) the bones of the legs;

(b) the bones of the arms;

(c) the top of the skull;

(d) the pit of the stomach;

(e) the reproductive organs;

(f) as though the breath were travelling up and down the spinal column, descending from the top of the skull to the tailbone on the inbreath, and then rising again from the tailbone to the top of the skull on the outbreath;

(g) as though inhaling and then exhaling through every pore of the skin.

When this is finished, keep breathing rhythmically, and imagine nwyfre flowing in from the universe around you to the following nervous centers of the body on each inbreath, and radiating from the same centers on each outbreath; give each center three such breaths. The centers are worked in this way in the following order:

(a) the forehead;

(b) the back of the head;

(c) the base of the brain, around the atlas vertebra where the spine meets the skull;

(d) the solar plexus;

(e) the sacrum and tailbone, at the base of the spine;

(f) the region of the navel;

(g) the reproductive organs.

Conclude this process by sweeping the entire body with currents of nwyfre, descending from head to toes on the inbreath, and ascending from toes to head on the outbreath. Do this seven times. Finish with one cycle of the same cleansing breath you use at the beginning and end of meditation.

SEVEN NWYFRE EXERCISES

These seven exercises were likewise taught in many mystery schools in earlier times. They should not be done within an hour of eating a meal, and have the most salutary effects when practiced in the morning, shortly after waking.

Each of these exercises depends on a particular kind of full or complete breathing, which exercises all the muscles of the trunk. To learn this form of breathing, lie upon your back on a comfortable surface, such as a bed. Place one hand upon your chest and the other upon your belly. Breathe in, and so direct the movements of the breath that your belly is pushed out first and your chest afterwards. Hold the breath for a short time, and then exhale, directing the movement so that your belly descends to its resting position first, and the chest afterwards. Repeat this, slowly and gently, until you have established a rhythm, and the breath appears to rise in a wave from the pit of your stomach to the top of your chest, and then recede in a wave that moves in the same direction, from bottom to top. This is the complete breath, and should be used in each of the following exercises.

In performing the exercises, you will at times need to hold your breath. This is to be done by holding the chest expanded and the diaphragm down, and not by closing the throat; the latter can cause damage to the sensitive tissues of the lungs. If you find your throat closing by habit, you can prevent it from doing so, when you reach the end of the inhalation, by continuing to try to breathe in even though your lungs are full. Do this gently, with just enough pressure to keep your throat open.

To begin the exercises themselves, stand upright with your feet parallel and about a foot distant from each other, your knees slightly bent, your arms hanging comfortably by your sides, and your spine straight without being stiff. This is the beginning position for each of the following movements.

Exercise 1

Draw in a complete breath slowly and steadily through the nose. Once you have finished inhaling it, hold it for as long as is comfortable. Then exhale vigorously through your mouth. Breathe in normally, and breathe out using the same cleansing breath you use to begin and end meditation.

Exercise 2

Draw in another complete breath through the nose, and hold it as before. While holding it, make your hands into loose fists and drum gently all over your chest, sides, shoulders, and upper back. (Women practicing this exercise should refrain from drumming on their breasts, but should be sure to drum just beneath them and immediately to the sides.) Then exhale vigorously through your mouth. Breathe in normally, and breathe out with the cleansing breath.

Exercise 3

Draw in another complete breath through the nose, and hold it. While holding the breath, sweep your arms slowly upward and outward from your sides, holding them straight but without tension, and let them rise up until your hands touch well above your head. Then let them descend slowly to your sides. Repeat this as many times as you can before holding your breath becomes uncomfortable. When finished, exhale vigorously through your mouth. Breathe in normally, and breathe out with the cleansing breath.

Exercise 4

Draw in another complete breath through the nose, and hold it. While holding the breath, bring your arms up in front until they extend straight out before you, palms facing one another. Slowly swing them outward to the sides until they are as far back as they can go, and then return them to their position out in front of you. Repeat this as many times as you can before holding your breath becomes uncomfortable. When finished, exhale vigorously through your mouth. Breathe in normally, and breathe out with the cleansing breath.

Exercise 5

Draw in another complete breath through the nose, and hold it. While holding the breath, bring your arms up in front until they extend straight out before you, palms facing one another, as in exercise 4. Then bend your elbows and draw your hands straight back to your sides, forming them into fists with a muscular effort, and turning them palms up. Push them forward again, relaxing the hands and returning to the position in front of you. Repeat this as many times as you can before holding your breath becomes uncomfortable. When finished, exhale vigorously through your mouth. Breathe in normally, and breathe out with the cleansing breath.

Exercise 6

Draw in another complete breath through the nose, and hold it. While holding the breath, place your hands on your hips as though grasping your sides, fingers forward and thumbs back. Bend forward at the waist, keeping your legs and hips steady, and breathing out through your mouth as you bend. Straighten up, inhaling as you do so, and then bend backward from the waist, keeping your legs and hips steady, and breathing out through your mouth as you bend. Straighten up, inhaling as you do so, and then bend to the right side, keeping your legs and hips steady, and breathing out through your mouth as you bend. Straighten up, inhaling as you do so, and then bend to the left side, again keeping your legs and hips steady, and breathing out through your mouth as you bend. Straighten up, inhaling as you do so, and breathe out with the cleansing breath.

Exercise 7

Draw in another complete breath through the nose, but instead of drawing it in steadily, do it in little "sniffs." Do not exhale between sniffs; instead, add one to another until your lungs are full. Hold briefly and then exhale vigorously through your mouth. Breathe in normally, and breathe out with the cleansing breath.

These exercises have a potent effect on the lungs, cleansing them of stale air and strengthening both the lung tissues themselves and the muscles throughout the trunk that assist breathing. They also increase the amount of nwyfre circulated through the body to many times that found in most people. Both these effects can be challenging for the unprepared body. For this reason, you are advised to begin by practicing these exercises once a week, and over the course of the three months you spend in this grade, work up to practicing them daily.

AWAKENING THE PALM CENTERS

Much of the practical work of the grades to come depends on the awakening of energy centers located in the palm of each hand. These centers are awakened in the following manner.

Once each day, preferably at the conclusion of your daily meditation, trace an inverted triangle on the palm of your left hand with the index finger of your right hand. Start the triangle at the base of your left palm just above the wrist-lines below your palm. Trace the triangle from there to the base of your left index finger, across to the base of your left little finger, and back to the point of beginning. Imagine yourself drawing this triangle in bright blue light, and when your finger returns to the point of beginning, imagine the triangle filled with the same blue light. This triangle, as in the Sphere of Protection ritual, represents the element of Water.

Next, still using your right index finger, draw a circle on the palm of your left hand. The circle begins at the initial point of the triangle and surrounds the entire palm. Imagine yourself drawing this circle in bright green light. When the finger returns to the point where it began, draw a straight line from there up your wrist about as long as your palm is tall. Bring your right index finger back to the point of origination for both symbols and imagine green light filling the circle. This green circle with its descending line, as in the Sphere of Protection ritual, represents the element of Earth.

Continue the process by tracing an upright triangle on the palm of your right hand with your left index finger. Start the triangle at a point just below the gap between your ring and middle fingers. Trace the triangle down to the base of your thumb, straight across to the outside edge of your palm, and back to the point of beginning. Imagine yourself drawing this triangle in bright red light; then place the point of your left index finger at the base of the triangle, just above your wrist, and imagine the triangle filled with the same red light. This triangle, as in the Sphere of Protection ritual, represents the element of Fire.

Next, still using your left index finger, draw a circle on the palm of your right hand, starting at the same point where you began the triangle and surrounding the entire palm. Imagine yourself drawing the circle in bright yellow light. When the finger returns to the point where it began, draw a straight line from there up between and to the tips of your second and third fingers. Place the tip of your left index finger on the base of your right palm—at a place equivalent to the one where you started the symbols on the right hand—and fill the circle with yellow light. The yellow circle with its ascending line, as in the Sphere of Protection ritual, represents the element of Air.

An esoteric teaching is hidden in these symbolic gestures. The right hand, which is symbolically related to the solar current, is used to awaken the center of the left hand, and the left hand, which is symbolically related to the telluric (earth) current, is used to awaken the right hand. Each hand transmits energy to the other, and the energies are of opposite polarity but equal power.

When you have traced the symbols on your hands, bring your hands together with the base of each palm pressed against the other. The fingers of the left hand should point forward, along a horizontal axis, while the fingers of the right

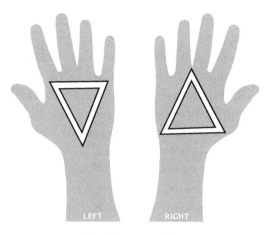

Fig. 25. *The Palm Centers of Water & Fire*

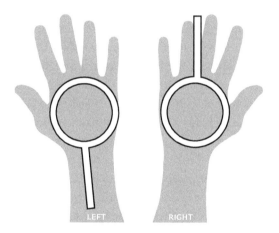

Fig. 26. *The Palm Centers of Earth & Air*

hand should point upwards, along a vertical axis. Hold them in this position while breathing slowly and evenly for a time, then rotate the fingers of the left hand to point upwards, separate the hands, and clap them together once, crisply and forcefully. This seals the energy centers and makes it possible for you to go about your day without leaking energy through your palm centers.

Charging the Palm Centers

When you have practiced awakening the palm centers daily for two or three weeks and the process is familiar to you, you may begin to charge the palm centers. This is done by awakening the centers and then drawing in nwyfre from the material elements.

Begin with the element of water. This is best done by a stream, river, lake, or seacoast, where water flows naturally; it can also be done during rainfall or, if no other option is available, by turning on a cold water tap and allowing the water to flow freely for a minute or so before beginning. Charging should never be done in the presence of stagnant or seriously polluted water, which would have negative consequences to the practitioner's health.

Perform the awakening process, tracing all four elemental symbols on the palms, then holding the palms together as just described and breathing slowly and steadily for a time. Then separate the hands, without clapping; let the right hand fall to the side, and extend the left palm toward the water. It should not actually touch the water, but for best results it should be close enough that you can feel the cooling effect of the water on the skin of your palm.

Now breathe in, imagining blue water energy flowing into your palm and charging it. Breathe out and visualize the charge remaining in your palm. Repeat this process three times the first time you practice this exercise, and then nine times thereafter. When you are finished, pause for a time, feeling the presence of the water energy in your palm, and then reverse the process: breathe in, feeling the water energy in your palm but not drawing any more in, and breathe out, imagining the water energy flowing out of your palm. Repeat this breathing out of the water energy as many times as you repeated the process of breathing it in; at the end of the process, all the water energy will have left your palm. When you are done, bring the energy centers at the base of your palms together, turn the left fingers upward, and clap once to seal the centers.

Next, on the same day or another, do the same process with the element of earth. This may be done with a large stone, especially a natural outcropping still rooted in the ground, or with fertile soil. It should not be done in any place where the soil has been damaged or polluted by human mishandling. The process is exactly the same as charging with the element of water.

The next step is to charge your right palm with the element of fire. You may use a flame of any size, from a candle flame to a bonfire, for this charging. Use the right palm instead of the left; except for this, the process is done exactly the same way as charging with water or earth.

Finally, charge your right palm with the element of air. This should be done with the wind; once you have awakened the energy centers by tracing the four symbols in your palms and holding the energy centers together for a time, raise your right hand into the air, your palm facing into the wind, and charge the palm with air energy from the wind. Use exactly the same process as you did with water, earth, and fire.

You should charge your palm centers at least three times with each of the four elements during the three months you spend on this grade. More than this is not necessary, but if you can manage more, it will benefit you in the work of the grades to come.

THE MABINOGION: MATH SON OF MATHONWY

HE FOURTH AND FINAL BRANCH of the Mabinogion is the richest and most complex of the Branches, as it not only completes the story of Pryderi the Mabon, but brings in an entire additional symbolism that frames the events of the other three Branches as a process of initiation. Thus in one sense, the events of this Branch reprise the seasonal cycle from *Calan Haf* (Belteinne, May 1) to *Calan Gaeaf* (Samhuinn, November 1) as represented in the heavens, mirroring the Third Branch's expression of the same half of the year on earth; in another sense, they trace the last portion of the life of Pryderi son of Pwyll, Lord of Dyfed, ending in his death in battle; yet on a deeper and a more important level, they describe the process of his initiation, and recapitulate the whole cycle of the year and of life of the Mabon Pryderi who becomes the Og Llew.

Among the oldest symbols of initiation is that of death and rebirth. The initiator is the slayer and the reviver of the candidate, who sheds the personality he has worn in the outer world and passes through a transition akin to the one that waits for all of us after death, before taking on a new form more appropriate to his awakening individuality. This happens in its proper order to Pryderi the Mabon, who is killed and reborn as Llew the Og: "anxiety," the literal meaning of the name Pryderi, has become "Lion," the Sun-symbol of the ancient mysteries. In his new character as an initiate, Llew must confront a series of challenges, culminating in a second experience of death, transformation and rebirth.

His first death delivers him from the outer world and makes him an initiate of the Lesser Mysteries; the challenges he is given by Arianrhod, "Silver Wheel," the goddess of the lunar current, represent the stages of the Lesser Mysteries that follow the first initiation; while his second death and rebirth recapitulates the whole cycle of the year, brings him into the Greater Mysteries, and gives him that kingship over himself that is the gift of all true initiation.

Yet the story told in this Branch does not begin with Llew, or even with Pryderi, but with Math son of Mathonwy, the wizard-king of North Wales, and the troubled affairs of his court. There are deep teachings hidden in the events that lead to the death of Pryderi and the birth of Llew, and the transformations of Gwydion and Gilfaethwy that follow. In particular, it is important to keep in mind that Gwydion, Llew's initiator, is far from perfect, and takes on the task of initiation at least in part to atone for his role in a terrible crime. In the story of Gwydion and Gilfaethwy are represented some part of the transformations of the soul as it contends with its own weaknesses and begins the path that leads to wisdom; in that story, Math functions as initiator, and then transmits that role to Gwydion.

Much is also woven into the relationship between Llew, his magically created bride Blodeuwedd, and his slayer and eventual victim Gronw, lord of the neighboring province of Penllyn. The part of the tale that begins with Llew's marriage to Blodeuwedd is full of references to the other branches of the Mabinogion— for example, the first appearance of Gronw in the tale is meant to hearken back to the hunting scene that opens the First Branch, with Gronw's behavior toward Blodeuwedd thus placed in strong contrast with that of Pwyll at Arawn's court. The very ancient mythic imagery of the contest of summer and winter for the living Earth is played out here as an initiation ritual in which, as normally happens in ceremonial enactments of the Greater Mysteries, the candidate takes on the role of the Summer King, undergoes a ceremonial death and transformation, and then is restored to life.

The translation that follows is again that of Lady Charlotte Guest, but has been corrected—as was the First Branch—to include a few details that were considered indelicate in her time but are necessary to the meaning of the tale.

MATH SON OF MATHONWY

Math the son of Mathonwy[1] was lord over Gwynedd, and Pryderi the son of Pwyll was lord over the one-and-twenty Cantrefs of the South; and these were

---

1. *Math son of Mathonwy*: "Treasure, son of Treasure-ruler."

the seven Cantrefs of Dyved, and the seven Cantrefs of Morganwg, the four Cantrefs of Ceredigiawn, and the three of Ystrad Tywi.[2]

At that time, Math the son of Mathonwy could not exist unless his feet were in the lap of a maiden, except only when he was prevented by the tumult of war. Now the maiden who was with him was Goewin,[3] the daughter of Pebin[4] of Dôl Pebin, in Arfon,[5] and she was the fairest maiden of her time who was known there.

And Math dwelt always at Caer Dathyl,[6] in Arfon, and was not able to go the circuit of the land, but Gilfaethwy[7] the son of Don, and Eneyd[8] the son of Don, his nephews, the sons of his sisters, with his household, went the circuit of the land in his stead.

Now the maiden was with Math continually, and Gilfaethwy the son of Don set his affections upon her, and loved her so that he knew not what he should do because of her, and therefrom behold his hue, and his aspect, and his spirits changed for love of her, so that it was not easy to know him.

One day his brother Gwydion[9] gazed steadfastly upon him. "Youth," said he, "what aileth thee?"

"Why," replied he, "what seest thou in me?"

"I see," said he, "that thou hast lost thy aspect and thy hue; what, therefore, aileth thee?"

"My lord brother," he answered, "that which aileth me, it will not profit me that I should own to any."

"What may it be, my soul?" said he.

---

2. Notice that the fourteen Cantrefs Pryderi ruled at the end of the First Branch have now become twenty-one; that is, he rules the seven aspects of himself in all three realms of being. The place names are actual locations in southern Wales.

3. *Goewin*: "lively, sprightly."

4. *Pebin*: "staunch, sturdy."

5. *Arfon*: one of the ancient provinces of northern Wales, its name means "over the isle of Anglesey."

6. *Caer Dathyl*: "Castle of Rejoicing."

7. *Gilfaethwy*: appropriately enough, "hidden weakness."

8. *Eneyd*: an older spelling of the word *enaid*, the body of Nwyfre. The meaning here is that Math's mind and spirit have risen to the spiritual realms, while his passions (Gilfaethwy) and life force (Eneyd) are still manifested on Earth.

9. *Gwydion*: traditionally, a punning name meant to suggest the Welsh words *gwyddon*, "loremaster," and *gwydiau*, "vices." The appropriateness of this double meaning will be clear as the story unfolds.

"Thou knowest," he said, "that Math the son of Mathonwy has this property, that if men whisper together, in a tone how low soever, if the wind meet it, it becomes known unto him."

"Yes," said Gwydion, "hold now thy peace, I know thy intent, thou lovest Goewin."

When he found that his brother knew his intent, he gave the heaviest sigh in the world.

"Be silent, my soul, and sigh not," he said.

"It is not thereby that thou wilt succeed. I will cause," said he, "if it cannot be otherwise, the rising of Gwynedd, and Powys, and Deheubarth,[10] to seek the maiden. Be thou of glad cheer therefore, and I will compass it."

So they went unto Math the son of Mathonwy.

"Lord," said Gwydion, "I have heard that there have come to the South some beasts, such as were never known in this island before."

"What are they called?" he asked.

"Pigs, lord."

"And what kind of animals are they?"

"They are small animals, and their flesh is better than the flesh of oxen."

"They are small, then?"

"And they change their names. Swine are they now called."

"Who owneth them?"

"Pryderi the son of Pwyll; they were sent him from Annwn, by Arawn the king of Annwn, and still they keep that name, half hog, half pig."

"Verily," asked he, "and by what means may they be obtained from him?"

"I will go, lord, as one of twelve, in the guise of bards, to seek the swine."

"But it may be that he will refuse you," said he.

"My journey will not be evil, lord," said he; "I will not come back without the swine."

"Gladly," said he, "go thou forward."

So he and Gilfaethwy went, and ten other men with them. And they came into Ceredigiawn, to the place that is now called Rhuddlan Teifi,[11] where the

---

10. The three parts of Wales. Gwydion is prepared to plunge all of Wales into war to help his brother force himself on Goewin.

11. *Rhuddlan Teifi*: "The red shore of the river Teifi." The journey has reached the world of physical incarnation.

palace of Pryderi was. In the guise of bards they came in, and they were received joyfully, and Gwydion was placed beside Pryderi that night.

"Of a truth," said Pryderi, "gladly would I have a tale from some of your men yonder."

"Lord," said Gwydion, "we have a custom that the first night that we come to the court of a great man, the chief of song recites. Gladly will I relate a tale." Now Gwydion was the best teller of tales in the world, and he diverted all the Court that night with pleasant discourse and with tales, so that he charmed every one in the Court, and it pleased Pryderi to talk with him.

And after this, "Lord," said he unto Pryderi, "were it more pleasing to thee, that another should discharge my errand unto thee, than that I should tell thee myself what it is?"

"No," he answered, "ample speech hast thou."

"Behold then, lord," said he, "my errand. It is to crave from thee the animals that were sent thee from Annwn."

"Verily," he replied, "that were the easiest thing in the world to grant, were there not a covenant between me and my land concerning them. And the covenant is that they shall not go from me, until they have produced double their number in the land."

"Lord," said he, "I can set thee free from those words, and this is the way I can do so; give me not the swine tonight, neither refuse them unto me, and tomorrow I will show thee an exchange for them."

And that night he and his fellows went unto their lodging, and they took counsel.

"Ah, my men," said he, "we shall not have the swine for the asking."

"Well," said they, "how may they be obtained?"

"I will cause them to be obtained," said Gwydion.

Then he betook himself to his arts, and began to work a charm. And he caused twelve chargers to appear, and twelve black greyhounds, each of them white-breasted, and having upon them twelve collars and twelve leashes, such as no one that saw them could know to be other than gold. And upon the horses twelve saddles, and every part which should have been of iron was entirely of gold, and the bridles were of the same workmanship. And with the horses and the dogs he came to Pryderi.

"Good day unto thee, lord," said he.

"Heaven prosper thee," said the other, "and greetings be unto thee."

"Lord," said he, "behold here is a release for thee from the word which thou spakest last evening concerning the swine; that thou wouldst neither give nor sell them. Thou mayest exchange them for that which is better. And I will give these twelve horses, all caparisoned as they are, with their saddles and their bridles, and these twelve greyhounds, with their collars and their leashes as thou seest, and the twelve gilded shields that thou beholdest yonder." Now these he had formed of fungus.

"Well," said he, "we will take counsel." And they consulted together, and determined to give the swine to Gwydion, and to take his horses and his dogs and his shields.

Then Gwydion and his men took their leave, and began to journey forth with the pigs.

"Ah, my comrades," said Gwydion, "it is needful that we journey with speed. The illusion will not last but from the one hour to the same to-morrow."

And that night they journeyed as far as the upper part of Ceredigiawn, to the place which, from that cause, is called Mochdref[12] still. And the next day they took their course through Melenydd, and came that night to the town which is likewise for that reason called Mochdrev between Keri and Arwystli. And thence they journeyed forward; and that night they came as far as that Commot in Powys, which also upon account thereof is called Mochnant,[13] and there tarried they that night. And they journeyed thence to the Cantref of Rhos, and the place where they were that night is still called Mochdrev.

"My men," said Gwydion, "we must push forward to the fastnesses of Gwynedd with these animals, for there is a gathering of hosts in pursuit of us." So they journeyed on to the highest town of Arllechwedd,[14] and there they made a sty for the swine, and therefore was the name of Creuwyryon[15] given to that town. And after they had made the sty for the swine, they proceeded to Math the son of Mathonwy, at Caer Dathyl. And when they came there, the country was rising. "What news is there here?" asked Gwydion.

"Pryderi is assembling one-and-twenty Cantrefs to pursue after you," answered they. "It is marvellous that you should have journeyed so slowly."

---

12. *Mochdref*: "Pig Town."

13. *Mochnant*: "Pig River." The other names in this paragraph, like these, are actual places in Wales.

14. This is near Harlech, where the action of the Second Branch began.

15. *Creuwyryon*: "Gwydion's Sty."

"Where are the animals whereof you went in quest?" said Math.

"They have had a sty made for them in the other Cantref below," said Gwydion.

Thereupon, lo, they heard the trumpets and the host in the land, and they arrayed themselves and set forward and came to Penardd in Arfon.

And at night Gwydion the son of Don, and Gilfaethwy his brother, returned to Caer Dathyl; and Gilfaethwy took Math the son of Mathonwy's couch. And while he turned out the other damsels from the room discourteously, he made Goewin unwillingly remain.

And when they saw the day on the morrow, they went back unto the place where Math the son of Mathonwy was with his host; and when they came there, the warriors were taking counsel in what district they should await the coming of Pryderi, and the men of the South. So they went in to the council. And it was resolved to wait in the strongholds of Gwynedd, in Arfon. So within the two Maenors they took their stand, Maenor Penardd and Maenor Coed Alun.[16] And there Pryderi attacked them, and there the combat took place. And great was the slaughter on both sides; but the men of the South were forced to flee. And they fled unto the place which is still called Nantcall.[17] And thither did they follow them, and they made a vast slaughter of them there, so that they fled again as far as the place called Dol Pen Maen,[18] and there they halted and sought to make peace.

And that he might have peace, Pryderi gave hostages, Gwrgi Gwastra[19] gave he and three-and-twenty others, sons of nobles. And after this they journeyed in peace even unto Traeth Mawr;[20] but as they went on together towards Melenryd,[21] the men on foot could not be restrained from shooting. Pryderi dispatched unto Math an embassy to pray him to forbid his people, and to leave it between him and Gwydion the son of Don, for that he had caused all this. And the messengers came to Math.

---

16. *Maenor Penardd* and *Maenor Coed Alun*: These are "the manor of the chief garden" and "the manor of the wood of harmony" respectively.

17. *Nantcall*: "Valley of the Wise."

18. *Dol Pen Maen*: "Vale of the Stone Head."

19. *Gwrgi Gwastra*: "Human Flesh, the Leveler." Pryderi has given his own body as "hostage" in the process of initiation that now begins.

20. *Traeth Mawr*: "The Great Shore."

21. *Melenryd*: "The Yellow Ford."

"Of a truth," said Math, "I call Heaven to witness, if it be pleasing unto Gwydion the son of Don, I will so leave it gladly. Never will I compel any to go to fight, but that we ourselves should do our utmost."

"Verily," said the messengers, "Pryderi saith that it were more fair that the man who did him this wrong should oppose his own body to his, and let his people remain unscathed."

"I declare to Heaven, I will not ask the men of Gwynedd to fight because of me. If I am allowed to fight Pryderi myself, gladly will I oppose my body to his." And this answer they took back to Pryderi.

"Truly," said Pryderi, "I shall require no one to demand my rights but myself."

Then these two came forth and armed themselves, and they fought. And by force of strength, and fierceness, and by the magic and charms of Gwydion, Pryderi was slain. And at Maen Tyriawc,[22] above Melenryd, was he buried, and there is his grave.

And the men of the South set forth in sorrow towards their own land; nor is it a marvel that they should grieve, seeing that they had lost their lord, and many of their best warriors, and for the most part their horses and their arms.

The men of Gwynedd went back joyful and in triumph.

"Lord," said Gwydion unto Math, "would it not be right for us to release the hostages of the men of the South, which they pledged unto us for peace? For we ought not to put them in prison."

"Let them then be set free," saith Math. So that youth,[23] and the other hostages that were with him, were set free to follow the men of the South.

Math himself went forward to Caer Dathyl. Gilfaethwy the son of Don, and they of the household that were with him, went to make the circuit of Gwynedd as they were wont, without coming to the Court. Math went into his chamber, and caused a place to be prepared for him whereon to recline, so that he might put his feet in the maiden's lap.

"Lord," said Goewin, "seek now another to hold thy feet, for I am now a wife."

"What meaneth this?" said he.

---

22. *Maen Tyriawc*: "Stone of Healing."

23. "That youth" is of course Pryderi, who has passed through the first symbolic death and rebirth, and resumes his life in the material world ("the South") while the results of his initiation unfold in the spiritual world ("the North").

"An attack, lord, was made unawares upon me; but I held not my peace, and there was no one in the Court who knew not of it. Now the attack was made by thy nephews, lord, the sons of thy sister, Gwydion the son of Don, and Gilfaethwy the son of Don; unto me they did wrong, and unto thee dishonour."

"Verily," he exclaimed, "I will do to the utmost of my power concerning this matter. But first I will cause thee to have compensation, and then will I have amends made unto myself. As for thee, I will take thee to be my wife, and the possession of my dominions will I give unto thy hands."

And Gwydion and Gilfaethwy came not near the Court, but stayed in the confines of the land until it was forbidden to give them meat and drink. At first they came not near unto Math, but at the last they came.

"Lord," said they, "good day to thee."

"Well," said he, "is it to make me compensation that ye are come?"

"Lord," they said, "we are at thy will."

"By my will I would not have lost my warriors, and so many arms as I have done. You cannot compensate me my shame, setting aside the death of Pryderi. But since ye come hither to be at my will, I shall begin your punishment forthwith."

Then he took his magic wand, and struck Gilfaethwy, so that he became a doe, and he seized upon the other hastily lest he should escape from him. And he struck him with the same magic wand, and he became a stag.[24]

"Since now ye are in bonds, I will that ye go forth together and be companions, and possess the nature of the animals whose form ye bear. And this day twelvemonth come hither unto me."

At the end of a year from that day, lo there was a loud noise under the chamber wall, and the barking of the dogs of the palace together with the noise.

"Look," said he, "what is without."

"Lord," said one, "I have looked; there are there two deer, and a fawn with them." Then he arose and went out. And when he came he beheld the three animals. And he lifted up his wand.

"As ye were deer last year, be ye wild swine each and either of you, for the year that is to come." And thereupon he struck them with the magic wand; and the doe became a wild boar, and the stag a wild sow. "The young one will I take and

---

24. That is, the two of them have fallen from the human level into animal incarnations in Abred. The "twelvemonth" term of the punishment is symbolic.

cause to be baptized." Now the name that he gave him was Hydwn.[25] "Go ye and be wild swine, each and either of you, and be ye of the nature of wild swine. And this day twelvemonth be ye here under the wall."

At the end of the year the barking of dogs was heard under the wall of the chamber. And the Court assembled, and thereupon he arose and went forth, and when he came forth he beheld three beasts. Now these were the beasts that he saw: two wild swine of the woods, and a well-grown young one with them. And he was very large for his age.

"Truly," said Math, "this one will I take and cause to be baptized." And he struck him with his magic wand, and he become a fine fair auburn-haired youth, and the name that he gave him was Hychdwn.[26] "Now as for you, as ye were wild hogs last year, be ye wolves each and either of you for the year that is to come." Thereupon he struck them with his magic wand, and the wild boar became a she-wolf, and the wild sow a wolf. "And be ye of like nature with the animals whose semblance ye bear, and return here this day twelvemonth beneath this wall."

And at the same day at the end of the year, he heard a clamour and a barking of dogs under the wall of the chamber. And he rose and went forth. And when he came, behold, he saw two wolves, and a strong cub with them.

"This one will I take," said Math, "and I will cause him to be baptized; there is a name prepared for him, and that is Bleiddwn.[27] Now these three, such are they:

> "The three sons of Gilfaethwy the false,
> The three faithful combatants,
> Bleiddwn, Hydwn, and Hychdwn the Tall."[28]

Then he struck the two with his magic wand, and they resumed their own nature. "Oh men," said he, "for the wrong that ye did unto me sufficient has been your punishment and your dishonour. Prepare now precious ointment for these men, and wash their heads, and equip them." And this was done.

And after they were equipped, they came unto him.

"Oh men," said he, "you have obtained peace, and you shall likewise have friendship. Give your counsel unto me, what maiden I shall seek."

---

25. *Hydwn*: from *hydd*, "stag."

26. *Hychdwn*: from *hwch*, "pig."

27. *Bleiddwn*: from *bleidd*, "wolf."

28. A Welsh bardic triad.

"Lord," said Gwydion the son of Don, "it is easy to give thee counsel; seek Arianrhod, the daughter of Don, thy niece, thy sister's daughter."

And they brought her unto him, and the maiden came in. "Ha, damsel," said he, "art thou a maiden?"

"I know not, lord, other than that I am." Then he took up his magic wand, and bent it.

"Step over this," said he, "and I shall know if thou art the maiden."

Then stepped she over the magic wand, and there appeared forthwith a fine chubby yellow-haired boy. And at the crying out of the boy, she went towards the door. And thereupon some small form was seen; but before anyone could get a second glimpse of it, Gwydion had taken it, and had flung a scarf of velvet around it and hidden it. Now the place where he hid it was the bottom of a chest at the foot of his bed.

"Verily," said Math the son of Mathonwy, concerning the fine yellow-haired boy, "I will cause this one to be baptized, and Dylan[29] is the name I will give him."

So they had the boy baptized, and as they baptized him he plunged into the sea. And immediately when he was in the sea, he took its nature, and swam as well as the best fish that was therein. And for that reason was he called Dylan, the son of the Wave. Beneath him no wave ever broke. And the blow whereby he came to his death, was struck by his uncle Gofannon.[30] The third fatal blow was it called.

As Gwydion lay one morning on his bed awake, he heard a cry in the chest at his feet; and though it was not loud, it was such that he could hear it. Then he arose in haste, and opened the chest: and when he opened it, he beheld an infant boy stretching out his arms from the folds of the scarf, and casting it aside. And he took up the boy in his arms, and carried him to a place where he knew there was a woman that could nurse him. And he agreed with the woman that she should take charge of the boy. And that year he was nursed.

And at the end of the year he seemed by his size as though he were two years old.[31] And the second year he was a big child, and able to go to the Court by himself. And when he came to the Court, Gwydion noticed him, and the boy became familiar with him, and loved him better than any one else. Then was

---

29. *Dylan*: a pun on *dy llanc*, "thy lad."

30. *Gofannon*: the Welsh blacksmith-god, the brother of Gwydion. The "third fatal blow" in the following sentence refers to another Welsh bardic triad.

31. Compare this to the rapid growth of Pryderi in the First Branch.

the boy reared at the Court until he was four years old, when he was as big as though he had been eight.

And one day Gwydion walked forth, and the boy followed him, and he went to the Castle of Arianrhod, having the boy with him; and when he came into the Court, Arianrhod arose to meet him, and greeted him and bade him welcome.

"Heaven prosper thee," said he.

"Who is the boy that followeth thee?" she asked.

"This youth, he is thy son," he answered.

"Alas," said she, "what has come unto thee that thou shouldst shame me thus? Wherefore dost thou seek my dishonour, and retain it so long as this?"

"Unless thou suffer dishonour greater than that of my bringing up such a boy as this, small will be thy disgrace."

"What is the name of the boy?" said she.

"Verily," he replied, "he has not yet a name."

"Well," she said, "I lay this destiny upon him, that he shall never have a name until he receives one from me."

"Heaven bears me witness," answered he, "that thou art a wicked woman. But the boy shall have a name how displeasing soever it may be unto thee. As for thee, that which afflicts thee is that thou art no longer called a damsel." And thereupon he went forth in wrath, and returned to Caer Dathyl and there he tarried that night.

And the next day he arose and took the boy with him, and went to walk on the seashore between that place and Aber Menei. And there he saw some sedges and seaweed, and he turned them into a boat. And out of dry sticks and sedges he made some Cordovan leather, and a great deal thereof, and he colored it in such a manner that no one ever saw leather more beautiful than it. Then he made a sail to the boat, and he and the boy went in it to the port of the castle of Arianrhod. And he began forming shoes and stitching them,[32] until he was observed from the castle. And when he knew that they of the castle were observing him, he disguised his aspect, and put another semblance upon himself, and upon the boy, so that they might not be known.

"What men are those in yonder boat?" said Arianrhod.

"They are cordwainers," answered they. "Go and see what kind of leather they have, and what kind of work they can do."

---

32. Compare this to Manawyddan's making of shoes in the Third Branch.

Fig. 27. The Mabinogion • *Arianrhod Lays a Destiny (Tynged) upon Her Son*

So they came unto them. And when they came he was coloring some Cordovan leather, and gilding it. And the messengers came and told her this.

"Well," said she, "take the measure of my foot, and desire the cordwainer to make shoes for me."

So he made the shoes for her, yet not according to the measure, but larger. The shoes then were brought unto her, and behold they were too large.

"These are too large," said she, "but he shall receive their value. Let him also make some that are smaller than they."

Then he made her others that were much smaller than her foot, and sent them unto her.

"Tell him that these will not go on my feet," said she. And they told him this.

"Verily," said he, "I will not make her any shoes, unless I see her foot." And this was told unto her.

"Truly," she answered, "I will go unto him."

So she went down to the boat, and when she came there, he was shaping shoes and the boy stitching them.

"Ah, lady," said he, "good day to thee."

"Heaven prosper thee," said she. "I marvel that thou canst not manage to make shoes according to a measure."

"I could not," he replied, "but now I shall be able."

Thereupon behold a wren stood upon the deck of the boat, and the boy shot at it, and hit it in the leg between the sinew and the bone. Then she smiled. "Verily," said she, "with a steady hand did the lion aim at it."

"Heaven reward thee not, but now has he got a name. And a good enough name it is. Llew Llaw Gyffes[33] be he called henceforth."

Then the work disappeared in seaweed and sedges, and he went on with it no further. And for that reason was he called the third Gold-shoemaker.[34]

"Of a truth," said she, "thou wilt not thrive the better for doing evil unto me."

"I have done thee no evil yet," said he. Then he restored the boy to his own form.

"Well," said she, "I will lay a destiny upon this boy, that he shall never have arms and armour until I invest him with them."

"By Heaven," said he, "let thy malice be what it may, he shall have arms."

---

33. *Llew Llaw Gyffes*: "Lion with the Steady Hand." Llew's golden hair explains the "lion" reference.

34. A reference to yet another triad.

Then they went towards Dinas Dinlleu,[35] and there he brought up Llew Llaw Gyffes, until he could manage any horse, and he was perfect in features, and strength, and stature. And then Gwydion saw that he languished through the want of horses and arms. And he called him unto him.

"Ah, youth," said he, "we will go to-morrow on an errand together. Be therefore more cheerful than thou art."

"That I will," said the youth.

Next morning, at the dawn of day, they arose. And they took way along the sea coast, up towards Bryn Aryen. And at the top of Cefn Clydno they equipped themselves with horses, and went towards the Castle of Arianrhod. And they changed their form, and pricked towards the gate in the semblance of two youths, but the aspect of Gwydion was more staid than that of the other.

"Porter," said he, "go thou in and say that there are here bards from Glamorgan." And the porter went in.

"The welcome of Heaven be unto them, let them in," said Arianrhod.

With great joy were they greeted. And the hall was arranged, and they went to meat. When meat was ended, Arianrhod discoursed with Gwydion of tales and stories. Now Gwydion was an excellent teller of tales. And when it was time to leave off feasting, a chamber was prepared for them, and they went to rest.

In the early twilight Gwydion arose, and he called unto him his magic and his power. And by the time that the day dawned, there resounded through the land uproar, and trumpets and shouts. When it was now day, they heard a knocking at the door of the chamber, and therewith Arianrhod asking that it might be opened. Up rose the youth and opened unto her, and she entered and a maiden with her.

"Ah, good men," she said, "in evil plight are we."

"Yes, truly," said Gwydion, "we have heard trumpets and shouts; what thinkest thou that they may mean?"

"Verily," said she, "we cannot see the color of the ocean by reason of all the ships, side by side. And they are making for the land with all the speed they can. And what can we do?" said she.

"Lady," said Gwydion, "there is none other counsel than to close the castle upon us, and to defend it as best we may."

"Truly," said she, "may Heaven reward you. And do you defend it. And here may you have plenty of arms."

---

35. *Dinas Dinlleu*: "Fortress of the Lion-man."

And thereupon went she forth for the arms, and behold she returned, and two maidens, and suits of armor for two men, with her.

"Lady," said he, "do you accoutre this stripling, and I will arm myself with the help of thy maidens. Lo, I hear the tumult of the men approaching."

"I will do so, gladly." So she armed him fully, and that right cheerfully.

"Hast thou finished arming the youth?" said he.

"I have finished," she answered.

"I likewise have finished," said Gwydion. "Let us now take off our arms, we have no need of them."

"Wherefore?" said she. "Here is the army around the house."

"Oh, lady, there is here no army."

"Oh," cried she, "whence then was this tumult?"

"The tumult was but to break thy prophecy and to obtain arms for thy son. And now has he got arms without any thanks unto thee."

"By Heaven," said Arianrhod, "thou art a wicked man. Many a youth might have lost his life through the uproar thou hast caused in this Cantref to-day. Now will I lay a destiny upon this youth," she said, "that he shall never have a wife of the race that now inhabits this earth."

"Verily," said he, "thou wast ever a malicious woman, and no one ought to support thee. A wife shall he have notwithstanding."

They went thereupon unto Math the son of Mathonwy, and complained unto him most bitterly of Arianrhod. Gwydion showed him also how he had procured arms for the youth.

"Well," said Math, "we will seek, I and thou, by charms and illusion, to form a wife for him out of flowers. He has now come to man's stature, and he is the comeliest youth that was ever beheld."

So they took the blossoms of the oak, and the blossoms of the broom, and the blossoms of the meadow-sweet, and produced from them a maiden, the fairest and most graceful that man ever saw. And they baptized her, and gave her the name of Blodeuwedd.[36]

After she had become his bride, and they had feasted, said Gwydion, "It is not easy for a man to maintain himself without possessions."

"Of a truth," said Math, "I will give the young man the best Cantref to hold."

"Lord," said he, "what Cantref is that?"

---

36. *Blodeuwedd*: "Formed of Flowers."

"The Cantref of Dinodig,"[37] he answered. Now it is called at this day Eivionydd and Ardudwy. And the place in the Cantref where he dwelt, was a palace of his in a spot called Mur y Castell,[38] on the confines of Ardudwy. There dwelt he and reigned, and both he and his sway were beloved by all.

One day he went forth to Caer Dathyl, to visit Math the son of Mathonwy. And on the day that he set out for Caer Dathyl, Blodeuwedd walked in the Court. And she heard the sound of a horn. And after the sound of the horn, behold a tired stag went by, with dogs and huntsmen following it. And after the dogs and the huntsmen there came a crowd of men on foot.

"Send a youth," said she, "to ask who yonder host may be."

So a youth went, and inquired who they were.

"Gronw Pebyr[39] is this, the lord of Penllyn,"[40] said they. And thus the youth told her.

Gronw Pebyr pursued the stag, and by the river Cynfael he overtook the stag and killed it. And what with flaying the stag and baiting his dogs, he was there until the night began to close in upon him. And as the day departed and the night drew near, he came to the gate of the Court.

"Verily," said Blodeuwedd, "the chieftain will speak ill of us if we let him at this hour depart to another land without inviting him in."

"Yes, truly, lady," said they, "it will be most fitting to invite him."

Then went messengers to meet him and bid him in. And he accepted her bidding gladly, and came to the Court, and Blodeuwedd went to meet him, and greeted him, and bade him welcome.

"Lady," said he, "Heaven repay thee thy kindness."

When they had disaccoutred themselves, they went to sit down. And Blodeuwedd looked upon him, and from the moment that she looked on him she became filled with love for him. And he gazed on her, and the same thought came unto him as unto her, so that he could not conceal from her that he loved her, but he declared unto her that he did so. Thereupon she was very joyful. And all their discourse that night was concerning the affection and love which they

---

37. *Dinodig*: the Cantref of northern Wales that includes Harlech, the castle from which Bran the Blessed ruled in the Second Branch. Llew has now taken Bran's place.

38. *Mur y Castell*: "The Wall of the Castle." Llew thus stands on the boundary between worlds.

39. *Gronw Pebyr*: "Crown the Sturdy."

40. *Penllyn*, "Head of the Lake," is the Cantref next to Dinodig.

felt one for the other, and which in no longer space than one evening had arisen. And that evening and night passed they in each other's company.

The next day he sought to depart. But she said, "I pray thee go not from me today." And that night he tarried also. And that night they consulted by what means they might always be together.

"There is none other counsel," said he, "but that thou strive to learn from Llew Llaw Gyffes in what manner he will meet his death. And this must thou do under the semblance of solicitude concerning him."

The next day Gronw sought to depart.

"Verily," said she, "I will counsel thee not to go from me to-day."

"At thy instance will I not go," said he, "albeit, I must say, there is danger that the chief who owns the palace may return home."

"Tomorrow," answered she, "will I indeed permit thee to go forth."

The next day he sought to go, and she hindered him not.

"Be mindful," said Gronw, "of what I have said unto thee, and converse with him fully, and that under the guise of the dalliance of love, and find out by what means he may come to his death."

That night Llew Llaw Gyffes returned to his home. And the day they spent in discourse, and minstrelsy, and feasting. And at night they went to rest, and he spoke to Blodeuwedd once, and he spoke to her a second time. But, for all this, he could not get from her one word.

"What aileth thee?" said he, "art thou well?"

"I was thinking," said she, "of that which thou didst never think of concerning me; for I was sorrowful as to thy death, lest thou shouldst go sooner than I."

"Heaven reward thy care for me," said he, "but until Heaven take me I shall not easily be slain."

"For the sake of Heaven, and for mine, show me how thou mightest be slain. My memory in guarding is better than thine."

"I will tell thee gladly," said he. "Not easily can I be slain, except by a wound. And the spear wherewith I am struck must be a year in the forming. And nothing must be done towards it except during the sacrifice on Sundays."

"Is this certain?" asked she.

"It is in truth," he answered. "And I cannot be slain within a house, nor without. I cannot be slain on horseback nor on foot."

"Verily," said she, "in what manner then canst thou be slain?"

"I will tell thee," said he. "By making a bath for me by the side of a river, and by putting a roof over the cauldron, and thatching it well and tightly, and bringing a buck,[41] and putting it beside the cauldron. Then if I place one foot on the buck's back, and the other on the edge of the cauldron, whosoever strikes me thus will cause my death."

"Well," said she, "I thank Heaven that it will be easy to avoid this."

No sooner had she held this discourse than she sent to Gronw Pebyr. Gronw toiled at making the spear, and that day twelvemonth it was ready. And that very day he caused her to be informed thereof.

"Lord," said Blodeuwedd unto Llew, "I have been thinking how it is possible that what thou didst tell me formerly can be true; wilt thou show me in what manner thou couldst stand at once upon the edge of a cauldron and upon a buck, if I prepare the bath for thee?"

"I will show thee," said he.

Then she sent unto Gronw, and bade him be in ambush on the hill which is now called Bryn Cyfergyr,[42] on the bank of the river Cynfael. She caused also to be collected all the goats that were in the Cantref, and had them brought to the other side of the river, opposite Bryn Cyfergyr.

And the next day she spoke thus.

"Lord," said she, "I have caused the roof and the bath to be prepared, and lo! they are ready."

"Well," said Llew, "we will go gladly to look at them."

The day after they came and looked at the bath.

"Wilt thou go into the bath, lord?" said she.

"Willingly will I go in," he answered. So into the bath he went, and he anointed himself.

"Lord," said she, "behold the animals which thou didst speak of as being called bucks."

"Well," said he, "cause one of them to be caught and brought here." And the buck was brought. Then Llew rose out of the bath, and put on his trousers, and he placed one foot on the edge of the bath and the other on the buck's back.

Thereupon Gronw rose up from the hill which is called Bryn Cyfergyr, and he rested on one knee, and flung the poisoned dart and struck him on the side, so that the shaft started out, but the head of the dart remained in. Then he flew

---

41. That is, a male goat. Llew thus stands between the goat and the cauldron, or as we would now say, on the cusp between the zodiacal signs Capricorn and Aquarius. The story has thus circled around to the half of the year explored in the First and Second Branches.

42. *Bryn Cyfergyr*: "Hill of Battle."

up in the form of an eagle and gave a fearful scream. And thenceforth was he no more seen.

As soon as he departed Gronw and Blodeuwedd went together unto the palace that night. And the next day Gronw arose and took possession of Ardudwy. And after he had overcome the land, he ruled over it, so that Ardudwy and Penllyn were both under his sway.

Then these tidings reached Math the son of Mathonwy. And heaviness and grief came upon Math, and much more upon Gwydion than upon him.

"Lord," said Gwydion, "I shall never rest until I have tidings of my nephew."

"Verily," said Math, "may Heaven be thy strength."

Then Gwydion set forth and began to go forward. And he went through Gwynedd and Powys to the confines.[43]

And when he had done so, he went into Arfon, and came to the house of a vassal, in Maenor Penardd.[44] And he alighted at the house, and stayed there that night. The man of the house and his house-hold came in, and last of all came there the swineherd.

Said the man of the house to the swineherd, "Well, youth, hath thy sow come in to-night?"

"She hath," said he, "and is this instant returned to the pigs."

"Where doth this sow go to?" said Gwydion.

"Every day, when the sty is opened, she goeth forth and none can catch sight of her, neither is it known whither she goeth more than if she sank into the earth."

"Wilt thou grant unto me," said Gwydion, "not to open the sty until I am beside the sty with thee?"

"This will I do, right gladly," he answered.

That night they went to rest; and as soon as the swineherd saw the light of day, he awoke Gwydion. And Gwydion arose and dressed himself, and went with the swineherd, and stood beside the sty. Then the swineherd opened the sty. And as soon as he opened it, behold she leaped forth, and set off with great speed. And Gwydion followed her, and she went against the course of a river, and made for a brook, which is now called Nant y Llew.[45] And there she halted

---

43. Gwynedd is north Wales, Powys central Wales. The material world, symbolized by south Wales, is not part of Gwydion's search.

44. Note that this is the site of the battle where Gwydion defeated Pryderi earlier in this Branch.

45. *Nant y Llew*: "Valley of the Lion" or "Valley of Llew."

and began feeding. And Gwydion came under the tree, and looked what it might be that the sow was feeding on. And he saw that she was eating putrid flesh and vermin. Then looked he up to the top of the tree, and as he looked he beheld on the top of the tree an eagle, and when the eagle shook itself, there fell vermin and putrid flesh from off it, and these the sow devoured. And it seemed to him that the eagle was Llew. And he sang an Englyn:

> "Oak that grows between the two banks;
>   Darkened is the sky and hill! Shall I not tell him by his wounds,
>   That this is Llew?"

Upon this the eagle came down until he reached the center of the tree. And Gwydion sang another Englyn:

> "Oak that grows in upland ground,
>   Is it not wetted by the rain? Has it not been drenched by nine score
>   tempests?
>   It bears in its branches Llew Llaw Gyffes!"

Then the eagle came down until he was on the lowest branch of the tree, and thereupon this Englyn did Gwydion sing:

> "Oak that grows beneath the steep;
>   Stately and majestic is its aspect! Shall I not speak it?
>   That Llew will come to my lap?"

And the eagle came down upon Gwydion's knee. And Gwydion struck him with his magic wand, so that he returned to his own form. No one ever saw a more piteous sight, for he was nothing but skin and bone.

Then he went unto Caer Dathyl, and there were brought unto him good physicians that were in Gwynedd, and before the end of the year he was quite healed.

"Lord," said he unto Math the son of Mathonwy, "it is full time now that I have retribution of him by whom I have suffered all this woe."

"Truly," said Math, "he will never be able to maintain himself in the possession of that which is thy right."

"Well," said Llew, "the sooner I have my right, the better shall I be pleased."

Then they called together the whole of Gwynedd, and set forth to Ardudwy. And Gwydion went on before and proceeded to Mur y Castell. And when Blodeuwedd heard that he was coming, she took her maidens with her, and fled to the mountain. And they passed through the river Cynfael, and went towards a court that there was upon the mountain, and through fear they could not proceed except with their faces looking backwards, so that unawares they fell into the lake.[46]

And they were all drowned except Blodeuwedd herself, and her Gwydion overtook.

And he said unto her, "I will not slay thee, but I will do unto thee worse than that. For I will turn thee into a bird; and because of the shame thou hast done unto Llew Llaw Gyffes, thou shalt never show thy face in the light of day henceforth; and that through fear of all the other birds. For it shall be their nature to attack thee, and to chase thee from wheresoever they may find thee. And thou shalt not lose thy name, but shalt be always called Blodeuwedd."

Now Blodeuwedd is an owl in the language of this present time, and for this reason is the owl hateful unto all birds. And even now the owl is called Blodeuwedd.

Then Gronw Pebyr withdrew unto Penllyn, and he dispatched thence an embassy. And the messengers he sent asked Llew Llaw Gyffes if he would take land, or domain, or gold, or silver, for the injury he had received.

"I will not, by my confession to Heaven," said he. "Behold this is the least that I will accept from him; that he come to the spot where I was when he wounded me with the dart, and that I stand where he did, and that with a dart I take my aim at him. And this is the very least that I will accept."

And this was told unto Gronw Pebyr.

"Verily," said he, "is it needful for me to do thus? My faithful warriors, and my household, and my foster-brothers, is there not one among you who will stand the blow in my stead?"

"There is not, verily," answered they. And because of their refusal to suffer one stroke for their lord, they are called the third disloyal tribe even unto this day.[47]

"Well," said he, "I will meet it."

Then they two went forth to the banks of the river Cynfael, and Gronw stood in the place where Llew Llaw Gyffes was when he struck him, and Llew in the place where Gronw was.

Then said Gronw Pebyr unto Llew, "Since it was through the wiles of a woman that I did unto thee as I have done, I adjure thee by Heaven to let me

---

46. This image is meant to suggest stars setting in the ocean.

47. Another reference to a Welsh bardic triad.

place between me and the blow, the slab of stone thou seest yonder on the river's bank."

"Verily," said Llew, "I will not refuse thee this."

"Ah," said he, "may Heaven reward thee."

So Gronw took the slab and placed it between him and the blow.

Then Llew flung the dart at him, and it pierced the slab and went through Gronw likewise, so that it pierced through his back. And thus was Gronw Pebyr slain. And there is still the slab on the bank of the river Cynfael, in Ardudwy, having the hole through it. And therefore is it even now called Llech Gronw.[48]

A second time did Llew Llaw Gyffes take possession of the land, and prosperously did he govern it. And, as the story relates, he was lord after this over Gwynedd. And thus ends this portion of the Mabinogi.

---

48. *Llech Gronw*: "Stone of Gronw."

DRUID PHILOSOPHY: COSMOS AND THE NATURE OF LAW

HIS FOURTH LECTURE on Druid philosophy, like the ones that precede it, presents a series of themes for meditation and study in the form of nine triads and their corresponding commentaries. Here, the structure of the Cosmos and the nature of the laws that govern it are the central themes of instruction. The explication and relation of these themes have two goals; the first is to present the student with a clearer sense of the structure and nature of the Cosmos as the Druid mysteries understand it, and the second is to equip the student with a set of perspectives that underlie the practical work of this and the later grades of this course.

As before, it is important to remember that the ideas and imagery presented in these lectures are intended as tools for the mind. They are meant to be used rather than to be believed. As you study these teachings, and explore the triads and their commentaries in your meditations, consider the ways in which the events you experience in your daily life reflect the principles discussed here, and think about how those principles might be put to use in practical ways when confronting the problems life brings to you.

One of the great distinctions between the mystery teachings of past and present, and the popular thought of the present day, may be traced by attending to the use of the word "chance." It is a commonplace of modern thought that chance rules many aspects of life, perhaps extending to all of it. The theory of evolution as propounded by Darwin and his successors, to name but one example, holds that chance variation in living things, subjected to the selective effects of chance events in the life of each plant or animal, give rise to the myriad wonderful adaptations that fit living things to one another and the world around them. Ordinary speech echoes this habit of thought, setting aside many an event as the product of mere chance, happenstance, and random influences from the surrounding world. It is no wonder that many sensitive souls, exposed repeatedly to such ideas, find themselves confronted by the prospect of a world in which mere chance governs all things, and human life with all its joys and sorrows is but a random play of molecules in a void.

The teachings of the wise of all ages contradict this gloomy prospect. From the perspective of the Druid mysteries, as of every other mystery teaching, we live in a Cosmos that is perpetually governed by laws, the existence of which is woven into the very being of the Cosmos and the reality of Awen. There is no blind chance, nor arbitrary decree in the Cosmos. There is no place or room for these, for law fills the whole field of cosmic activity. Nor is there disorder or inharmony in the Cosmos; rather, everything is in a state of balance, subtle and powerful beyond our conceiving. As for chaos, that bugbear of the mind, it does not exist.

The following three triads express the nature of law in the Cosmos according to the teachings of the Druid mysteries:

Triad I.

Three modes of law that shape the Cosmos: Awen, which is one in number; the Cosmic Laws or Creative Principles, which are seven in number; and the laws that govern the processes of Nature in manifestation, which are infinite in number.

Triad II.

Three orders of manifestation of law in the three circles of existence: in Ceugant, in the order of eternal unity; in Gwynfydd, in the order of logical necessity; and in Abred, in the order of manifestation as phenomena in time.

Triad III.

Three principles in which law is equally manifested: substance, motion, and consciousness.

TRIAD I.

Three modes of law that shape the Cosmos: Awen, which is one in number; the Cosmic Laws or Creative Principles, which are seven in number; and the laws that govern the processes of Nature in manifestation, which are infinite in number.

According to the teachings of the mysteries, all things in the Cosmos are subject to law, and the recognition of this principle brings clarity to many things that popular thinking leaves obscure and muddled. As the mists of the morning disappear before the rays of the rising sun, so do the superstitious fears and cruel doctrines commonly believed by the uninitiated vanish with the recognition of cosmic order. In a universe governed by eternal laws there is no place for the chance events portrayed by popular unbelief or the arbitrary decrees of an angry and jealous deity portrayed by popular belief, even when these are dressed in the ornate robes of philosophy or theology. Before the light of understanding, these things melt away.

The ordinary human mind, even without the benefit of the initiate's training, is able to discover the existence of law in the universe, in every phase of its manifestation. The rising and setting of the sun, the flow of the tides, the laws of gravitation and mechanics, and the orderly pattern of Nature in all her phases, show to the perceptive mind the presence of law in the Cosmos. These laws of nature cannot be broken; we can ignore them, but only at the cost of suffering the inevitable consequences. No one breaks the law of gravitation by stepping over a cliff. Equally, no one breaks the law of gravitation by thinking through its consequences, finding some other law of nature that provides an upward force to counter gravitation's downward pull, and rising gracefully into the sky in a balloon. The law remains the same; the difference lies in our response to it.

With the benefit of initiation, or in some cases by ordinary study pursued with great intentness and discipline, it is possible to recognize a second set of laws distinct from the ordinary laws of nature. These are the seven Cosmic Laws or creative principles taught in the Mystery schools of the western world: the Laws of Unity, Polarity, Balance, Causation, Vibration, Correspondence, and Circularity, to give them the names that are assigned to them in the Druid mysteries. Just as individual phenomena, whether in matter, life, or mind, are subject to the myriad laws of Nature, so the laws of Nature themselves are subject to the seven Cosmic Laws; and these, in turn, are subject to Awen, which is the One Law that governs all law.

These laws are not the result of the arbitrary choice of some divine being. They are inherent in the very nature of the Cosmos. No deity had to decide in advance that two and two would make four, or that a straight line would be the shortest distance between two given points, or that the laws of Nature would be as they are and not otherwise. Cosmic Laws are not made—they are inherent in the Cosmos, and inseparable from it; they are that which brings the Cosmos into being, as expressions of Awen reflected in the infinite potentiality of Annwn.

Every intelligent conception of the Cosmos must of necessity include the conception of law. The very origin of the word "Cosmos" shows the underlying thought in the minds of the ancient Greek philosopher-initiates, members of the Pythagorean Brotherhood, who first used this term. The word is derived from the archaic Greek word *konieo*, "to take care of," and the Pythagorean philosophers used it first in the sense of "order," and later in the broader sense of "the world as a manifestation of order and arrangement, as opposed to chaos." Its antithesis is the word "chaos," which is also derived from ancient Greek and has two meanings in that language: first, "a yawning empty space"; and second, "confusion, or a mass without order or laws; a confused mixture without order or regularity."

Thus the term chaos is opposite in meaning to Cosmos. When we postulate a Cosmos without order, or one in which law sometimes governs and sometimes does not, we are simply applying the term Cosmos to what is really chaos. There can be no such thing as an universe half Cosmos and half chaos. Order and chaos are antithetical. Law and chance are antithetical. The three basic principles of thought reveal this fact. Let us consider them for a moment:

A. The Principle of Identity: "Each thing, relation, or quality is always the same as itself, no matter how different the conditions in which it may happen to occur."

B. The Principle of Contradiction: "No thing, relation, or quality can, at the same time and place, both be and not be."

C. The Principle of the Excluded Middle: "Each thing, relation, or quality must either be or not be; there is no third option."

These are established axioms of logic. A leading modern authority on logic, Prof. Jevons, says of them: "Students are seldom able to see at first their full meaning and importance. All arguments may be explained when these self-evident laws are granted; and it is not too much to say that the whole of logic will be plain to those who will constantly use these laws as the key."

Therefore we must either hold that the Cosmos is under law, or else that it is not. If it is not, then chance or arbitrary decree rule the universe—and the Cosmos is but chaos. There is no alternative—there can be no half-and-half about the matter. Which is it? We need scarcely to assure the student that modern scientific thought, and the common sense of all ages, both agree perfectly with the teachings of the ancient Druids, to the effect that the Cosmos is governed by law in every detail, and as a whole; and that there is universal order, balance, and harmony manifested through it.

Triad II.

Three orders of manifestation of law in the three circles of existence: in Ceugant, in the order of eternal unity; in Gwynfydd, in the order of logical necessity; and in Abred, in the order of manifestation as phenomena in time.

While law pervades the Cosmos, it manifests itself in the three circles of existence in different ways. In Ceugant, the highest of the circles, law expresses itself in "the order of eternal unity," that is, as a single gesture or expression of the Eternal, which may be glimpsed by created beings but not understood by them. In the circle of Gwynfydd, the "luminous life" to which initiation tends, law is understood as a sequence of logical necessity that, unfolding from first principles instantly self-evident to the mind, proceeds outward to explain the laws governing every phenomenon of matter, life and mind on every plane of being.

It is in the circle of Abred, the realm of embodied existence in which each of us presently dwells, that the understanding of law becomes more complex and, it may be, more difficult. We have proved above that the Cosmos must be governed by law, and that there is in it no space or place for chaos, but the everyday experiences of life in the world we know may betimes seem to contradict that proof. What is normally called chance seems to play so great a role in the ordering of things, and to overset the apparently reasonable expectations of so many people, that the Druid teaching of the primacy of law may seem folly—as, indeed, it has seemed down through the centuries to many who could or would not learn to see past the facade of events to the firm structure of law that governs them.

The role of Law in a Cosmos that seems to be governed by chance can be best understood by exploring the concept of chance, in order to dispel the popular misconceptions that surround the nature and meaning of this much-used word. Chance is generally held to mean "an accident; something happening without a cause; a supposed agent or mode of activity, causing events, that is other than a force, law, or purpose." The English word was derived originally from the Latin word *cadentia*, meaning "the falling of the dice." The strict meaning of "chance" is "without cause," and it is quite often used in this sense, to suggest that a chance event had no determinate cause at all.

With the advancing knowledge of the universal prevalence of causality, brought about by the researches of science, chance in the original sense of the term is no longer regarded as a reality. The word is now employed by scientists to mean "the unknown or unforeseen cause or causes of an event." Chance is but a mere name, and really nothing in itself; a conception of our minds, and only a convenient way of speaking, whereby we would express that such effects as are commonly attributed to chance, were produced by true and proper causes not yet known to us. The highest modern philosophical thought agrees with the Druid teaching that in the Cosmos there is no chance. Where law governs, there can be no chance in the strict sense of the word; no "accidents," no "happenings," that come into being without a cause. Even the cast of the dice is now seen to be as much the result of strictly unfolding cause and effect as is the motion of the sun, planets and tides. To phrase the whole matter neatly, in philosophical thought, casualty[49] has been superseded by causality.

The key to understanding the role of law in the world of Abred is to recognize that the effects of causes unfold over time, in an orderly sequence. Cause and effect are connected logically, but separated by some interval of time, however short or long. When the interval is brief, the connection of cause to effect is clear to us, but when the interval is long as human consciousness measures time, the connection between cause and effect may escape us. The effect that seems to spring out of nowhere may be the result of a cause long past, just as the cause that seems to have yielded no result simply has not yet had the time proper to the manifestation of its effect.

In the circle of Abred, all things proceed in a continuous stream or procession of events, and it is this that we call time. All events flow from previous

---

49. The word "casualty" has the same root as the word "casual," and its original meaning was "something that just happens" without any particular cause or order.

events, and likewise result in subsequent events which flow from them. There is always a "something before" and a "something after" every event. Every event has causes, and is in itself one of the causes for that which must follow after it. Just as no link in a continuous chain can escape having a preceding and succeeding link, so no event can fail to have precedent and subsequent events connected with and related to it. No event in Abred can be isolated from the stream of events.

More broadly, no event, no thing, and no being, can stand alone in the Cosmos. Every thing and every event is interdependent, from the very nature of the Cosmos itself. The nature of the interdependence uniting all events, things, and beings is experienced differently in the three circles of existence: in Ceugant, as a fundamental unity that admits of no separation; in Gwynfydd, as an unfoldment of logical necessity that the perceiving mind can understand and, understanding, rejoice in knowing that perfect harmony, balance, and justice guide all things; in Abred, finally, as a sequence of cause and effect in which every event is determined by its precedent causes and, in turn, determines its subsequent effects.

Here again we see that there can be no such thing as "chance" or "accident" in the Cosmos. Nothing ever "merely happens," in the usual sense of the phrase. Everything, every event, every happening, has its preceding causes, and from it will emerge the succeeding effects—all being links in the continuous chain of Law. Now and again we recognize these things dimly in everyday life, and call them the workings of cause and effect. Still, that process may be understood on a far broader scale, and it is to this final reflection we now turn.

Modern scientific thought generally holds the conception that everything is an effect of precedent causes and, at the same time, the cause of the effects which arise from it.[50] According to this conception, each thing is a link in an endless chain of cause and effect; every event in time, or thing in space, has its own causes, and at the same time is the cause of succeeding events in time, or things in space. This way of thinking may seem to be very similar to the sequence of cause and effect in the Druid teaching, but there is an important difference: the Druid teaching does not hold that the chain of cause and effect is beginningless and endless. On the contrary, the Druid teaching holds that the Cosmos emerged from Annwn at the dawn of the Cosmic Day—therefore, this

---

50. The comments that follow are less true of modern scientific thought, which currently traces all chains of cause and effect back to the Big Bang, than they were when these lessons were originally composed.

particular Cosmos had a beginning in time; and likewise, it will have an ending in time, when it again is resolved into Annwn. Awen is the only eternal reality.

From the beginning, everything that takes place in the Cosmos proceeds according to cause and effect. What you are today—what happens this moment—is the necessary result of all that has gone before. What will be tomorrow, a year hence, or a million years hence, will be the necessary result of all the things and events that exist at this moment. Everything proceeds from what has gone before, and from every thing develop the seeds of what is to come. Everything is a blossom, and contains within itself the seeds of future blossoms. Every event is but a phase in the One Event that is the Cosmos. Every thing is but a part of the One Thing that is the Cosmos. Thus nothing is really separate from anything else; there is ultimately only One Thing.

At any particular moment in the Cosmic Day—for example, at the moment that you read these lines—certain things are at certain places, subject to certain conditions, and acting and being acted upon in certain ways. All this results from a chain of cause and effect that reaches back to the first glimmer of the Cosmic Dawn. Likewise, at any moment in the future—a year hence, or a million years hence—there will be certain things in certain places, under certain conditions, acting and being acted upon in certain ways. All that is proceeds from all that has gone before. And from all that is will flow all that shall be even unto the coming of the Cosmic Night.

These things are certain, not because some being arbitrarily decreed that they would happen, but because of the operation of constant natural principles. Cause produces effect; everything has its precedent, and will have its subsequent. The seeds of the future exist in the present, just as the seeds of the present existed in the past. No thing or event is arbitrary, separate, disconnected, independent. We are all parts of a Cosmic Whole.

TRIAD III.

Three principles in which law is equally manifested: substance, motion, and consciousness.

Most thinkers, modern as well as ancient, accept that the rule of law governs substance and motion. More controversial is the claim that the same rule governs the life of the mind. Many people feel that applying the rule of law to the mental side of existence, and seeing cause and effect as applying to the mind and will, would make free will impossible and reduce the individual to the status of a machine. Theologians in particular struggle vainly to overcome the apparently forced choice between a universe of law, in which free will is nonexistent, and a universe that permits free will and is therefore reduced to mere chaos.

The entire difficulty, however, is illusory. Freedom of the will is not the absence of cause and effect, but an effect that has its appropriate causes. This may be seen in everyday life in the awakening of choice in each individual. An infant's actions are very nearly as predictable as those of a machine, but as the infant grows into childhood, and the child toward adulthood, increasing experience of the world gives a basis for reflection, and increasing capacity for reflection opens the door to choices that are not simply mechanical reactions to events. The mind, as it matures, learns to weigh one cause against another and to assess the promptings of the passions and the habits instilled by upbringing in the light of experience and reason.

The theologians get into trouble because they confuse law with predestination. They recognize the logical absurdity of holding someone morally responsible for doing what for all eternity he has been predestined to do. When determination is distinguished from pre-determination, a new light dawns. Despite their reluctance to admit cause and effect into the mental sphere, teachers of every religion act as though the mind were subject to law, advocating the training of the mind according to some particular scheme of mental laws, and proposing rewards and punishments as motivations for action. If the will is entirely free, how could these motivations affect it? All education and training of the mind implies the existence of cause and effect on the mental level of being.

TRIAD IV.

Three great planes of manifestation: the material plane, the astral plane, and the spiritual plane.

TRIAD V.

Three levels of the astral plane: the halls of light, the halls of thought, and the halls of the hollow forms.

TRIAD VI.

Three aspects of the astral body: the body of vitality, the animal form, and the magical mirror of the Cosmos.

Triad IV.

Three great planes of manifestation: the material plane, the astral plane, and the spiritual plane.

There is much confusion in the use of the term "plane" in occult writings, for it is employed in various ways, due to the difficulty of expressing conceptions of those aspects of human experience not limited to the material. The word "plane" in occult writings has a meaning apparently at variance with its more normal usage. In ordinary language a "plane" is a "perfectly level, flat, and smooth surface." In geometry and astronomy it is sometimes used in an abstract or ideal sense, to indicate an ideal surface supposed to cut or pass through a solid body or in various directions; as the plane of an ecliptic, the plane of a planet's orbit, and so forth. It is also used in a figurative sense, implying "a level, or field of consciousness or action" as in such phrases as "on the plane of reason;" "on the plane of common sense," and the like. This last usage is the one that gave rise to its occult usage.

But the student is cautioned against confusing the term "plane" with any conception of "place." A plane is not a place. Every plane exists in each particular place or, more exactly, every particular place exists simultaneously on all the planes; for the planes interpenetrate each other. A plane has no dimensions in space, and rather more resembles a state or condition than a place. It cannot be measured in terms of space or time; rather, it is capable of measurement by degrees in the scale of vibrations. These states or degrees of vibration interpenetrate each other, without interference, like many analogous physical phenomena. For instance, a dozen or more currents of electricity may pass along the same wire at the same time without interfering with each other, and may then register each on its special instrument, providing that the rate of alternation of current—that is, of vibration—be different in each case. In the same way, light, heat, radio waves, X rays, and many other vibrations may manifest and remain present in a single room at the same time.

On the physical plane of the Cosmos occur the various manifestations of the physical world—this is the familiar world of matter and energy. It is the plane best known to us, for all of our physical activities are performed on one or another of its sub-planes. On these planes there are manifestations of matter of degrees unrecognized by the ordinary senses of humanity, as well as the familiar forms and degrees. Likewise there are forces and energies of which most of us are totally ignorant, but are known and understood by the initiates who have risen above the ordinary level through their own exertions.

On the spiritual plane of the Cosmos, similarly, occur the various manifestations of the mental world, only the faintest and lowest manifestations of which are known to the humanity of today. Most of what passes for mental activity among human beings belongs to the intermediate plane, the astral plane, which will be discussed in more detail below. The mind is only truly active on its own plane, the spiritual plane, when it passes beyond forms and images into pure intuitions of meaning and value. Abstract thought of a more ordinary kind, such as is experienced when reasoning concerning mathematics and the truths of philosophy, stands on the border between the spiritual and astral planes, and may partake more of one or the other depending on the extent to which it moves toward the formless or toward form.

Triad V.

Three levels of the astral plane: the halls of light, the halls of thought, and the halls of the hollow forms.

It is the astral plane on which occurs most of what we are normally pleased to call mental activities, and it is on this plane likewise that most of the work of any mystery school is accomplished. The term "astral" (from a Greek word meaning "star") is of ancient usage in western occult traditions. Among the old occult philosophers, the heavens were held to be the habitation of beings whose embodiments were a more ethereal and finer nature than those of our material world. In the regions above the earth, among the planets and stars, disembodied entities and supernatural beings were held to abide.

Today the term is used with various shades of meaning by different schools of occultism, and students commonly become confused as a consequence of this looseness of meaning. Some schools use the term "astral plane" to designate what these lessons call the lower sub-planes of the astral, using other terms to designate the higher planes, which latter are often confounded with the lower sub-planes of the spiritual plane. Other schools include everything above the material plane, from the lower astral to the upper spiritual sub-planes, under the general term of the astral plane. The teachings communicated in these lessons apply the term "astral plane" to the intermediate plane of the Cosmos—the plane lying between the material and the spiritual—including the higher as well as the lower astral sub-planes. This has been the standard usage of the term in most occult schools, and is worth preserving, as it clarifies the important distinction between the realm of substantial form—the realm of insubstantial form—and the realm of pure and formless spirit.

There are many sub-planes on the astral plane, and many of these bear close analogies to corresponding planes known to us on the material plane. There are also sub-planes containing modes of existence which differ from those familiar to us, and which bear the same relationship to the latter that the black keys on the piano keyboard bear to the white keys. On these "black-key" sub-planes dwell entities strange to human sight and thought, but which nevertheless form a part of the universal manifestation of life. These entities are nonhuman; they never were human, and never will be human. Their evolution has been, and will continue, along different lines than ours. We shall consider these entities in a later lesson.

In learning what we may call the subtle geography of the astral plane, we may begin with the highest set of sub-planes, those closest to and most strongly influenced by the spiritual plane. The Druid name for these is the Halls of Light. Here dwell high and profoundly illuminated beings, both those who were once embodied in human form and those who were never human. In the present age of the world, for reasons that will be discussed in a future lesson, human souls reach up to these sub-planes only in the rarest of circumstances, and for this reason little will be said of them here.

The middle sub-planes of the astral planes, intermediate between the spiritual and material planes, are the levels in which those experiences that are normally called mental, internal, or imaginary take place. The Druid name for these sub-planes is the Halls of Thought. These are the sub-planes in which thought currents operate, and also in which the astral bodies of the embodied, and the auric colors are visible to those who have developed the gift of seeing them. These sub-planes both influence and are influenced by the material plane, and they are often experienced by persons whose psychic faculties have become sharpened by one means or another and who have developed the power of clairvoyance—that gift the ancient Druids called the Second Sight.

On these middle sub-planes of the astral plane are manifested the thought waves, thought currents, thought-forms, etc., which produce the phenomena of mentalism.[51] Thoughts and mental states manifest themselves on these sub-planes in objective form. When a person concentrates on a thought or emotional state, whether intentionally or otherwise, that state causes the mind to emanate waves and currents of thought-force which spread outwards in

---

51. Mentalism: At the time when these lessons were originally compiled, this was the general term for all the applications of the powers of the mind. A lecture on the basic practices of mentalism is included in a later lesson.

constantly widening circles in every direction. In this way great thought-clouds are formed which hover around places to which they are attracted. Thought-clouds of the same general character have a tendency to coalesce and mingle and blend with each other, and to move persons who resonate them toward places in which similar thoughts or feelings are being radiated. Certain of the applications of practical enchantment operate by using thought influences of this kind to attract those who resonate with similar thoughts and feelings. Cities, towns and smaller places—even businesses, office buildings, houses, and rooms have their own particular astral atmosphere that influence thought and feeling; these may be felt by anyone who learns to pay attention to such influences, and seen clearly by those who possess the Second Sight.

Akin to these thought radiations are what are sometimes known as thought-forms, which are thought radiations of great density and power of cohesion, which are also charged with the strong will or ardent desire of the persons who project them them—and which are often effectually vitalized by the nwyfre of the person who projected them, and infused a part of his own vitality into them. Thought-forms of this kind represent another tool of magical practice, and indeed the art of talismans—of which so many hints have been dropped and so little effective teaching circulated—is little more than the art of creating powerful thought-forms and linking them to an appropriate physical object to give them permanence.

Lacking such an anchor in the material plane, thought vibrations and thought-forms abide on the middle and lower sub-planes of the astral plane until, having used up the energy originally given them and finding no more, they finally disintegrate. In the interval, they tend to coalesce with similar forms and gather around places in which the vibrations are harmonious to their own. This is why some places have mental atmospheres of vice, others of greed, others of industry, others of the reverse. In short, thought atmospheres exist everywhere on these astral sub-planes, just as material atmospheres of greater or lesser density exist everywhere on the material plane. One is just as real as is the other. They have all the correspondences one might expect. Those who are able to develop the Second Sight, or simply learn to pay attention to the ordinary sensitivity to thought atmospheres that all of us have innately, find in the phenomena of thought atmospheres a source of never-failing interest; it is very often possible to know the most secret activities, past or present, of people living, working, or engaged in other activities in a certain place, solely from the nature of the thought atmosphere present in that place.

At times this sensitivity becomes a burden and a source of unwelcome knowledge, so gross and base are the emotions and feelings manifesting in the dark, heavy suffocating thought atmospheres in certain places—so horrible some of the thought-forms that appear there. These may be effectually banished by the Sphere of Protection and other magical workings, while on a simpler level, repeated mental states and activities of a contrary nature to these unwelcome presences tend to repel them and scatter them away from one's vicinity.

Closer still to the material plane, on the lowest set of sub-planes of the astral plane, is found what has been called the "scrap pile of the Astral," and, indeed, that term of the workshop very aptly expresses the matter; the Druid name for these sub-planes is the Halls of the Hollow Forms. On these sub-plane are to be found the discarded astral materials of the astral bodies which have been "sloughed off" by entities at the end of an incarnation. In time, these astral forms are resolved into their original elements and dissolved into the astral substance of the Cosmos, but for some time after the death of the physical body, the forms remain.

It is important to remember that these remnants of astral bodies, discarded and disintegrating, have long since lost all connection to the souls which formerly inhabited them. They are mere shells, without soul or minds of their own, and preserving only a slight degree of vitality or nwyfre. They are astral corpses, just as much of a corpse as is the discarded physical body. But, just as a physical corpse may be aroused into a moment of apparent life by a strong electric current, and will roll its eyes, move its limbs, and even utter groans—so may these astral corpses be "galvanized" by the nwyfre of a Spiritualist medium,[52] if the conditions be favorable, and may be partly materialized so as to appear as a shadowy form, acting, moving and even speaking. The only mind present in the shell, however, is supplied by the thoughts of the medium or the persons present at the seance. It is for this reason that the phantoms that appear at seances, real as they sometimes are, so rarely possess any knowledge or wisdom unknown to the medium; their personalities and memories are supplied to them, often but not always unconsciously, by the medium who evokes them.

These astral corpses also become visible under certain conditions, often around graveyards, battlefields, and the like, and are thought to be the ghosts of those who formerly inhabited them. They are, however, most often nothing but the densest layer of the astral body—its "shell," so to speak—and are no more to

---

52. Nowadays a New Age trance channeler would be a comparable phenomenon.

be regarded as the deceased person himself than is the physical body lying in the grave. Both are discarded coverings, both are corpses.

It happens relatively often to untrained or poorly trained psychics that they happen to wander on to these sub-planes of the astral. It is not a welcome event to roam in this charnel house of the astral plane. Most people find the encounter with this part of the astral an extremely unpleasant experience, for these sub-planes are pervaded with a quality of denseness and materiality, making travel there resemble nothing so much as pushing one's way through some unclean and viscous fluid, while some of the inhabitants and influences of these planes are dangerous to encounter.

There are indeed inhabitants of these lowest sub-planes of the astral, inhabitants who were once human beings. They are not consigned to this unwelcome fate as punishment; they have chosen it themselves. For countless centuries, among those who practice magic, there have been those who have been led astray by the fear of death and the pride of power, and refuse to pass through the transformations spoken of in the previous lesson—those transformations that lead from one life to another and, by means of the natural resonance of the soul with those conditions most attuned to its character, send one person to a life in the animal realm, another to a life in a new human body, and still another to the liberation of Gwynfydd. Those who have not mastered the flow of nwyfre have no choice in this matter, but it is possible for an initiate to develop his astral shell to such a degree of solidity and resistance that it continues to hold the higher principles of the self within itself after the death of the physical body.

This process is distinct from, and more specific than, though it sometimes accompanies, the refusal of the One Life discussed in the previous lesson of this course. It represents a particular perversion of the path of initiation—the use of certain highly specialized disciplines to create an astral form that will endure after physical death. Those who choose this path gain their wish; they continue to exist on the astral plane after death expels them from the physical plane; yet the nature of their embodiment is such that they can only exist on the lowest sub-planes of the astral, in the Halls of the Hollow Forms.

There they remain, for upon the death of the material body, the astral form they have constructed as a refuge becomes a prison; until the last of the nwyfre with which they charged that form is exhausted—a process that may take years, decades, or centuries, depending on the skill and potency of their original efforts—they are constrained to linger on these lowermost sub-planes of the astral, dwelling among the decaying remains of countless astral bodies. Their sole desire in this condition is to find some way to return to the world of matter, whence arises one of the dangers of necromancy—that ancient art of which today's Spiritualism is too often a modern manifestation.[53]

TRIAD VI.

Three aspects of the astral body: the body of vitality, the animal form, and the magical mirror of the Cosmos.

The astral body has not previously been discussed in detail in this course, for it is not something that the uninitiated or the beginning student needs to explore, and in fact a premature focus on the astral body and its properties can be the cause of many unwelcome pathologies of spiritual training and development. At this stage in your training, it becomes important to understand how the three elements of the personality—the *bywyd*, the *nwyd*, and the *hunan*—relate to the astral world, and more generally to the three planes described above.

Each of these elements of the personality is a composite of astral and spiritual forces, and the astral portion of that composite may usefully be described as a body. In the case of the *bywyd* or vital and biological aspect of the personality, the corresponding astral body is called the body of vitality. This is the lattice or framework of nwyfre on which the dense matter of the corff or material body is formed, and which provides the latter with its vitality and animation.

In the case of the *nwyd* or passionate aspect of the personality, the corresponding astral body is called the animal form. The nwyd is the predominant level of the personality in the animal, as the bywyd is in the plant; the animal and plant alike have a collective *hunan* rather than a personal one—there is a collective hunan for each species, an "oversoul" if you will, which provides that reasonable guidance to the passionate self of the individual animal that we call instinct. The oversoul of the plant includes a nwyd as well as a hunan, accounting for many of the legends of dryads and plant spirits who have passions and emotions as well as thought and speech.

The animal form in the human astral body takes its name from a tradition among Druids, found also among Welsh villagers and other Celtic peoples. This tradition holds that when a human being has neglected the life of reason and wisdom, and lived a life more proper to an animal, and will therefore be reborn in an animal form, one with the Second Sight can see the animal that person will become, like a spectral shape near or surrounding him; the Welsh word for

---

53. Again, a comparison with some aspects of the New Age movement is not inappropriate.

this shape is *cydfil*. The author George Macdonald in his fine children's story *The Princess and Curdie* has made use of this legend, equipping his hero with the ability to see both the animal form of human beings who are descending to the animal level, and the human form of animals who are ascending to the human level. This is not merely a fiction; there are those living today who have the same ability.[54]

The animal form is thus malleable, changing its shape and character in response to changes in the character of the person to whom it belongs. It is the portion of the astral body least affected either by the material body or corff below it, or the spiritual body or elaeth above it, and thus partakes more than the others of the dreamlike, variable quality of the astral.

In the case of the hunan or thinking, conscious self, the corresponding astral body is called the magical mirror of the Cosmos, or the sphere of sensation. This body forms an egg or elongate sphere surrounding the material body on all sides at a distance of several feet. It is called the magical mirror of the Cosmos because in it are reflected all the powers and potencies of the Cosmos. Thought as we normally experience consists of the mind moving from image to image reflected on this magical mirror. In the uninitiated, the sphere of sensation is commonly clouded by the influences of the nwyd and the distorted projections of other minds; much of the work of initiation thus consists of purifying the magical mirror of these clouds, so that the hunan may perceive the images of the Cosmos reflected there, and think true and clear thoughts. The regular practice of the Sphere of Protection exercise has as one of its central purposes precisely this purification of the magical mirror of the Cosmos.

The sphere of sensation of one person can also be seen from outside by another person, provided the latter has developed the power of clairvoyant observation. The most common form by which the perception of the sphere of sensation manifests is in the perception of auric colors. These are in the nature of emanations or radiations from the entirety of the astral body, which are projected onto the surface of the magical mirror of the Cosmos. The body of vitality has its own forces which flow freely from it, particularly when the vitality of the person is strong. This is the "human magnetism" of the magnetic healers and others, and which serves to arouse strength and vigor to those to whom it is applied. The majority of the colors seen in the magical mirror of the Cosmos are rather an emanation of the mental states, feelings and emotions of the person's

---

54. A statement as true today as it was when these lessons were originally compiled.

mind. The mirror manifests various colors, particularly around the head, the colors corresponding to the character of the mental states being manifested, or those habitual to the person. For instance:

Red indicates the animal passions, such as lust and anger. Blue represents religious emotion—light blue denoting what is generally called "spirituality," but which in reality is but a refined form of religious feeling. Spirituality is more a matter of knowledge and life development, rather than feeling or emotion. Green denotes jealousy in certain shades, and in others represents tact, agreeableness, diplomacy, or deceit. Gray denotes selfishness. Yellow, intellectuality in its various degrees and forms. Black is the astral color of hate, malice and vengeful emotion. Persons in whom the faculty of astral sensing is well developed may see these auric colors plainly, and are thereby informed as to the mental characteristics of the person under observation.

Triad VII.

Three laws governing the individual on the plane of personality: the law of habit, the law of desire, and the law of fear.

Triad VIII.

Three laws governing the individual on the plane of will: the law of character, the law of effort, and the law of grace.

Triad IX.

Three laws governing the individual on the plane of individuality: the law of balance, the law of harmony, and the law of love.

Triad VII.

Three laws governing the individual on the plane of personality: the law of habit, the law of desire, and the law of fear.

While on the personal plane, the individual always acts and chooses in accordance with habit, desire, and fear. The individual on the plane of personality, like the animal, acts and chooses according to the sum of his habits, desires and fears, the strongest motives always dominating and determining the choice.

There need be no consistency among the habits, desires, and fears in the individual on the personal plane; sometimes habit will take the lead, sometimes desire, and sometimes fear; at one time one desire will be made the basis for choice, and at another time, a different desire will play that role.

The personal man thus is at the mercy of his mental states. These mental states manifest as traits, tendencies, temperament, nature, disposition, and indeed all we describe as personality. Different persons are attracted by different things, in different degrees, and respond in different ways and in different degrees. Each person thus has a collection of feelings, desires, wants, inclinations, likes and dislikes, habits of thought, capacity for thought, degree and character of will, and so forth. Each has a subconscious collection of stored-up impressions, memories, inherited traits, and the like, alongside the conscious mental faculties—in fact, nine-tenths of all mental activities arise from the subconscious region. Each person has a collection of seed-thoughts which constitute its share in the experiences of its ancestors. Each has a store of impressions and experiences which have modified it accordingly. The result of heredity, environment and experience creates a personality according to which one acts and chooses. This personality, at any particular moment, is just what a person is at that particular moment. And as he is, so will he act and choose. He always acts and chooses by reason of what he is. On the personal plane, he cannot act differently. And what he is—his personality of the moment—always has as its motive power the sum or average of his desires and fears.

It may be said that on the level of personality, people act in accordance with the line of the greatest satisfaction. What will be the greatest satisfaction for any person depends entirely upon the nature of the person—his personality—which is regulated by his tendencies, disposition, inherited qualities, results of his experience, environment, education, training, and history, all of which, of course, have other causes behind them. Whatever gives to the person the greatest satisfaction at the moment of action or choice, that will he do or choose. This is the rule—test it most rigidly by applying it to your own acts and decisions, and those of others. But in so testing, do not overlook the effect of habit as crystallized desire; nor the effect of fear as negative desire. When two desires are otherwise equal in strength, the one most habitual will win the day.

The element of fear, or aversion, is but a desire not to experience something, or to avoid, or get away from something. Compulsion by others may result in action through fear. One often refrains from manifesting a desire because he fears to pay the price. The most desirable thing, according to the judgment of the moment, is always chosen—the most undesirable thing of the moment is always avoided. Sometimes this necessitates compromise, but in the end we do what we like to do—we do what we want most, and avoid what we want least.

Did you ever make a choice, or perform an act which gave you the least satisfaction, or which you knew to be the most undesirable under all the circumstances of the case? If you did so—why did you do it? If you yield to the suggestions, desires, reason or will of another person, against your own inclination and judgment—what is this but the "line of least resistance," which gave you the least trouble or dissatisfaction at the moment, and in which habit, desire, or fear had its usual effect?

In the case of hypnotic influence, or the domination of one's will by another by any means, the rule is not broken, for the stronger person's will influences and arouses the desire of the weaker person. Even in this case, habit, desire or fear is the motive of action or choice.

In considering this subject, remember that the strongest motives always dominate and decide the matter. We often are forced to find a compromise among our conflicting desires. Then again, wisdom, experience and intelligence enable us to gain a clearer appreciation of the desirability of objects and acts, and thus play an important part in the choice. Imagination gives us a wider range of choice, by presenting a greater number of objects before us for choice.

Thus the nature of each person's habits, desires and fears determine his acts. This explains many actions in a strange way. For instance, one man is kind because it gives his nature the greatest satisfaction, just as another gains the greatest satisfaction by being otherwise. One finds satisfaction in doing his duty, while another finds satisfaction in escaping it. One finds satisfaction in virtue, another in vice. One finds it in selfishness, another in serving others. One finds more satisfaction in giving his life for his country; another finds it in running away and hiding. One finds the greatest satisfaction in giving; another, in getting. One finds the greatest satisfaction in being moral; another in the reverse. One takes the greatest pleasure in being a good citizen; another finds his satisfaction in the opposite. Each acts according to his nature and personality—just as a cat and dog act according to their natures.

The main point of difference between the human being and the cat or dog is that the human being has the capacity to change his nature, while the cat or the dog have not yet developed this capacity. It is unfortunately true that in a great many human beings, that capacity goes unused, and even unnoticed, during the whole span of life from birth to death. Nonetheless, it exists, and it may be awakened in anyone, by the simple but potent act of paying attention and reflecting on experience. Once this begins to occur, the individual begins to pass from the plane of personality to the planes beyond.

TRIAD VIII.

Three laws governing the individual on the plane of will: the law of character, the law of effort, and the law of grace.

The roles of habit, desire, and fear must be understood, so that you may come to a realization, perhaps for the first time, of what an important part these three things play in your own choices and actions—how much in thrall to these things you may be even now. One who realizes his bonds is in a position to work to rid himself of them. It is only when the slave realizes that he is a slave, that thoughts of freedom come to him. There is a plane above that of personality, and that is the plane of individuality. The transition from one to the other takes place by means of an intermediate state which may be called the plane of will.

When the individual sets out to attain individuality, he enters upon the plane of will, and rises above the plane of desire, which is the plane of personality. Desire and will are opposite poles, negative and positive respectively, of the same principle—the center of balance being reason. On the plane of will, though the forces of habit, desire, and fear remain effective, they are no longer an assortment of random forces as often as not pulling in different directions. They coalesce into a unity, which we may call character.

Character is the summation of the habits, desires, and fears acquired in previous lives, or in other words the sum total of the soul's previous experience, when subjected to the influence of reflective consciousness. Just as the heat of a furnace melts disparate metals into liquid form and causes them to fuse together into an alloy, possessing properties none of the original metals had when they were separate, the capacity of the mind to reflect on its actions and experiences fuses the disparate and confused raw materials of personality into character. As this takes place, the soul gradually ceases to be buffeted this way and that by the alternating blows of habits, desires, and fears that at times, nay, very often contradict one another; as these contending influences take their place in the unity of character, the struggle ceases and the individual becomes able to choose his direction in life.

Such an individual may learn to create desire by will, as well as to restrain and master desire by will. Furthermore—and this is among the great secrets—he eventually learns to will to will, to deliberately choose to will one thing over another, for the sake of gaining strength of will and the capacity to will more strongly and steadily. In this way, he rises from the plane of desire to the plane of will, and subjects the lower laws of habit, desire, and fear to the higher laws of character, effort and grace. This ascent can be made only once the creation of character is well advanced. Before this the individual can only desire to will, or fear not to will. Afterward, he can will to will, and pass thence from strength to strength.

All this requires effort; it may not be attained except by continued exertion. To enter onto the plane of will is to enter into a field of labor where every attainment must be earned by the sweat of one's brow. As the habit of exertion becomes part of character, the efforts already made become automatic, but new efforts then present themselves; it is not by a single step, but by a long journey, that the individual passes from the plane of personality to that of individuality. Still, there is another influence that comes into play as the ascent proceeds.

There are many other powers in the Cosmos than that of the striving individual soul, and some among those powers work for the uplifting of the individual. It thus happens that when the aspirant reaches the limits of his strength in some task and stretches out a despairing hand toward a goal that seems impossible to reach, he feels that hand suddenly taken in a firm though unseen grip, and finds himself drawn upwards irresistibly by a strength not his own. The phenomenon of grace, as this factor is called in the language of ordinary religion, is a reality often met with in the work of the mystery schools; it cannot be predicted, commanded, or earned; it comes and goes of its own accord, or rather, by the wills of those great beings whose work is experienced by human beings in this way, according to rules and reasons we do not know—very probably, that we cannot know. All the seeker can do is accept it with gratitude, and strive onward.

TRIAD IX.

Three laws governing the individual on the plane of individuality: the law of balance, the law of harmony, and the law of love.

With the full awakening of individuality, character being fully established as a vehicle for the soul and its aspirations, and effort and grace both having achieved their fruition, other influences come into play. Little of constructive value may be said about them here. According to the Druid teachings, the individuality thus awakened has transmuted the burdens of the personality into strengths. It no longer needs to contend with the warring forces that make life on the plane of personality so troubled, and require so much effort to tame on the plane of will. On the plane of individuality, the work that awaits is to integrate the microcosm with the macrocosm—the self with the Cosmos that surrounds it.

The first task to be accomplished is that of balance—of finding and maintaining that state of moving and active equilibrium in which the poise of the self is not upset by the changing currents and ever-varying forces of the Cosmos. This task, it is said, requires the equivalent of many lives, for the attainment of perfect balance requires a profound knowledge both of the self on all its levels, and likewise of the Cosmos on all its corresponding levels. As this knowledge is gained, the individual awakens into power; just as a machine delicately balanced can transform the pressure of a fingertip into immense force, the self delicately balanced becomes able to exert force on itself and on the Cosmos.

That force is expressed, in turn, in the second task of the awakened individuality, which is harmony. The implied reference to music here is deliberate, for it is indeed as though each soul has the capacity to add its own music to the great symphony of the Cosmos, provided only that it first learns to play the instrument that evolution has crafted for it across so many ages. Thereafter the law that governs it is the law of love—or more precisely that scarcely imaginable mode of being that is dimly shadowed forth for us, here in the realm of human life and the soul's adolescence, as the experience of love.

It must never be forgotten that it is an illusion that leads so many people to think of the realm of the spirit as something simple, vague, and formless. In reality, it is the realm of material existence that is relatively simple, vague, and formless, and that of the spirit that is rich in complexity, precise in manifestation, and intricate in its many forms, levels, and expressions. All that we know here in the Circle of Abred are the blurred and uncertain reflections of the realities of Gwynfydd, which are themselves reflections of the supernal unity and perfection of Ceugant. Thus the ascent of the soul through the circles of being leads, not to something less than life as it is known to us, but to something more—something immeasurably grander.

THE MAGICAL MEMORY: MEMORY OF SOUND

ANY PEOPLE ARE in the habit of using the word "perception" to mean experiencing something by the sense of sight, but the term is equally applicable to experiencing something through the medium of the sense of hearing. There is a great difference in individuals in how well they retain impressions through these two senses. Some remember far more readily that which they see, while others find it much easier to recall something by the impression received from hearing. One man will remember an old acquaintance at once as soon as he sees him, while another will not recognize the face of the stranger, but will remember him at once when he speaks. We have known cases in which persons who had not been seen or heard of for years were recognized by one-time friends by their voices, heard over the telephone. We remember a case reported in the daily papers of a detective failing to recognize a noted criminal through his wonderful disguise and makeup, but who identified and arrested his man at once when the latter spoke, although it had been ten years or more since the detective last heard his voice. We have known men and women who recognized a former schoolmate whom they had not seen since childhood, simply by remembering the voice, although the childish treble had been replaced by the mature tones of the man or woman.

With most people, impressions received through the eye are grasped more rapidly, but the memory seems to hold better that which enters the mind by means of the ear. Some people remember what they have heard much more readily than what they have read. Some writers hold, however, that in the case of remembering the words of lectures and the like, the ear is best aided by the eye, by remembering the appearance, gestures, and expressions of the speaker, and we are inclined to agree with this view. But the lecture seems to be much more "alive" when we hear it than when we afterwards read it in print. Perhaps the best plan is to hear and then read the lecture, and thus get the benefit of both sense memories.

Many musicians, of course, have trained their sense of hearing to a remarkable degree, and the musical ear can detect at once the slightest disharmony, or the most trifling variation from the proper note on the violin. But many others have also developed this faculty to a wonderful degree. Machinists can detect the slightest variation from the clear tone resulting from the tapping of a piece of machinery with a hammer. Railroad men can detect from the slight difference in the sound whether anything is the matter with the wheels or track while the train is running at a high rate of speed. Engineers will detect the slightest change in the song of the engines, and knowing that something is wrong somewhere will shut off the power at once. Old river pilots will recognize the whistle of any boat on the river, and the tones of the different church bells are recognized by residents of a large city. Telegraphers recognize the different styles of the various operators on their lines, and will detect the "fist" of a new operator in a moment, merely from the almost imperceptible difference in the "tick" of the instrument.

In ages long since past, when written language was almost unknown, the knowledge and experience of one generation was passed along from parent to child, from teacher to pupil, from mouth to ear. The utmost power of attention and concentration was employed by the hearer, for what was thus taught was retained and preserved intact and afterward delivered, in turn, to the child or pupil of the hearer. After many repetitions, the students could repeat teaching of great length without the omission or change of a single word. The poems of the ancient Greeks were thus passed along from generation to generation. Thus were the sagas of the Norsemen transmitted. And in like manner were the philosophies of ancient Persia and India handed down along the ages. Oriental teachers distrusted stone and papyrus, and preferred that their sacred teachings be indelibly recorded in the brains of their pupils, and thus endure as a living truth.

It is related that, over two thousand years ago, the first emperor of all China became jealous of his ancestors and of the greatness of the past history of his nation. He sought to destroy all the historical, religious and philosophical records of the past, so that in the future, history might be thought to have begun with his reign. He burned every written or graven record in the empire, including all the works of Confucius. Many books perished forever, but the works of

Confucius endure intact, thanks to the wonderful power of memory possessed by one elderly sage, who stored away in his mind the teachings received in his youth, and kept this knowledge secure until after the death of the iconoclastic Emperor, when the new Emperor had the works of the great Chinese philosophers reproduced from the old sage's dictation. So perfect was his memory that when, long years after, there was found an old Confucian manuscript that had somehow escaped the fires of the former Emperor, it was found that the old sage had not missed a single word of the text.

The same custom maintains in India, where many scholars have stored away in their minds the great Vedas, which have been handed down from a time when writing was unknown in India. The entire Sanskrit language survives entirely in the form of the Vedas and the many religious and philosophical commentaries upon them, of which not only the mere words, but the accent, inflection and pronunciation as well, are carefully preserved. Many Hindu scholars can recite the whole of the Vedas, containing nearly one million words. It takes years to accomplish the task of committing this to memory, a few lines being learned every day, much rehearsing and revieing being done. The lesson is taught entirely by word of mouth, no reference to manuscript being permitted. The Kabbalah or secret mystical teaching of the Jews was thus transmitted; many of the ancient Greeks and Romans were adepts in this form of memory, and instances are cited where citizens could repeat word for word every important speech they had heard. Of course the ancient Druids were widely famed for their abilities in this regard, for they considered it sacrilege to write down any of their teachings, and so relied on word of mouth to transmit those teachings in the form of verses from teacher to pupil, up to twenty years being devoted in some cases to the proper education of a Druid in this manner.

The sheer capacity of a memory trained in this way extends far beyond what most people today believe the human memory can hold. There are Hindu priests and folk storytellers now living who can repeat accurately the entire text of the *Mahabharata*, the world's longest and grandest epic poem, which comprises 300,000 lines of verse. The minstrels of some eastern European countries of the present day have by heart immensely long epic poems, and the Algonquin Indians committed to memory and repeated accurately mystic legends of almost interminable length. The ancient laws of Iceland were not written or printed, but were carried in the minds of the judges and lawyers of that land, and their sagas relate that the lawyers of that day were able to carry in their minds not only the laws themselves but also the innumerable number of precedents which had grown around the law.

Among the lessons learnt from studying these prodigies of memory is the importance of reciting a text to be memorized, and not simply reading it in silence. Reading aloud will prove a great help in committing to memory that which is being read, and also in impressing upon the mind the meaning of the words. Longeve says: "Reading aloud gives a power of analysis which silent reading can never know. The eye runs over the page, skips tedious bits, glides over dangerous spots. But the ear hears everything. The ear makes no cuts. The ear is delicate, sensitive and clairvoyant to a degree inconceivable by the eye. A word which glanced at, passed unnoticed, assumes vast proportions when read aloud."

EXERCISES IN EAR PERCEPTION

Great differences are noticeable among individuals regarding the development of the sense of hearing. Some have a very keen ear for sounds in general, or sounds appertaining to certain lines of occupation, etc., but have but a very moderate, or even poor, degree of perception of musical tones, while on the other hand many musicians are notorious for their dullness of perception of nonmusical sounds. Then again, some are able to distinguish certain kinds of sounds very readily, and scarcely notice others.

Our statement, in a previous lesson, that attention and interest is necessary before the mind will register a clear impression which can be readily reproduced, is particularly true in the case of impressions received through the sense of hearing. Good authorities have stated that "half of the deafness that exists is the result of inattention." This being the case it will readily be seen that the best way to cultivate improved ear perception is to cultivate attention and interest. This, perhaps, will be more easily understood when we remember that in many cases we are almost perfectly oblivious to the sounds around us, being intently occupied with some other subject. In which case the sounds enter our ears freely, but the mind, being otherwise occupied, fails to notice the impressions received. In many instances, however, we will be able to remember things which were said which at the time we failed to hear. This results from the subconscious functions of the mind, of which we have spoken elsewhere.

It is a pity that the training of the sense of hearing has been so much neglected in modern times. It is capable of affording us great pleasure and enjoyment as well as rendering us great service if educated and trained that we may receive from it the advantages which it is capable of affording. The sense of hearing may be more highly trained and developed than perhaps any of the other senses. It may be developed by exercise and culture, just as it deteriorates by neglect and inattention. The Indian has developed such a wonderful sense of hearing, by prolonged practice from earliest youth, that he is enabled to hear the sound of the footsteps of his approaching enemy by placing his ear to the ground. The mere rustling of a leaf or the cracking of a twig is distinctly heard by him. The leader of an orchestra will detect the faintest disharmony or departure from time or tune in his orchestra, and will be able to detect the faulty performer without hesitation. The blind, being thrown back on their other senses, have developed these to a wonderful degree. They have so sharpened their sense of hearing, or rather the sense of attention and interest in sounds, that they can tell when they are passing a stationary object by the sound of their own footsteps, and can discriminate between a lamp-post and a man standing still, by the same means.

We give below several exercises intended to develop the sense of hearing by practice. These exercises are intended principally as suggestions to the student, that he may be able to take advantage of the opportunities around him in his daily occupation calculated to develop this sense.

Exercise 1

When passing along the street, endeavor to notice and retain for a few moments the scraps of conversation of the passersby that you chance to overhear. You will be surprised at the number and variety of disconnected sentences you will be able to hear and retain in the course of a walk of a few blocks. It is all a matter of attention and interest. This exercise is, of course, valuable only in the way of practice, as the remarks overheard will probably be of no importance, unless you are a student of human nature.

Exercise 2

Endeavor to distinguish between the voices of people you meet, and to remember the voice if you hear it again. Everyone has a different voice, and it is quite interesting to study the different types of voices and their characteristics. You will notice that every man has his own way of pronouncing and accenting certain words. You will also notice that persons from different countries, and from different parts of our own country, have different tones and peculiarities in speech. We have known traveling men who almost invariably could determine from what part of the country a person came, merely by hearing him speak.

Then a person's character is often revealed by his voice, and the student of the subject will be able to form a very good idea of the speaker's mental make-up in this way. It may pay you to devote a little time and attention to this subject, in odd moments.

Exercise 3

An interesting exercise is that of standing where you cannot see the persons speaking, and endeavoring to distinguish their voices and to identify each speaker in turn. We have heard of a game of this sort, where a number of people sit behind a screen or curtain and speak a few words, endeavoring to disguise their voices. Those in front of the screen guess at the identity of the speaker. The result is said to be amusing, many finding it very difficult to recognize the voices of their best friends and relatives, while others who have paid more attention to voices will be able to identify the owner of every voice.

Exercise 4

We knew a young woman employed in a large office building who could detect the slight difference in sound between the footsteps of every man having an office along the same long corridor. She claimed that each step had its own characteristics, and even went so far as to assert that the character of the walker revealed itself by the sound he made in placing his feet on the floor. There is a field here for one who wishes to study character while at the same time developing his sense of hearing.

Exercise 5

You will find it interesting and helpful to endeavor to remember the precise words that have been addressed to you during the course of the day just past. Very few people are able to correctly repeat that which has been said to them only a few moments before. Inattention is largely the cause. All employers know how little dependence can be placed in the attention and memory of the average employee in this respect. By cultivating your attention and memory along these lines, you may find it of advantage to you in every department of daily life.

Exercise 6

A useful exercise is that of listening to a simple piece of music, or a catchy tune, and then endeavoring to hum it over or whistle it. As simple as this may seem to be, it will prove to be a great help in ear training, and it will also develop the attention to sounds. Those who will practice it, will find that they are developing a new interest in tune, and will be able to enjoy music better than ever before.

Exercise 7

You should attend as many lectures, sermons, and talks as you can, and, paying strict attention to each one, endeavor afterwards to jot down what you can remember of what you have heard. Review the lecture and analyze it, and repeat as far as possible the words used. This is not only of value in developing ear perception and memory, but is one of the best possible means of becoming an expert speaker. Students who sit long under a favorite professor will gradually acquire more or less of his style, and listening to good speakers will gradually develop within the mind of the listener a power of expression far superior to that formerly possessed. This is particularly true if the student will endeavor to repeat sentences and expressions which he has heard. When one trains himself to memorize portions of the addresses of good speakers, and to repeat them as accurately as possible, not only the words but the tone and expression as well, he will find that he is developing within himself powers of delivery and expression which will prove quite useful in life.

Exercise 8

The best method of training the memory to retain and recall that which has been heard, is that used by the ancient Druids and other people in the transmission of their sacred teachings and philosophies. The keynote and secret of their wonderful system is small beginnings, gradual increase, and frequent reviews. The Druid teachers are said to have begun by repeating a single line of their sacred verses to the student. The latter memorizes this line thoroughly, imprinting both the words and their meaning upon his mind indelibly, so that he knows every word in the line as if it stood out before him. He can repeat the line backward or forward and knows the position of each word. Then he learns another line the next day, after which he reviews the first line, following it up with the second one just learned, thus joining then together in his mind. The next day a third line is added, the first two being reviewed and the third joined to them. And so on, one line each day, and constant review and joining together of the new line and the old ones. The review is, of course, the important thing, as it causes the student to go over and over the lines previously learned, each time the impression being deepened. These frequent repetitions also serve to rub smooth the line by which each line has been soldered to the succeeding and preceding ones, and makes the whole appear as if it had been learned at one time, thus giving a completeness to the composite impression. Later on, the student is able to take up two lines a day, then three and so on until an almost incredible capacity has been acquired. But teachers of this method warn against attempting too many lines a day for some time, as the mind must be gradually trained to the work.

To the student of this work, who desires to develop along these lines, we would advise that he have some friend help him in the work, reading a line to him the first day, and then repeating it until it is firmly fixed in his mind. Then the next day having him review the first line and learn the second, and then reviewing both. Proceed in this fashion, keeping to a single line a day for a month or so before attempting more. The student may choose any text for this purpose, whether prose or poetry, so long as it is one that holds his interest and attention.

After hearing a line read the first time, the student should endeavor to repeat it. If he cannot repeat it clearly and plainly, he should have it re-read to him after a few minutes, and so on until he knows it thoroughly. He should then repeat it a number of times, until he thinks he knows it, and then he may try to say it backward. If he has so fixed it in his mind that he can make a mental picture of the words, he will have little difficulty after once acquiring the knack.

The second day he will repeat the line already learned, before he attempts the second line, and then, after learning the second line thoroughly in the way above stated, he should join the two together. On succeeding days he will add a line each day—one new line each day, remembering that the review is the thing that is the most important for him. He must think of the meaning of the words, as well as the mere words themselves, endeavoring to form a mental picture of what is being described. Do not attempt too much at the start. The one line a day will soon give you as much as you can well review without too much effort. Do not let the apparent simplicity and "easiness" of the task give you a poor idea of the plan. This is the same plan whereby the Hindu student or chela learns to commit to memory books equal in size to the Bible. Little by little, with constant reviewing, does he acquire this art.

In this exercise, if you find your interest fading, take up some new poem or subject, for a change, not forgetting to review the old lines from time to time.

This change will give new zest to the exercise, and will enable you to go back to the old lines with renewed interest.

COMPLETION EXERCISES: ORIENTING THE SELF

HESE EXERCISES, like the completion exercises of the preceding grades, are intended to be performed during the transition between this grade and the next. You should begin them when you have finished the other work of this grade.

The student of the Mysteries who has practiced the preceding lessons with diligence will by this time have advanced to the stage in which, in the ancient parlance, he "has found himself," has discovered that his real self is something far different from anything that he ever had imagined it to be. Instead of being an entity with distinct characteristics and personal peculiarities, he discovers that it is something of pure potentiality. We do not mean for a moment that the self exists only in a potential sense—on the contrary, it is real in the most extreme and positive sense.

Its quality of being is endowed with such a degree of actuality that all else seems to fade into relative non-existence compared to it. The statement "I Am Not" can never be truly stated about the self—it is first, last and always a something of which the positive "I AM" can and must be asserted. It is only when we come to examine the nature, attributes and qualities of this "I AM" self, that we are forced to use the terms of potentiality instead of actuality. Let us consider this a little further, for in its understanding lies the solution of many occult paradoxes.

In the first place, if we pay close attention to our experience of ourselves, and understand the terms that philosophers use to talk about the self, we will see that the formulas for establishing the self, and the practice of the exercises that arise from them, have drawn a distinction between the self and the usual attributes, characteristics and personal peculiarities which are popularly supposed to belong to it. Setting aside as the "Not I" first one feeling and then another; first one emotion and then another; first one characteristic and then another; first one personal peculiarity and then another; and placing them in turn in the "Not I" category—the student finds that after he has stripped the self of all the attributes of Personality, there is still something left which, while definitely existing is yet incapable of being described, expressed or designated in rational terms—an unknown x forming the other side of all the complex equations of the self. As to the existence of this unknown x, there is no doubt in the Druid teachings, even though the modern philosophies differ about the matter. Moreover, it is a fact which may be determined by the direct experience of anyone who practices the exercises of these lessons in the proper way. The "I AM" will always be found at the center of the self, and will always respond "I Am!"

But when we attempt to describe this ultimate "I"—when we attempt to identify it with attributes, qualities, or peculiarities, whether those we normally assign to ourselves or some other, we find ourselves at sea, for these things all belong to the plane of personality, while the "I" transcends personality, and cannot be expressed or designated in the terms of the latter. Nevertheless there is a way of identifying the "I." The philosophy of the self—both that taught within the mysteries, and that taught outside them—gives us a term whereby we may discuss and consider the "I," or ultimate element of the self. This "I," which we have described as the unknown x of the equation of the self, is identical with the highest conception of that which has been called the will. Thus the x equals the will. Let us then try to understand the "I" by considering what the highest human thought reports regarding the will. By studying the symbol we may understand the reality.

Setting aside the popular conceptions of the will, we find that the highest philosophical and psychological thought uses the term "the will" to designate the underlying essence of our being—the fundamental life-mind-spirit principle of the self. The ancient philosophers of the East so used the term; Buddhist philosophy so employs it; we find it so used by eminent thinkers all through the history of philosophical thought; Schopenhauer, Nietsche and Wundt used the term in this sense. The Druid teachings likewise identify the principle of will with spirit—the essence—the "beingness" of Being. The will is that essence or spirit, in the Cosmos and in the individual, which is ever moving, changing its manifestations, flowing, evolving, proceeding, desiring, attaining, seeking, accomplishing. It contains within itself the potentiality of Everything, but it itself cannot be said to be any of the things it manifests.

Thus do we find that the self or "I" is, in its deepest human analysis, will. Thus we find in turn that will is a potential manifestation of the activity of the whole Cosmos—the manifestation of the will to be in the form of becoming— the essence which may mould itself into any and all forms—the basic activity of being which may manifest how and as it pleases, within the limits placed on or, rather, within it by Awen.

Running back from cause to prior cause, and to still more remote preceding causes of his desires, the individual finds himself at last confronting the Cosmic Will. Retracing his path back to the present, he finds himself confronting his personal will which is moved by desire. In other words, he finds a chain of desire extending from the Cosmic Will to the personal will—a chain of countless links, having a beginning in will, and ending in will—an endless chain, because it is a circle. Thereupon he learns the first lesson of the Secret of the Excluded Middle, and thenceforth strives to realize the union of the two ends of will. What is this union? Simply that will can become the cause of will.

From the realization of this union arises the individual will—the positive will of the self. In this process the law of cause and effect is not violated, but will is made the cause of will—the cause and effect merge. When this is attained, the door is open to the hidden realms of mastery.

The journey to this attainment may be started by means of the following exercises.

Completion Exercise 1

First take up the standard position of meditation, and perform the usual preliminaries of relaxation and breathing. Then consider one action you have performed in the previous twenty-four hours. The action you choose does not have to be an important or unusual action—any action at all may be used as a basis for this exercise, and in fact those actions that are most habitual and seemingly unimportant are often the most useful for the purpose of this work. Consider the action in detail—what exactly it consisted of, first on the physical plane; then on the plane of ordinary thinking and feeling, the astral plane; then on the plane of abstract realization, the spiritual plane, should you be able to lift your mind so far. Consider how the action relates to the rest of the day on which you performed it; consider how it relates to the rest of your life. Note what you think about the action, what you feel about it, what consequences it had and will have for yourself and for others.

When you have considered the action in all these ways, ask yourself: why did I do this action? In asking this you are not seeking praise or blame, but understanding. Your task is to mentally note all the reasons why you did the action in question. If there are many reasons, you may need to note them down on paper in order to keep track of them all! When you believe you have understood the reasons behind the action you performed, see if there is any common thread that connects the various reasons, or some other reason that provides the context or the explanation that makes them make sense to you.

Perform this exercise at least once each day during the time you spend in transition from this grade to the next. Examine a different action each time, and try to make the actions as varied as possible, so that you examine a broad selection of the actions and decisions you make in the course of your everyday life. As you do so, if you notice that certain reasons appear over and over again, make a note of this. When you find that the reasons you discover for any given action are among those you have considered while examining other actions, proceed to the second Completion Exercise.

Completion Exercise 2

Once again, take up the standard posture of meditation, and perform the usual preliminaries of relaxation and breathing. When you have finished these, turn your attention to your life as a whole, as far as you have lived it to date, as a single action expressed in many particulars. As you did with the individual actions you examined in the first Completion Exercise, seek a good general grasp of the shape and direction of your life on the three planes of being; consider how it relates to the other people with whom you interact, and how it relates to the Cosmos as a whole. Spend several sessions exploring these questions.

When you feel you have a clear sense of the life you have lived so far, ask yourself: what is the motive or reason that explains this life? If I had chosen such a life, what would be its purpose or its goal? To what end does it appear to be directed? Pursued to that end, what will it accomplish and what meaning and value will it express?

Perform this exercise at least once a day until you are ready to begin the exercises of the *Gradd y Gwyddon y Ffordd*, the Grade of the Loremaster of the Path.

JOHN MICHAEL GREER is Grand Archdruid Emeritus of the Ancient Order of Druids in America. He is the author of more than thirty books on a wide range of subjects, including The Druid Grove Handbook: A Guide to Ritual in the Ancient Order of Druids in America *(Lorain Press, 2011);* The Celtic Golden Dawn: An Original & Complete Curriculum of Druidical Study *(Llewellyn Publications, 2013);* The Gnostic Celtic Church: A Manual and Book of Liturgy *(Lorian Press, 2013);* Paths of Wisdom: Cabala in the Western Tradition *(Llewellyn, 1996);* Inside A Magical Lodge: Group Ritual in the Western Tradition *(Llewellyn, 1998);* The Art And Practice Of Geomancy: Divination, Magic, and Earth Wisdom of the Renaissance *(Weiser, 2009); and* After Progress: Reason and Religion at the End of the Industrial Age *(New Society Publishers, 2015). He is also the translator of Giordano Bruno,* On the Shadows of the Ideas *(Azoth Press, 2017); with Mark Anthony Mikituk of Éliphas Lévi,* The Doctrine and Ritual of High Magic *(TarcherPerigee, 2017); and with Christopher Warnock, of* The Picatrix: The Occult Classic of Astrological Magic *(Adocentyn Press, 2010–11). Additionally, he is the editor of the new edition of Israel Regardie's* The Golden Dawn: The Original Account of the Teachings, Rites, and Ceremonies of the Hermetic Order *(Llewellyn, 2016). He lives in Cumberland, Maryland, an old red brick mill town in the north central Appalachians, with his wife Sara. You may follow his weekly blogging at* Ecosophia: Toward an Ecological Spirituality *(www.ecosophia.net).*

About the Publisher

Azoth Press *is a small independent publishing house which makes its home in the Pacific Northwest. Our purpose is to create extraordinary books by practicing magicians for the practicing magician, with a standard of knowledge influenced by years of dedicated occult study and magical experience. We hope that our books will contribute to the practitioner's evolution and transformation, and also add to the magician's library a collection of unique, hand-made tomes meant to last for generations. Magical books should be Hermetic and talismanic works of art produced by the conjunction of well-written, well-researched, and enlightening content with beautiful design and elegant binding. In line with our goal of creating such magical volumes for practitioners and scholars of the Great Work, all Azoth Press limited-edition books are hand-bound by artisans with decades of experience in the fields of printing and master bookbinding. Each book is manufactured not only to a high æsthetic standard to please the eye and hand, but also to a demanding standard of artisanship and materials, so that each rare volume may be handed down, read, and used in their practice by generations of magicians to come. Please visit our website at* azothpress.com *and follow us on Facebook at* www.facebook.com/AzothPress/.

CPSIA information can be obtained
at www.ICGtesting.com
Printed in the USA
LVHW080112281222
736048LV00011B/653